The Genocide
Contagion

Studies in Genocide: Religion, History, and Human Rights

Series Editor: Alan L. Berger, Raddock Family Eminent Scholar Chair of Holocaust Studies, Florida Atlantic University

Genocide is a recurring scourge and a crime against humanity, the effects of which are felt globally. Books in this series are original and sophisticated analyses describing, interpreting, and articulating lessons from historical as well as current genocides. Written from a range of scholarly perspectives, the works in this series articulate patterns of genocide and offer suggestions about early warning signs that may help prevent the crime.

Jihad and Genocide, by Richard Rubenstein
Balkan Genocides: Holocaust and Ethnic Cleansing in the Twentieth Century, by Paul Mojzes
Native America and the Question of Genocide, by Alex Alvarez
The Genocide Contagion: How We Commit and Confront Holocaust and Genocide, by Israel W. Charny

The Genocide Contagion

How We Commit and Confront Holocaust and Genocide

ISRAEL W. CHARNY

ROWMAN & LITTLEFIELD
Lanham • Boulder • New York • London

Published by Rowman & Littlefield
A wholly owned subsidary of The Rowman & Littlefield Publishing Group, Inc.
4501 Forbes Boulevard, Suite 200, Lanham, Maryland 20706
www.rowman.com

Unit A, Whitacre Mews, 26-34 Stannary Street, London SE11 4AB, United Kingdom

British Library Cataloguing in Publication Information Available

Library of Congress Cataloging-in-Publication Data
Names: Charny, Israel W., author.
Title: The genocide contagion : how we commit and confront holocaust and genocide /
 Israel W. Charny.
Other titles: G'enosaid. English
Description: Lanham : Rowman & Littlefield, [2016] | Series: Studies in genocide:
 religion, history, and human rights | Originally published in 2011 in Hebrew as:
 G'enosaid : U-vi'arta ha-ra' mi-kirbekha : Sho'ah ve-retsah 'am ke-ma'aśe yadenu,
 bene-adam. | Includes bibliographical references and index.
Identifiers: LCCN 2016013457 (print) | LCCN 2016020519 (ebook) | ISBN
 9781442254350 (cloth : alk. paper) | ISBN 9781442254367 (electronic)
Subjects: LCSH: Genocide—History—20th century. | Holocaust, Jewish (1939–1945)—
 Psychological aspects. | Holocaust, Jewish (1939–1945)—Moral and ethical aspects. |
 Genocide.
Classification: LCC HV6322.7 .C46313 2016 (print) | LCC HV6322.7 (ebook) | DDC
 364.15/1—dc23
LC record available at https://lccn.loc.gov/2016013457

Printed in the United States of America

To my wife, Judith Katz-Charny, our six children,
and our thirteen (currently) grandchildren.
Wishes to each for a healthy and productive life

Contents

Introduction

YAIR AURON

The first time it was reported that our friends were being butchered there was a cry of horror. Then a hundred were butchered. But when a thousand were butchered and there was no end to the butchery, a blanket of silence spread.

When evil-doing comes like falling rain, nobody calls out "stop!" When crimes begin to pile up, they become invisible. When sufferings become unendurable the cries are no longer heard. The cries too fall like rain in summer.[1]

—Bertolt Brecht

This book explores aspects of human behavior that lead people to commit genocide. It considers the Holocaust and other genocides as the actions of human beings, examines the psychology of *genocidaires* (perpetrators of genocide), and asks whether we are capable of overcoming the evil within ourselves. These issues give us, as human beings, no rest. They force us to ask ourselves a long list of complex moral, ethical, and psychological questions. I hope this book will make us more self-aware. Throughout, I invite the reader to consider doing exercises presented in a section at the end of the book titled "Independent Study." The independent study questions are designed to help us ask ourselves tough questions and seriously consider not only how we harm others but also how we work to preserve lives. Some readers will want to repeat these exercises when they finish reading the book.

THE SERIES

This book was originally published in Hebrew in Israel as part of the Open University's series on genocide. Outside Israel it is now published in the Rowman & Littlefield Studies in Genocide series, edited by Alan L. Berger. The Open University series on genocide consists of twelve volumes, each of which can stand alone in its own right but is also part of a larger whole. In order to provide readers with the necessary context and background, each book in the series begins with a brief introduction reviewing critical terms and concepts relevant to genocide and providing readers with a common terminology. If the book is devoted to a specific case of genocide, the introduction also contextualizes the particular genocide under discussion with a brief exploration of genocide in general. Genocide as a general phenomenon is discussed in greater depth in the first book in the series, *Reflections on the Inconceivable: Theoretical Aspects in Genocide Studies.*

CONCEPTS AND TERMINOLOGY

Genocide

Genocide is the most extreme of all crimes against humanity. Although there have been mass killings throughout human history, some argue that the twentieth century witnessed more genocides than any other, which is why it has been referred to as "the century of genocide," "the century of evil," and "the century of violence." With the multiple genocides of the twentieth century, we have witnessed severe blows to human rights, extreme displays of indifference to human suffering, and severe moral breakdowns of humanity—of these, some consider the Holocaust to be the greatest moral breakdown ever.

Nonetheless, we must always remember that horrific acts of genocide occurred well before the Holocaust and, even more shockingly, have continued since. In the 1990s alone, when more people in the world were well informed about the Holocaust than at any other time in the past, and when the world reiterated its promise of "Never Again," we witnessed genocides in the former Yugoslavia and Rwanda, and these two genocides could have been prevented.

Many definitions of genocide have been proposed over the years. Despite its deficiencies, which will be discussed below, the books in this series use the standard definition employed by institutions of the United Nations.

The word "genocide" derives from two words: *genos*, ancient Greek for "race," and *caedere*, Latin for "to slaughter or murder." The term was coined during World War II by the Polish Jewish lawyer Raphael Lemkin (1901–1959), who is considered the founding father of the United Nations Convention on the Prevention and Punishment of the Crime of Genocide. Lemkin lost most of his family in the Holocaust. He fled Poland and eventually settled in the United States, where he dedicated the rest of his life to studying genocide and working to incorporate crimes of genocide into international criminal law. Lemkin first used the term in the context of the Nazi extermination of European Jewry with reference to the racially motivated killing of a people. However, Lemkin himself had a broader view of genocide that even includes "cultural genocide." The definition in the UN Convention already expands the crime of genocide beyond concepts of race to include mass extermination that is nationally, ethnically, or religiously motivated. During and following the war, Lemkin continued to grapple with the definition of genocide, expanding its scope. He repeatedly emphasized that the crime of genocide does not always entail the immediate and absolute destruction of a group of victims; rather, genocide can also be committed by means of a series of planned actions aimed at the gradual destruction of the national and economic infrastructure, the language, and the culture of a specific group.

In international law as expounded by Lemkin, genocide is a *generic* classification referring to the extermination of a people. Today, the term is commonly used in statutes, international covenants, judicial rulings, and academic and journalistic literature to refer to the killing of a particular national, ethnic, racial, or religious group. In the view of many, genocide also includes the murder of individuals solely because of their membership in a political group and with the aim of harming and eradicating the group as a whole (this form of genocide is not included in the UN Convention).

A QUESTION OF TERMINOLOGY

Scholars are engaged in a never-ending, meaningful, and often bitter debate regarding the difference between the terms "Holocaust" and "genocide." Some argue for a clear distinction between the two concepts, maintaining that although the term "genocide" encompasses certain aspects of the Holocaust, the term "Holocaust" refers to a unique event in human history that was an exceptional, total, all-encompassing crime that transcends genocide. Such scholars emphasize the fact that the Nazi genocide of the Jews was directed against an entire people, irrespective of their location and the historical circumstances in which they lived. Other scholars regard the Holocaust as falling under the general category of genocide despite its unique characteristics. These scholars argue that *every* act of genocide is unique in its own way and that, in this respect, the Holocaust is no different.

Historians, politicians, and legal experts also have different opinions when it comes to applying the term "genocide" to some of the mass killings that took place in the twentieth century, including a number of internal, politically motivated killings, such as those committed by Stalin in the Soviet Union. One such debate relates to the question of whether the events that took place in the former Yugoslavia should be classified as genocide or merely as a series of "genocidal acts." Similarly, under American pressure, the UN Security Council refused to classify the events that took place in Rwanda in the spring of 1994 as genocide—not because of disagreements as to the nature of the events themselves but because the Council was reluctant to get involved. The case of Rwanda was even more problematic because millions of people around the world were watching the atrocities as they unfolded live on their living room TV sets. Internal US government documents from the period made explicit use of the term "genocide." Nonetheless, the United Nations recognized the massacres as genocide only after the events.

Such terminological debates led, among other things, to the coining of the term "politicide" to describe politically motivated mass murders. To be precise, genocide and politicide should not necessarily be understood as two distinct phenomena: mass killings may be simultaneously genocide and politicide. Indeed, the Stalinist regime in the Soviet Union, the Maoist regime in China, and the Pol Pot regime in Cambodia all committed internal mass killings for political reasons (politicide) that were also mass murders aimed at exterminating specific ethnic groups (genocide).

Some scholars propose using the term "ethnocide" to describe mass murder for cultural reasons—that is, the intentional destruction of the culture of an ethnic, national, religious, or other group not necessarily involving physical extermination.

In light of the multiplicity of large-scale crimes and the many different classifications and definitions that have been proposed to relate to them, some people have called for employing a broader term, "democide" (from the Greek *demos*, meaning "population" or "people"), to encompass all murders carried out by a government, regardless of whether the victims belong to a particular group. Democide encompasses the concepts of genocide, politicide, and mass murder, as well as acts of state terrorism. If we apply this comprehensive definition, the number of people who have been killed through acts of democide in the twentieth century reaches incomprehensible levels. According to American scholar Rudolph J. Rummel, acts that can be classified as democide took the lives of over 169 million people the world over between 1900 and 1987, a figure even more unfathomable considering that it does not include soldiers or civilians killed in wars.[2] Rummel later revised his estimate for the entire twentieth century (including the mass killings of the final decade of the century in Rwanda, Yugoslavia, East Timor, and elsewhere) to 262 million! Regardless of the debates over semantics and terminology, we must never lose sight of the fact that every act of genocide is an extreme crime of mass murder of innocent people belonging to a particular national, ethnic, racial, or religious group.

THE UN CONVENTION ON THE PREVENTION AND PUNISHMENT OF THE CRIME OF GENOCIDE

On December 9, 1948, in the wake of Nazi war crimes and the extermination of the Jews in particular, the United Nations General Assembly unanimously adopted the Convention on the Prevention and Punishment of the Crime of Genocide. The contracting parties to the Convention confirmed that "genocide, whether committed in time of peace or in time of war, is a crime under international law which they undertake to prevent and to punish." Article 2 of the Convention defines genocide as follows:

> Any of the following acts committed with intent to destroy, in whole or in part, a national, ethnical, racial or religious group, as such:
> Killing members of the group;
> Causing serious bodily or mental harm to members of the group;
> Deliberately inflicting on the group conditions of life calculated to bring about its physical destruction in whole or in part;
> Imposing measures intended to prevent births within the group;
> Forcibly transferring children of the group to another group.

Like many other countries, Israel signed the Convention shortly after its original formulation; the government then enacted Israel's Crime of Genocide (Prevention and Punishment) Law of 1950. In this law, the Israeli legislators adopted the Convention's definition of the crime but were more stringent in stipulating punitive measures. The UN Convention does not specify the punishment of perpetrators of genocide, thus leaving loopholes that have enabled many of the people who stood trial for acts of genocide to go unpunished. In contrast, the Israeli statute unequivocally specifies that "a person guilty of genocide shall be punished by death" (except under certain circumstances not defined by the statute). Israeli legislators stipulated the same punishment for individuals found guilty under the Nazis and Nazi Collaborators Punishment Law of 1950, which was first carried out against the Nazi war criminal Adolf Eichmann.

Implementation of the UN Convention

A question of major significance is whether the United Nations and the international community are doing enough to prevent the recurrence of genocide. Some call for the amendment of the Convention to provide the United Nations with adequate tools not only to offer some level of assistance to victims after the fact but also to actually prevent genocide. To this end, the International Criminal Court (ICC) was established at the Rome Conference of July 1998. The ICC is authorized to try individuals on charges of genocide. The court was established in July 2002, after the decision was ratified by sixty countries (which did not include the United States or Israel). Only time will tell whether the establishment of the ICC was a significant step in the right direction.

PERPETRATORS, VICTIMS, AND THIRD PARTIES

Every act of genocide involves three main social groups: the perpetrators, their victims, and third parties—that is, people who neither take part in the killing nor are among its victims but who witness the events and must choose how to react to the atrocities as they unfold.

Acts of genocide can only be committed when the balance of power in a society is such that the perpetrators have complete power over their victims. The crystallization of such power relations requires that the rest of the world—that is, people who are neither perpetrators nor victims—behave in a certain manner. These "others" can be divided into three groups:

> Those who collaborate with the murderers (the accomplices) for a number of reasons, including a belief that it is best to maintain positive relations with the murderers because of the power they possess.

> Those who help the victims: These individuals always constitute a minority of the population and tend to be motivated by moral considerations. (In Israel, such individuals are known as "Righteous among the Nations." Those recognized by Yad Vashem as Righteous among the Nations are non-Jews who risked their lives to save the lives of Jews during the Holocaust.)

> Those who remain silent and indifferent (the bystanders): These individuals typically constitute a group that is much larger than either of the other two.

This breakdown raises a question of the utmost importance: Should bystanders be regarded as at least partially responsible for crimes they witnessed and did nothing to prevent?

Most countries in the world have remained indifferent in the face of mass extermination; major powers, such as the United States, are no exception. In an influential study, before she became US ambassador to the United Nations, American foreign policy advisor Samantha Power analyzed the attitude of the United States toward various acts of genocide committed in the twentieth century, including the Armenian Genocide, the Holocaust, and the genocides in Cambodia, Yugoslavia, and Rwanda. "What is most shocking," she concluded, "is that US policy makers did almost nothing to deter the crime. Because America's 'vital national interests' were not considered imperiled by mere genocide, senior U.S. officials did not give genocide the moral attention it warranted."[3]

In *Trauma and Recovery: The Aftermath of Violence—from Domestic Abuse to Political Terror*, American professor of psychiatry Judith Lewis Herman explores the effect of different types of violence on former combat soldiers, Holocaust survivors, prisoners of war, abused women, and victims of incest.

The ordinary response to atrocities is to banish them from consciousness. Certain violations of the social compact are too terrible to utter aloud: this is the meaning of the word unspeakable.

Atrocities, however, refuse to be buried. Equally as powerful as the desire to deny atrocities is the conviction that denial does not work. Folk wisdom is filled with ghosts who refuse to rest in their graves until their stories are told. Murder will out. Remembering and telling the truth about terrible events are prerequisites both for the restoration of the social order and for the healing of individual victims. . . .

To study psychological trauma is to come face to face both with human vulnerability in the natural world and with the capacity for evil in human nature. To study psychological trauma means bearing witness to horrible events. When the events are natural disasters or "acts of God," those who bear witness sympathize readily with the victim. But when the traumatic events are of human design, those who bear witness are caught in the conflict between victim and perpetrator. It is morally impossible to remain neutral in this conflict. The bystander is forced to take sides.

It is very tempting to take the side of the perpetrator. All the perpetrator asks is that the bystander do nothing. He appeals to the universal desire to see, hear, and speak no evil. The victim, on the contrary, asks the bystander to share the burden of the pain. The victim demands action, engagement, and remembering.[4]

It can be argued that through their passivity, bystanders—perhaps unintentionally—provide support for perpetrators but never for victims. When we choose not to take a stand, we are actually taking the side of the perpetrator. From a moral perspective, we thus cannot simply stand by while crimes of genocide are perpetrated. Justifications such as "nothing could be done to stop it" are also unacceptable. Injustice does not cease to be injustice when it is visited upon someone else. As the Bible teaches, "Neither shalt thou stand idly by when thy neighbor's blood is shed" (Leviticus 19:16). Bystanders, too, bear responsibility and perhaps also blame—at least morally—for such killings.

REFLECTIONS ON GENOCIDE EDUCATION AROUND THE WORLD

Teaching about genocide forces us to confront a variety of weighty philosophical and didactic issues. In the context of Holocaust education, Elie Wiesel raises a poignant question that can be applied to genocide education as well:

How do you teach events that contradict accepted knowledge, experiences that go beyond imagination? How do you tell children, big and small, that society could lose its mind and start murdering its own soul and its own future? How do you unveil horrors without offering at the same time some measure of hope? Hope in what? In whom? In progress, in science and literature, in God?[5]

While Holocaust education has already secured a place within academic and educational frameworks in countries around the world, the broader field of genocide studies, which is immensely important in its own right, is still in its first stages of development. Without a doubt, the knowledge possessed by people in most countries about other cases of genocide that took place during the twentieth century typically pales in comparison with what they know about the Holocaust. Some go as far as to argue that most genocides committed during the past century (except, of course, the Holocaust) can be thought of as "forgotten" or "unknown," like those that took place in the more distant past.

That being said, we must also acknowledge that the past two to three decades have witnessed a marked increase in general awareness regarding the genocides that have taken place around the world. Concurrently progress, though limited, has been made in the field of genocide education (in the specific field of Holocaust education, much greater progress has been made). Careful observation of the development of genocide education around the world reflects that progress is often driven by the initiatives of select people who are dedicated to the cause. They are passionate, dedicated activists who make it their lives' work and simply refuse to let the subject lie dormant. Not surprisingly, many such efforts have been led by Jews interested in developing the field of genocide education, in addition to the field of Holocaust education, out of a unique sense of empathy with the suffering of other peoples. We agree with such activists that, in addition to the contribution they make to the study of genocide in general, comparative studies (or genocide studies) also stand to contribute to the study of the Holocaust in ways that are simply impossible to achieve in Holocaust studies alone.

ON THE UNIVERSAL VALUE OF HUMAN LIFE

For more than thirty years, Israelis and other people around the world have engaged in bitter debates over the genocides that have befallen other

peoples. At the heart of these debates lies the controversial assertion that
the Holocaust was a completely unique event, despite the fact that its special
importance for Jews is actually unrelated to its uniqueness. This is not to say
that the Holocaust was not unique among genocides—indeed, the Holocaust
was a one-of-a-kind "industry of death" based on a racist theory and ideology aimed at exterminating all members of the Jewish people, wherever they
lived. However, its major significance lies in its deep entrenchment in Jewish
historical consciousness, where it continues to play a decisive role.

Ironically, notwithstanding the Jewish tradition of sensitivity to the suffering of others, indifference toward and denial of genocides that have befallen others also runs deeply within Israeli culture. In some cases, such lack
of recognition can have a decisive impact on victims' efforts to rehabilitate
themselves and cope with their tragedy, a process that may last a long time
and, in some instances, indefinitely. Primo Levi's *The Drowned and the Saved*
recounts how SS soldiers used to amuse themselves by cynically assuring prisoners that even if some of them survived the Nazi camps, no one would ever
believe their stories about what had taken place within. Levi also provides an
account of a recurring nightmare from which almost all survivors suffered in
the camps, one that differed somewhat from person to person but was identical in its overall message:

> They had returned home and with passion and relief were describing their past
> sufferings, addressing themselves to a loved one, and were not believed, indeed
> were not even listened to. In the most typical (and cruelest) form, the interlocu-
> tor turned and left in silence.[6]

We should be asking ourselves difficult questions. How do we respond to
other victims' just demands that we help them as best as we can to ensure
that their murderers and the offspring of their murderers acknowledge these
crimes? How do we relate to their demands that the world recognize the dual-
injustice they have suffered—the genocide itself and others' disregard for it
after the fact?

One aim of the genocide book series is to increase the sensitivity of students, scholars, and other readers to the phenomenon of genocide. Another
is to encourage them to question their own opinions and their sense of
responsibility regarding such acts of injustice and to consider possible ways

of taking action to prevent them, whether as individuals or in conjunction with other members of their own social reference groups. The fundamental principle underlying this book series is the universal value of human life, wherever it is found.

THE APPROACH OF ISRAEL CHARNY

This book was written by Professor Israel Charny, a clinical psychologist and family therapist and a pioneer and eminent scholar in the field of genocide studies. In 1980 Charny founded the Institute on the Holocaust and Genocide in Jerusalem. This marked perhaps the first official usages of the terms "Holocaust" and "genocide" in conjunction with one another (another was in the title of the academic journal *Holocaust and Genocide Studies*, established by Professor Yehuda Bauer soon afterward).[7]

Charny proposes a humanistic definition of the term "genocide" as the unrestrained killing of human beings based on any aspect of their identity—national, ethnic, racial, religious, political, geographical, or ideological. Charny maintains, "There never can be any identity process that in itself justifies the murder of men, women, and children because they are 'anti' some 'ism,' or because in their physical characteristics they are high- or low-cheekboned, short- or long-eared, or green or orange colored."[8]

Charny believes that his humanistic definition of genocide will endure, notwithstanding attempts to define genocide as the destruction of a specific ethnic, national, religious, or other group identity. According to Charny, genocide must be assigned a broader definition because the issue being addressed is the preservation of human lives. His definition of genocide as the conscious and unnecessary destruction of a sizable group of people encompasses *all* instances in which large numbers of people are put to death by others—except in cases in which there is clear evidence that the perpetrators acted in self-defense. Regardless of the shortcomings of international law and the scholarly debates over terminology, he suggests that this is the broad definition dictated by common sense.

Charny also explores the processes leading up to genocide. Today, most official bodies define genocide as the intentional murder of a sizable portion of a particular group for reasons justified by the ideology of the perpetrators. The processes leading up to these catastrophic events can be assessed from a number of perspectives related to the organization of societies and states, as well as the degree to which such bodies are committed to preserving or destroying human lives. Charny observes that the decline into genocide typically occurs during wartime or other periods of major stress on a society. The final push toward genocide is often related to perceptions that a particular group threatens the survival of the society as a whole. In some cases, the targeted group in fact does not constitute a true foe but becomes an alleged enemy which society unites and mobilizes against and then struggles to eradicate.

Charny compares the processes that lead to genocide to a cancer that starts in one part of the body and spreads to and kills off other parts of the body as well. Although the body possesses an immune system capable of fighting cancer, it is often unsuccessful in doing so, allowing the illness to run rampant throughout the body. This may ultimately result not only in the destruction of parts of the body under attack but in the death of the organism as a whole. Society, like the human body, has elements that attempt to assume greater control by killing off other parts; it also has forces capable of preventing such violent takeovers. If these forces are unsuccessful, the ultimate outcome is extremely destructive.

Continuing his humanistic definition of genocide, Charny proposes a generic definition of the term:

> Genocide in the generic sense means the mass killing of substantial numbers of human beings, when not in the course of military action against the military forces of an avowed enemy, under conditions of the essential defenselessness of the victim.[9]

Charny proposes a unique approach, focusing on the dynamics that facilitate the evolution and implementation of genocide, in contrast to most of the Israeli scholarship on the subject, which highlights the injustices committed and the suffering of the victims. He also forces readers to look within themselves and to consider whether they possess the necessary humanity (*menschlichkeit*) to meet the challenge.

Auschwitz Was Not Another Planet—It Is This World of Ours
Yehiel Dinur (Katzetnik)

Auschwitz was not another planet—it is this world of ours.
It is the site of a dress rehearsal of the atom.
The finger [that] will pull the atomic trigger that can bring chaos upon the world
    is not the finger of god but the finger of man.
I—Man—Created Auschwitz.[10]

Note by author: "Katzetnik," meaning concentration camp inmate, is the pen name adopted by Holocaust survivor Yehiel Dinur, who became a well-known prolific writer on the Holocaust. His most famous moment came when he collapsed while bearing witness at the Eichmann Trial. In his moving testimony, he declared, "Auschwitz was another planet!"

The excerpt given here is from a televised appearance he made after returning from Europe, where he had undergone intensive psychotherapy (including the use of LSD) by a well-known psychiatrist in Holland who specialized in treating trauma of captivity, terrorist attacks, and the like. Katzetnik had asked for treatment because of his continual post-Holocaust posttraumatic suffering.

The statement he made is an amazing declaration by a Holocaust survivor of concern for the world and acceptance of responsibility as a human being.

Preface

When we consider genocide, we must always be mindful of our own roles as human beings in the phenomenon, not only as victims but as perpetrators of evil.

The exploration of genocide must always be undertaken first and foremost from the vantage point of history. It is also crucial, however, to consider the role of the people involved in the context of the social institutions at work, as well as the psychology and sociology of the perpetrators and facilitators. This book illuminates some of the psychological aspects of genocide.

1. The psychology of social organizations and institutions, such as armies, police forces, legal systems, theological systems, and health-care systems, as well as systems of government, including political leaders. These social components are dynamic forces that justify violence and determine history no less than broader historical processes, such as the rise and fall of nations and cultures.
2. The psychology of individuals. We strive to understand the role of human beings in these systems and within broader social collectives (peoples, tribes, and other groups) as they march forward ceremoniously toward shedding the blood of their fellow man.
3. The psychology of perpetrators. We study those who perpetrate genocide, not only in the context of processes initiated by leaders, institutions, and

social groups but as a result of processes at play deep within their own individual psyches. In every generation there are those who rise up and slaughter large numbers of their fellow human beings. We must therefore seek ways to redirect this tendency, not only because we may find ourselves as victims but because, as human beings, we too become a party to acts of wrongdoing against others.

Even in Israel, where there is tremendous sensitivity to the Holocaust, the Israeli literature contains a plethora of books on the Holocaust but only a few on the mass murders that have befallen other peoples. Moreover, most of these books focus on the victims, only a few explore the major perpetrators, and virtually none address the simple citizens involved in the process, including the lower-tier leaders who typically constitute the bulk of those who actually carry out the murders.

This book raises a particularly grim question: Who among us is psychologically capable of taking part in genocide, and who among us is not? How can it be that in every case of genocide, a decisive majority of citizens "followed orders" and agreed to murder the victims, collaborated with the murderers, or stood by and allowed the killing to happen? This book also looks into the psychological dynamics of those who refused orders and declined to take part. Long before genocide takes place, is it possible to identify the individual characteristics that provide a fertile ground for the emergence of a willingness to kill? And what qualities of temperament, personality, and behavior do those who refrain from taking part share?

These questions raise another more fundamental question related to the fundamental nature of humankind. Are people innately good at heart, or is it true, as the biblical passage suggests, that "man's heart is evil from his youth" (Genesis 8:21)? And if people are in fact aggressive, violent, and bloodthirsty by nature, can they be transformed by forces such as love, cultural heritage, and ethical education into proponents of good who will strive to prolong their own lives and the lives of others?

This book differs from others on genocide and the Holocaust in that it focuses primarily on the aggressors, victimizers, and murderers instead of on the victims or the national experience of the persecuted. It attempts to shed light on the psychology of emotions and thought processes of the murderers themselves. What were the experiences of the perpetrators, not just in the course of their horrifying actions but during their lives beforehand, when there were few indications of what they would become later in acts of genocide. The book explores important aspects of people's thinking and emotional experiences in their everyday lives, as well as in social situations in which they are instructed and given the power to abuse or kill others (excluding clearly justified military activities against an attacking enemy).

Today hundreds of academics identify themselves as scholars of genocide studies, and an emerging field boasts a growing number of professional associations, conferences, and academic journals. Moreover, many intellectuals and scholars who do not necessarily classify themselves as genocide experts also engage the subject in a meaningful manner in their areas of scholarship, such as history, law, international relations, psychology, social work, medicine, theater, and art.

The US government today recognizes the danger of genocide and has announced that it intends to make efforts to prevent it.[1] The United Nations has also recently started to pay more attention to instances of genocide and has established a special office to address the issue under the direct authority of the secretary-general. A permanent international criminal court has been set up, and an increasing number of legal proceedings and pieces of legislation in countries around the world address the issues of genocide, crimes against humanity, and atrocity crimes.[2]

ACKNOWLEDGMENTS

I would like to express my gratitude to those who have graced me with their help and productive collaboration over the years. I extend a special thanks to Dr. Daphna Fromer, who many years ago helped me teach a course on the psychology of aggression and evil at Tel Aviv University. For that course we wrote a book on the foundations of evil, which the present book develops more extensively.

I would also like to thank my many colleagues in Israel and abroad who today are active in the new and ever-expanding academic field of genocide studies.

For encouraging me to write this book, I am especially grateful to Professor Yair Auron, whose remarkable work as a genocide studies educator and scholar is referred to in the book and is clearly evident in the series of books that he has edited, as well as in several of his own valuable works.

I also want to express my appreciation for the encouragement and critical reviews of the manuscript by Professor Yoel Elizur, Professor Elihu Richter, and my dear friend Marc I. Sherman, MLS, who for many years has provided me with invaluable assistance on matters of bibliography and databases, as well as "zany" and humorous creative ideas.

And, finally, many thanks to my professional assistant, Karen Wolberger, MPH, for her dedicated and fine work and fun-to-work-together work.

The index was prepared jointly by the author, Marc Sherman, and Karen Wolberger, under the direction of Marc Sherman.

SOURCE CREDITS

We are grateful to the copyright holders who granted their permission to use the items that appear in this book.

Page 1: Bertolt Brecht. (1935). "When Evil-Doing Comes Like Falling Rain." In *Poems, 1913–1956*, edited by John Willet and Ralph Manheim. London: Methuen, 1979. © Bertolt-Brecht-Erben / Suhrkamp Verlag.

Pages 19–20: "Al zot" ("About this"), Natan Alterman © Acum and writer.

Page 42: Saguy Green, "How Could They Kill Small Children?," *Haaretz English Edition*, October 26, 2010, Gallery Section, Copyright © "Ha'aretz" Daily News Paper Ltd.

Page 158: Excerpts from Benyamin Neuberger, "Our Holocaust—and Others'," *Haaretz English Edition*, April 28, 2006. Courtesy of Benyamin Neuberger.

We have endeavored to trace the copyright owners of all the external material. We sincerely apologize for any omission or error and upon notification will be pleased to rectify it in future editions.

1

Who Are We as Human Beings?

How Do Ordinary People Commit Violence?

NATAN ALTERMAN AND DAVID BEN-GURION ON WAR CRIMES BY ISRAELIS

> He cut through the conquered city on his jeep
> A stalwart lad, armed to the teeth, . . . a lion of a youth!
> And on the desert road
> An old man and a woman
> Pressed against the wall in fear of him
>
> The lad smiled with his milky teeth:
> "I'll try the machinegun" . . . and he fired
> The old man barely held his head in his hands . . .
> And his blood covered the wall
>
> For our finest sons and daughters,
> And we with them
> Some as active accomplices, others in silent acquiescence,
> Muttering "necessity" or "revenge,"
> Slide and are pulled into the sphere of war criminals
>
> —Natan Alterman

19

Israel's first prime minister, David Ben-Gurion, wrote to Alterman about the poem:

> November 21, 1948
> Dear Alterman,
>   Bless you for the moral strength and courage of your expression in your column in *Davar* [newspaper]. . . . You are a voice—true and loyal—for the human conscience. If this conscience will not beat in our hearts and be heard in days such as this, we will not deserve the greatness that has come our way thus far.
>   I request your permission to reprint your column by the Israel Ministry of Defense and to distribute it to every soldier in the Israeli army.
>   With deep respect and thanks,
>   D. Ben-Gurion[1]

I AM A HUMAN BUT AM I?
Man Genocider
A poem by Israel W. Charny

> I am a son of Adam
> Who am I?
> A peace-loving man grateful for the gift of my life?
> A serial mass genocider?
> An accomplice to mass murders?
> An all-too available victim?
> A bystander getting away with a box seat on the madness of it all?
>
> Long before the Government or Party or Church
> Tell me it's good to get rid of those maggots,
> And I go to do it
> What do I look like in my everyday life?
> Do I wear a tie? Do I speak nicely?
> Do I love my children?
> Am I fun to be with?
>
> *Je Tue, donc Je Suis!*
> *I kill, therefore I Am!*
> I beat you, Descartes—mine is more powerful
> You die. I live.

You die because I command your death
Of course I command my life
I told you I am the Commander. I am Eternal. Immortal. Superior.

My people are Chosen,
And we are the Superior ones
Your seminars on Holocaust and Genocide, films, books, TV programs,
    sermons, conferences,
even laws and courts can't stop us
We are Death, and Death always wins
Only we live, precisely because we are Death
We are Your Death[2]

We do not understand fully the *mechanism of destruction*. That may be
the essence of the tragedy, writes Holocaust survivor and Nobel laureate Elie
Wiesel:

> The executioner had greater imagination than his victims, for he always knew
> more than what was known to them. The process worked with terrifying ef-
> ficiency. A true industry of death was established in which all the participants
> were in their places. The murderers murdered, the onlookers looked, and the
> victims, including children, were tossed into the ovens. It was as if things had
> been meant to happen this way since the world was created.[3]

Whenever we find ourselves faced with pictures of the terrifying atrocities
and the unbearable stories from "there"—the Holocaust that befell the Jews
during World War II—one of our natural reactions is to think that this could
not have happened, that human beings could never have done such things
to other human beings. However, when we examine the record of human
history, we quickly learn that *many* other peoples also have suffered and continue to suffer from genocide, each taking place in its own way.

Our confusion grows when we get a glimpse of "them," the murderers
who, to our great surprise, for the most part appear to be everyday normal
people, including worried parents and dedicated children, with emotions,
loves, and hatreds of their own. Could someone who looks just like the next-
door neighbor commit acts so horrifying as the merciless torture and mass

murder of women, children, and the elderly? How can human beings do such things to other human beings without becoming shocked and outraged? Can humans be transformed into cruel murderers, and if so, what causes this transformation in normal people, or in "ordinary men," to use a concept popularized by historian Christopher Browning[4] and others?[5]

This book explores a variety of mechanisms and dynamics familiar to psychology and the social sciences to help us better understand at least part of the difficult truth. In each case, we provide a definition and description of the mechanism that exists *in all of us* that, if not effectively controlled, can release our inner potential for evil. We also examine the manifestations of these mechanisms in our everyday lives and how, under certain historical circumstances, they may emerge and be translated into acts of genocide.

In all societies, we find psychological mechanisms and dynamics that can be channeled into mutually reinforcing synergistic processes in conjunction with one another to produce the ability to do harm to others. Over and over we must emphasize that most cases of mass murder involve the perpetration of evil by normal, everyday people. Typically, most of the murderers themselves have no intention of doing wrong. Rather, they are pulled into the atrocities they commit by a powerful dynamic shaped by an array of mechanisms and developments that lead them in the direction of continuous radicalization of their behaviors.

All societies and all individuals must ask themselves whether they have taken the measures necessary to protect themselves successfully against the two complementary basic elements of victimization—whose common denominator is doing harm to life, one's own or another's!

1. Developing the ability to fight for one's own life in order to avoid being led too easily to one's death
2. Never consenting to do serious harm to others (with the exception of genuinely justified self-defense)

Without a doubt, human society today requires renewed ethical values and a strong legal system to defend the sanctity of human life and the right of every person to live.

HOW COULD THEY DO SUCH A THING?

This book strives to gain a better understanding of the psychology of genocide in order to provide better answers to a number of questions: **How could they do such a thing?** Or, stated more broadly, How could we as human beings, who see ourselves as created in "God's image," do such a thing? And finally, the most difficult question of all: **Am I, or are other members of my nation, or is my nation as a whole capable of doing such a thing?**

I, the author, believe that I would not be capable of lending my hand to the murder of others. I also believe about my nation that the likelihood that Israel would commit a systematic large-scale genocide is low. But the potential is there in all human beings and societies.

Today it is clear that all individuals, nations, and states must ask themselves these questions. Very few countries in the world, including the world's democracies, are untainted by genocidal bloodshed.[6] For example, the United States carried out massacres of the Native American population within its borders and, two centuries later, of civilians in Vietnam. Canada slaughtered French settlers in the eighteenth century, as well as members of the First Nations population within its borders. Israel carried out mass murders in Arab villages such as Deir Yassin during Israel's War of Independence in 1948 and Kfar Qasim during the Sinai War in 1956, and killed Egyptian prisoners of war during the 1973 Arab-Israeli War. *In light of the prevalence of the phenomenon, it is incumbent upon all readers to engage in the unpleasant exercise of asking whether or not they themselves would be capable of taking the lives of large numbers of people—that is, of committing genocide.*

Moreover, as we come to better understand the human mind and why human beings are capable of committing murder, we also learn much about our willingness to do harm to others in our everyday lives, as members of groups and communities and as citizens of countries. This book differs from the bulk of existing writing on perpetrators of genocide—a topic that in its own right lags far beyond the literature on victims—because it focuses, first of all, on the basic *everyday* dynamics from which genocide evolves. Its premise is that social phenomena such as persecution, discrimination, and genocide all begin with seemingly minor psychological dynamics, such as the readiness to insult, humiliate, defame, and discriminate against other individuals and other ethnic, religious, or national groups. In this context, readers are asked to consider whether they themselves ever degrade, humiliate, mock, ridicule, discriminate against, persecute, delegitimize, harm, or injure others. This question can make many of us quite uncomfortable in that it can force us to contend with unpleasant truths about ourselves and, in any number of cases, about our behavior in our private lives. Simultaneously, our honest inquiry into ourselves will shed light on the willingness of the human race as a whole to commit genocide.

Without a doubt, the choice of whether or not to kill another human being is a soul-deep moral decision. Obviously it does not turn on the contents or understanding of any one book. Indeed, conceivably one can also read books about genocide in order to learn how to promote the phenomenon and to create the conditions that enable human beings to commit crimes of the most heinous nature. *The decision to refrain from harming others and from killing unarmed people is a moral decision of the highest level. It is a decision to respect the ultimate sanctity of life.*

Of course, totalitarian regimes also include some citizens who refuse to follow orders to kill, and "wise" fascist regimes find ways of bringing such individuals into an alliance with those committing the crimes. They do so by taking effective measures to overcome their resistance, such as gradually integrating them into the killing process to enable them to grow accustomed to it and to prevent them from experiencing emotional trauma. This process, known as desensitization, is based on a system of gradual exposure to initially disturbing stimuli.

Learning cognitively about human evil does not necessarily prevent people from doing evil themselves. *The decision to oppose actively the destruction of human life and to work for its preservation is a critical moral choice to be made by every individual, every group, and every people.*

▪ See Independent Study 1 ▪

As explained in the introduction, an "Independent Study" section is included at the end of the book to help readers consider whether they might participate in genocide or work to preserve life. Readers may review the independent study questions as they read or when finished with the book.

ARE PERPETRATORS OF GENOCIDE "NORMAL" PEOPLE?

It is difficult to grasp that only a small percentage of the murderers during the Holocaust were actually sadistic or cruel in character. Most were "ordinary men," to use the terminology of Browning,[7] or "normal people," to use the terminology of the scholars of psychology who preceded him. The first scholars to teach us about the surprisingly "normal" nature of the murderers during the Holocaust included clinical psychologist Gustave Gilbert[8] and psychiatrist Douglas Kelley,[9] both staff members of the Nuremberg Tribunal that tried the Nazi elite at the end of World War II.

In 1969, I gave my first lecture before the Israel Psychological Association in Jerusalem on the normal nature of the murderers during the Holocaust. During the 1970s and 1980s, I formulated a theory on the murderous sides of the personality of the "normal" person and proposed a new model for psychological and psychiatric diagnosis. This model suggests that all cases be assessed according to the damage a person does not only to him- or herself but also to others.

On this basis, individual psychological health is a combination of a person's ability to refrain both from harming him- or herself *and* from taking action that damages or undermines the healthy functioning of others.[10]

I maintain that psychological health is based on love and respect for one's own life and the lives of others and that damaging a person's ability to function—whether one's own or another's—is the clearest manifestation of psychological disorder. The psychiatric-psychological establishment tends to emphasize reduced capacity and disorder mainly in the functioning of the individual under examination. Even when a person does harm to others, the standard psychological diagnosis tends to emphasize the fact that the person is excluding himself from society and making himself vulnerable to severe repercussions and punitive actions over the heinous immoral behaviors of the person. In other words, it is not a person's actions vis-à-vis the others that determines psychological health but rather the damage the person causes him- or herself. In contrast, from the outset the diagnosis demanded by my proposal rests on a principle anchored both in morality and in health science: all that promotes human life is "healthy," and all that harms or destroys human life is "pathological." Note that on this basis damage done to the life of another person serves as a foundation, in and of itself, for diagnosing psychological disorders without "proving" that the person in question is also harming him- or herself.

Does a definition of emotional disturbance mean that genocidal murderers should be "treated" protectively because they are ill? It is certainly true that some psychologically disturbed individuals are unaware of their actions or incapable of controlling them. In such situations it is justifiable at times to understand, say, a onetime violent episode that erupts in an emotional outburst. However, such understanding cannot be extended to any systematic murderous violence that is part of a cruel and exploitative way of life. Individuals subject to an eruption of emotional violence may be deserving of some protection and clemency as psychiatric patients due to their inability to control the symptoms of their psychological disorders. But individuals exhibiting repetitive and systematic violent behavior must be punished for their way of life and their unforgivable criminal actions. From a philosophical and political standpoint as well, well-regulated societies cannot legally sanction systematic persecution and murder of others.

During the Holocaust, as well as during the numerous other genocides that have taken place over the course of human history, perpetrators have committed inhumane acts that must be clearly denounced and defined as unhealthy, unacceptable, deviant, and criminal. This should be true in all intellectual disciplines and, of course, in the field of psychology, with its major emphasis on categorizing behaviors as *normal* or *abnormal.* But as noted, studies to date reveal that most perpetrators of genocide are *not* "sick," "crazy," or "disturbed," based on the present classification of mental illness, which emphasizes the individual's disturbed behavior to him- or herself. As a result, nothing in current psychological terminology clearly classifies genocidal behavior as psychologically "abnormal." I believe we are obligated to change both the language we use and our standard system of diagnosis, and for this reason I proposed the new model of psychological and psychiatric diagnosis that assesses not only *self*-destructiveness but also the potential for causing harm to *others.*

In addition, the new model teaches us a most important lesson about the fundamental nature of human beings in general, and not just about particular groups who perpetrate genocide in their evilest hour. This lesson, which we Jews—who think highly of our culture as presenting advanced moral codes—

also must internalize, is that all "normal" people have a potential to commit genocide that needs to be countered.

TO WHAT EXTENT ARE HUMAN BEINGS INHERENTLY WILLING TO KILL?

As noted, in addition to exploring the dynamics underlying acts of mass murder, this book aims to penetrate to greater truth about our human race. Most interesting here is the extent to which human beings are inherently willing to kill other human beings. Each animal species displays different innate traits. For example, some canine breeds have a potential for extreme aggressiveness to the point that some societies prohibit people from raising these breeds altogether, at least not without muzzles and other restraints. Could the same be true about human beings? Could man have genetic traits that carry a built-in potential for violence as well? Historically, on the other side of the fence, perhaps the fact that a certain tribe in the Pacific Ocean has lived in continuous peace with others is indicative also of a genetically transmitted unwillingness to engage in violence.[11] Might the German people, who sparked two bloody world wars during the twentieth century, after previously committing the first genocide of the century against the Herero people of southwestern Africa,[12] have a genetic predisposition for violence? For the time being, these are questions for which we simply do not have answers. Not only is there no reasonable scientific evidence, but there are also no sound theories regarding such traits in the human genetic system.

We do know that culture plays an important role in molding either peaceful or violent behaviors. Peaceful societies that maintain values such as respect for human life and for the "other" are less likely to be drawn into violence as a collective way of life, although no society can be completely insulated from violent episodes. However, societies that praise aggression and belligerence and embrace theories of superiority and the conquest of other peoples are more likely to seek and find reasons for wars and for the persecution of others.

Within the cultural mosaics of all peoples, methods of government are of great significance. The manner in which a society organizes itself on the level of governance and politics is undoubtedly a critical component of national collective character. However, this structural-organizational aspect is not always entirely consistent with a given people's overall cultural heritage but sometimes adds a new dimension. A tyrannical military regime sometimes espouses values of peace and social justice. Alternatively, regimes based on democratic laws may adopt—typically in the name of democracy and freedom—policies of belligerence and conquest. A readiness to kill others may form part of a wartime strategy, or it may be a more direct formulation of a genocidal goal to exterminate a population perceived as an enemy people. But we dare not forget that people who are sentenced to death care little about whether their extermination is the result of military strategy or the direct outcome of a genocidal goal planned by a culture or government.

To better understand the phenomenon of genocide and to prevent it in the future, we must analyze and understand as thoroughly as possible the various factors that increase and decrease its likelihood.

From a philosophical perspective, an inconsistency between stated goals of peace and the sanctity of life and the means by which they are to be achieved—for example, a policy of weapons development and export—is liable to result in increased violence. Thus, many thinkers, including the preeminent genocide scholar Leo Kuper, believe that the development and use of the nuclear bomb during World War II was an act of genocide, even if the war itself was a just war against a cruel enemy.[13]

Clearly, proponents of democracy and freedom who are willing to murder others who oppose the values they hold sacred are just as despicable as murderous fascists. The United States is known to have aided a number of mass-murdering regimes, such as those of Chile's Augusto Pinochet, who killed several thousand of his opponents,[14] and the Indonesian government, which killed approximately 1 million supposed communists between 1965 and 1966 and more than 100,000 East Timorese between 1975 and 1979.[15] In the Vietnam War, the United States also attempted to support proponents of democracy against communists. Of course, other "socialist-democratic" regimes have massacred their enemies at home and abroad. At the same time, it is important to note that some tyrannical regimes, such as those lead by Benito Mussolini in Italy during World War II and by Fidel Castro in Cuba, have governed in the name of fascist philosophies, while refraining from the larger-scale killing of civilians. In other words, tyrannical regimes are also capable of limiting the means they adopt to achieve their goals.

University of Hawaii political science professor Rudolph J. Rummel is the world's leading scholar on the statistics of genocide,[16] a clearly "impossible" subject since perpetrators of genocide only rarely leave behind systematic

data, such as the numbers tattooed on the arms of Jewish prisoners at Auschwitz or the Cambodian execution log from the central prison at Tuol Sleng
(but no records were left in the many killing fields). With the return of a nonlethal regime to power following a genocidal episode, survivors, aid organizations, and human rights groups may sometimes be capable of recreating what
transpired to a certain extent, but not in all cases. Rummel assembled his data
from a variety of sources and computed three different estimate levels: high,
mid-level, and low. Ultimately, he himself adopted the mid-level estimates for
the purpose of reaching his conclusions. Rummel concluded, overall, that by
the end of the twentieth century, some 262 million people had died as victims
of genocide.[17]

Rummel also considers whether these shocking numbers can serve as a
factual basis to better understand the circumstances that may increase or
decrease the likelihood of genocide. Unfortunately, he fails to assess other
important dimensions, such as the role of a dominant church within a given
society, its political status, and the nature of its response to the genocidal
murders of the regime. He also has not examined the prevailing values of
different cultures. Despite these blind spots, his comparison between democratic and totalitarian regimes yields an unequivocal empirical conclusion
of incomparable importance: although democratic regimes may periodically
commit genocide to a limited extent, **genocide is most likely to be committed by nondemocratic regimes**.[18]

With regard to the fundamental dynamic underlying processes of mass
murder, Rummel regards power and the quest for it as the primary corrupt-
ing force in human psychology and politics, as expressed by the well-known
axiom "Power corrupts. Absolute power corrupts absolutely."[19]

ERICH FROMM

If you begin your resistance to a Hitler only after he has won his victory, then you've lost before you've even begun. For to offer resistance, you have to have an inner core, a conviction. You have to have faith in yourself, to be able to think critically, to be an independent human being, a human being and not a sheep. . . . [A]nyone who takes this path will learn to resist not only the great tyrannies, like Hitler's, but also the "small tyrannies," the creeping tyrannies of bureaucratization and alienation in everyday life.[20]

IF A SYSTEM OF DEATH CAMPS WERE SET UP IN THE UNITED STATES / STANLEY MILGRAM

I would say, on the basis of having observed a thousand people in the experiment and having my own intuition shaped and informed by these experiments, that if a system of death camps were set up in the United States of the sort we had seen in Nazi Germany, one would be able to find sufficient personnel for those camps in any medium-sized American town.[21]

2

The Foundations of Evil in Human Nature

When we examine the people who commit genocide, we discover that alongside those who, by their very nature so to speak, perpetrate evil against others, there are many other "ordinary" members of society who will agree to kill or to assist in killing.

In addition to the satanic figures who typically head genocide-initiating hierarchies, such as Hitler, Stalin, and Pol Pot, and those who play less senior roles, such as "Ivan the Terrible," a notorious camp guard during the Holocaust, and Dr. Shirō Ishii during Japan's genocide in China, probably a majority of people—whose actions prior to and following the genocidal events show no clear predisposition toward cruelty or aggression—will allow, assist, or participate in genocide. We certainly need to understand their criminal actions as well as the murdering done by the big killers.

We also want to develop a better insight into which people are more and less likely to play roles in harming others in the future. But as noted, efforts to understand genocide by identifying different types of people with characteristic psychologies to date have yielded only limited findings. To try to understand the actions of the "ordinary" members of society, we must move from identifying **types of people** to examining the **contexts and conditions** in which ordinary people are likely to perpetrate evil against others. In addition, we must look at the **psychological processes at the core of the human psyche** that determine our responses to these contexts and conditions.

In the chapters that follow we will discuss twelve "foundations of evil," all of which are behavioral dynamics that can be regarded as essentially "normal" and common and initially even contribute positively to human life and self-defense. The role of these dynamics, however, remains positive only up to a certain point, after which people are drawn into types of behavior that result in increasingly severe harm to others.

We will study each of these dynamics, one at a time, as a potential source of harmful and disturbing behavior in our everyday lives. It turns out that many individuals responsible for harming others often are completely unaware of how—while acting out, in their entirely legitimate self-interest, the most basic of natural desires to protect themselves from the dangers of life—they allow themselves to travel down a road of radicalization to do harm to others. Our discussion of these different dynamics will make use of examples both from everyday life and from the radicalization of these processes in specific and well-known instances of genocide.

Below is a list of dynamic processes that constitute foundations of evil. Regretfully, all are human, all are common, all are necessary for our everyday functioning as human beings, and all, without exception, are practiced by every one of us. It is important to remember that they are all also dangerous. These dynamic processes, beyond a certain point, lead people toward the potential evil that lies within them. They tend to function in conjunction with one another, mutually reinforcing each other, thereby significantly multiplying their strength.

Foundations of Evil
1. Projecting onto others and sacrificing them as scapegoats
2. The human need for power and the inherent dangers of addiction to power
3. Defense of territory and human interests by dehumanizing others
4. Doing what is expected of me, being like everyone else
5. "Going with the flow"
6. Seeing while remaining unseen
7. The lure of the "golden calf"
8. Desires for excessive power and taking pleasure in controlling others: adopting the roles of jailers-authorities who keep people in their places
9. Total commitment to a divine call of ideology

10. Sacrificing the other—the ultimate sacrifice is taking the life of another person for one's own benefit
11. "These things never happened"—denying wrongdoing to others
12. Innocence and the flawed management of mind processes

A MULTIFACTOR MODEL FOR UNDERSTANDING THE HUMAN CAPACITY TO COMMIT GENOCIDE

What are the dynamics that in conjunction with each other and under the right circumstances make human beings willing and able to commit genocide?

In all societies there are people who are brutal and bloodthirsty and who murder others for a variety of reasons. All societies have a number of immoral individuals and "psychopaths" who crave killing other individuals, and it is our obligation to identify them and prevent them from doing so. However, the psychological studies at our disposal indicate that the percentage of people who are truly cruel is relatively small in comparison to the decisive majority that takes part in committing genocide.

Indeed, most people are neither cruel nor immoral at heart. What, then, causes them to be drawn into and swept up by genocide and actually to contribute to its perpetration—to participate directly, assist in the process, or stand passively and self-interestedly by while the killing unfolds? It is not surprising that during historical events in which genocide takes place, we see heartless, evil figures playing starring roles in the horrifying spectacle. It *is* surprising—and frankly even more frightening—that most genocidal killings are carried out by rank-and-file citizens who are neither cruel nor evil in their everyday lives.

The psychological and psychosocial mechanisms that we will now explore exist naturally in human beings and can draw ordinary men and women toward their inherent potential for evil and destruction—unless they control these dynamics and stop them from overpowering them. These foundations of evil and the dynamics they produce make up the basic components of the multifactor model we propose below. For instance, when we consider the human quest for power, we keep in mind that most of us like to experience power in a variety of contexts, such as in athletic or academic competitions, romantic pursuits, and many of life's other meaningful and fun challenges. However, if we do not keep ourselves focused on the positive aspects of our goals and fail to develop controls over the nature and intensity of our competitive instincts, we may find ourselves ultimately thirsting for destructive power more than for the healthy achievement we sought. (This is an important discovery for many good people who undergo successful psychotherapy and discover that too much striving for power and correspondingly too little clean devotion to the purposes of their work color their work lives.)

According to this model, each of the dynamics can be linked with the others in a synergetic process in which each reinforces the other, resulting in even greater destructiveness.

Here is a prosaic illustration of this cumulative effect in an example of the possible combined impact of three dynamics on the lives of a married couple:

- Projection: A man is being unfaithful to his wife. Because he allows himself to do so, he actually believes that she is also being unfaithful to him. He fails to understand that in this way he is justifying his own infidelity, which in any case he excuses as "normal" for men in general but not for women.
- The Desire to and Pleasure of Controlling Others: Deep down, a man may regard his wife as his property and demand her subservience and complete loyalty. Now he has a further reason to justify the normality of his infidelity.
- Denying Wrongdoing to Others: The preceding two dynamics also may operate in conjunction with a third dynamic of denial or discounting of the wrong we have done others. The man may believe that he is doing nothing wrong and that it is his wife who is distancing herself and pushing him away when he tries to get close to her.

The overall result of the combined mechanisms will likely be a husband who suspects his wife of infidelity largely because of his own infidelity, denies the significance of his own infidelity, and is accusing of her. Each component dynamic reinforces the other. The husband's behavior will bring about an ever-growing sense of alienation and anger in the relationship. (Yes, the very same story may be seen in a wife when she is the unfaithful one, not to mention if and when both spouses are simultaneously unfaithful.)

Psychologist James Waller developed a multifactor model that focuses on the role of psychosocial processes as opposed to psychological mechanisms in the everyday lives of individuals.[1] There are no significant disagreements between my model and Waller's. The major difference is that whereas

Waller emphasizes the social processes that lead individuals to commit genocide, I stress everyday behaviors of individuals that, when reinforced and linked together by social processes, lead "ordinary" people to become mass murderers. Nonetheless, there are also many commonalities between Waller's model and the foundations of evil in the individual presented above. Most importantly for our discussion here, both models acknowledge that, under certain circumstances, normal people can become accomplices to genocide. Waller also posits that, deep down, aspects of our human nature predispose us to committing evil, although he phrases the basic default in more physiological terms as an aspect of brain wiring, and I look at it more as a psychological process or way of processing experience that nature has set in us: "The possibility for genocide is hard-wired into the human brain. In other words, some of the fundamental characteristics of the human brain that have developed to help us survive both as individuals and as groups can give rise, under certain conditions, to extraordinary evil—that is, genocide and mass murder."[2] At the same time, Waller emphasizes that the above potential turns into a reality particularly under certain structural conditions—and I am in full agreement. Thus he writes, "Social processes can bring to a head that simple ordinary people turn into mass killers."[3] Waller also concludes that it is both individuals and societies that can become accustomed to accepting and commissioning evil acts.

THE FOUNDATIONS OF EVIL: HEALTHY, BENEFICIAL DYNAMICS THAT SPIN OUT OF CONTROL

The chapters that follow present fundamental aspects of the human personality that may be considered "healthy," owing both to their widespread natural occurrence and to the beneficial roles they typically play in our everyday lives. Preventing significant use of these psychological mechanisms would end up depriving us of important contributions to the psychological immune system we need to endure the pressures of life. It would also deprive us of many experiences that provide us with a sense of self-confidence, competence, meaning, and motivation.

In chapter 3 we will consider our ability to evade responsibility, our desire and need to exercise power over others, and our tendency to characterize others as inferior to us. Because of the social stigma with which they are associated, we find it difficult to view these elements of evil as dynamics that are also instinctive and beneficial. Yet, as we will see, to a certain extent, in their essence people's needs for power are "normal" (that is to say, common and natural), beneficial, and, in some cases, critical for human functioning and survival.

Thus, the act of projecting responsibility onto someone else is beneficial to a certain degree and in some situations unavoidable. It is a natural human response to unload some of our burdens. Honest people, however, take measures to balance out this tendency and to take responsibility when they are truly responsible.

Things are even clearer when it comes to the exercise of power. Without a doubt the desire for power is natural, as we must all attain a considerable amount of it to contend with the many challenges and misfortunes with which life presents us. Indeed, insufficient power often causes people to fail in different realms of life—including both love and work. Problems arise, however, when people possess an excessive affinity for power. Individuals in such situations attempt to acquire too much power and become intoxicated by it. It is abundantly clear that excessive power and its side-effects—self-importance and arrogance, as well as domination, humiliation, tyranny, and persecution of others—contribute heavily to evil and suffering in the world.

Next, we discuss the manner in which people attempt to defend what they perceive as their territory and their interests by dehumanizing others. Again, although it would appear that this dynamic is immoral and a source of evil, the role it plays *before* taking on its problematic dimension is actually natural and necessary. Humans instinctively attempt to recognize those to whom they are similar and with whom they might enjoy close relationships and to distinguish them from strangers who may in fact turn out to be dangerous enemies—just as a foreign substance introduced to the human body is identified and stimulates a hostile response on the part of the immune system. Such responses are our body's means of defending itself, both positively, as when our bodies fight off a dangerous foreign body, and negatively, as when our bodies mistakenly identify and attack a healthy part of itself, resulting in auto-immune disorders which we know can be quite serious. On a collective level, all social groups must be able to identify and fight off potential real enemies. From this perspective, the identification of others as suspicious foreigners, as opposed to "one of ours," is often rational and necessary. However, when this dynamic takes the form of discriminatory prejudice against other national or ethnic groups and brands others as fundamentally inferior or subhuman, it ceases to be self-defense and enters the realm of racism and discrimination.

In chapter 4, we meet people who behave like everyone else and attempt to act as others expect them to act—in accordance with the cultural norms of the society in which they live. Such people are naturally willing to be part of a majority that follow rules with exemplary obedience. We also meet people who try to avoid getting into trouble of any kind by seeing what is going on around them but keeping to themselves, as if invisible. In contexts of genocide, such individuals typically function as accomplices or bystanders. However, under certain conditions they are also capable of becoming direct participants in the action going on around them, for when participation is exciting and intoxicating for "everyone," even the shy and the reserved may be enticed to join the group dancing around the "golden calf" of mass action. After all, such individuals are busier "getting along" than they are committed to moral positions that oppose the suffering of others.

Nonetheless, the tendency to act according to the expectations of others and to emulate the majority is not without its benefits for the individual and for society. It is generally positive for people to participate in public endeavors, to accept authority, and to do what is asked of them. Without social consensus, reasonable levels of acceptance of authority, and agreed-upon frameworks for participation in public processes, all societies would collapse. However, when conforming to the majority negates our ability to think independently, express contradictory opinions, and make our own authentic decisions regarding what is acceptable and unacceptable behavior, we become robots at the service of any fascist goal set forth by the leadership. Clearly, those individuals who are interested first and foremost in ensuring that they do not stand out for not doing what is expected of them and/or want to do whatever others are doing will emerge as followers of the orgiastic cults of the collective. They are the people who are likely to be blind and enthusiastic participants in serious acts of destruction and evil, if their society goes on to perpetrate those. And so many societies have done just that.

Chapter 5 addresses dynamics characterized by more explicit "SS-style measures," that is, when people openly set themselves up as "masters" and use their status to control others. Again we note that such roles too are widespread throughout societies and are not inherently wrongful. Examples of such leadership positions abound in perfectly normal life and include department heads in universities, clinics, and hospitals; managers in high-tech companies; CEOs; chief engineers of spacecraft launches; rabbis, priests, and other religious leaders; schoolteachers; and also parents—in their basic role as leaders and educators of their own children. Many people who fill positions of authority have no intention of acting as arrogant "masters" and strictly ruling those under their power. However, the opportunity to exercise authority over others all too often may fuel a desire for more power and a tendency toward bossiness and even tyranny. A widespread example of this dynamic is seen in parents who tyrannize their children, causing enormous harm within families. Obviously people occupying more public positions can do immense damage.

Social psychologist Philip Zimbardo's well-known prison simulation study sheds a great deal of light on the dynamic of excessive use of force. That is not to say that anyone who receives a leadership position of authority has a lust for power and an intention to use it inappropriately. In many cases the opposite is true. Many people rising to significant leadership posts commit themselves to bettering the lives of others and succeed in their efforts. Obviously we are very much in need of real leaders in various realms of life, and a chronic shortage of leadership would result in significant damage. We have already noted the problematic behavior of mothers and fathers who tyrannize their children, but another phenomenon that is actually more widespread in Western society in our time is an absence of sufficient parental guidance. The lack of authority within families is the source of innumerable psychological and psychiatric problems for children and a cause of the breakdown of the family unit as a whole. Willingness to lead is a good thing. The true test, however, is the manner in which a leadership position is filled. Here is yet another example of a psychological dynamic that is beneficial and desirable at its core but has the potential to destroy when used improperly and taken to excess.

Dedication to ideology is also a natural dynamic. People search for ideals, guidance, and fulfillment of their core beliefs and values. Without ideology, we are weak; our lives are empty. Without guiding ideas and purposes, we find ourselves drifting through life with no real meaning, like a boat without a motor on a stormy sea. People like to espouse their collective identities with fervor, and this often proves beneficial to individuals and society alike. Examples include the thunderous cheering of fans at a sporting event, enthusiastic membership in a political movement, or dedication to a national pioneering project. In all these cases, the collective goal and experience intensify the participants' sense of power. Unfortunately, the same mechanism of zeal stemming from collective participation also functions just as easily when the aims are persecution and extermination, inquisition, celebration of the guillotine, or sending thousands of victims off to concentration camps.

Again I stress that many people have no intention of doing harm to others and, given the opportunity, would decisively refuse to join a movement or adopt a belief system that lists the destruction of human lives as an aim. However, many are enticed into joining movements or belief systems that are ostensibly based on an explicit endorsement of "positive" principles such as freedom, equality, and democracy and fail to take notice of the emergence of other more destructive, murderous plans and goals of the movement they join.

The most troubling aspect of human nature is that after joining such a movement, and after genocide emerges as the movement's main activity—as in the barbaric turn of events under Hitler or the atrocities committed under Stalin, whose guiding communist ideology settled on the "transfer" and extermination of large numbers of minorities in the former Soviet Union—many "believers" are no longer able to see the truth and to refuse to participate in the destruction being undertaken in their name. Many are also frightened of ceasing to take part in the killing because that is what their society and its leaders are dictating. Totalitarian societies and immoral organizations typically do not look favorably upon those who choose to leave their ranks.

We go on to study a powerful mechanism we call "sacrificing." The concept of sacrifice is familiar from the ritual sacrifices once practiced by the Jewish people and also by others, any number of whom did not limit themselves to the sacrifice of animals. This phenomenon gives us a penetrating understanding of genocidal activity, as if one person is telling another, "You will die by my hand. I will sacrifice you, for your sacrifice will protect me from the fate of death."

Of course, most of us view this approach as immoral. Nonetheless, here too we find a natural basis for the phenomenon, and without much effort, most of us can understand the logic of the following line of reason: If I can truly save myself by having someone else harmed in my stead, perhaps I will do so. In this way, the sacrifice of others also has its roots in human nature. If people could really save themselves from death and remain alive by sacrificing others, who knows how many would be willing to do so. Of course, for the rational mind it is crystal clear that we cannot evade our own death by having others die in our stead. And our moral selves know, instinctively, that to do so would be wrong. However, our "primitive mind," which plays a major role in deciding far too many issues in our lives, finds the magical metaphor of sacrifice—someone else dying in our place—quite enticing.

In chapter 6, we return to false claims of doing no wrong and, often enough, blatant denials that any wrongdoing has been done. The claim that an action or event never took place is rooted in the universal mechanism of humans trying to deny their own certain future deaths. Just as some anesthesia medications wipe out past, recent, or current memory, we all appear to have a considerable "loss" of the knowledge that we are going to die at some point. Obviously we are all basically aware of this fact, but we tend not to appreciate its reality and great significance during most of our lives and in most of our experiences. We typically say that it is "unpleasant" to know that we are fated to die. It is much simpler to ignore the truth. It is similarly also quite "unpleasant" for us to know and acknowledge when we have caused serious trouble in the lives of other people or that we have gone so far as to take their lives. It is much simpler to deny.

Chapter 6 continues with a discussion of other dynamics of behaviors that are not at all motivated by malevolent intentions and occur completely naturally in people but can lead them to do harm to themselves and to others. In such situations people often regret their actions, but by then it is usually too late. We look at how horrible acts can result unexpectedly and even unbeknownst to those involved because our natural behavioral mechanisms, without any aim to do harm, include going to extremes, and such radicalization can lead us to destructive actions we did not plan on or intend. Thus a driver who enjoys driving fast and is curious to know how it would feel to drive even faster goes to such an extreme that he loses control of the vehicle and causes an accident.

The model presented here can be thought of as a model of energy. Many activities typically require significant amounts of energy, but after a certain quantitative threshold is reached, a destructive force can erupt. This is why food becomes scorched, why spacecraft explode, and why some people suffer heart attacks or strokes.

We explore five enticing dynamics that, if experienced without sufficient caution and limitations, can end in adversity or disaster. They include "going all the way"; completing a gestalt; testing boundaries; indulging in the pleasures of risk-taking; and finally, and particularly lethally, pursuing an attraction to going to the brink of destruction and to our eventual fate, where "all is folly" reigns—hurray for nihilism and nothingness.

I must emphasize that none of this discussion is intended to justify the damage and destruction that we humans cause unintentionally while being swept up in these natural processes. Nor is it intended to offer understanding and sympathy to those who make critical mistakes that result in the destruction of human life, even though there are cases where the damage develops as a true tragedy. As human beings we have a responsibility to exercise extreme caution in our actions, particularly when there are signs that human life may weigh in the balance. Our duty to preserve human life requires us to consider the possible outcomes of our actions in advance and to refrain from dubious actions until we are certain that we can keep their destructive effects in check. Common sense tells us that too much of anything can lead to overload, outbursts, and collisions and that we must remain in control of our urges and experiences.

This book is committed to the concept that there can be no justification for the destruction of life with the exception of truly justified self-defense. Working to preserve life imbues us with a wonderful sense of decency and meaning. Human beings are charged with the sacred work of building and preserving life. Those who really do nurture and safeguard life are awestruck by the very miracle of life. Albert Camus captured this sentiment in an essay published shortly after World War II:

> The years we have just gone through have killed something in us. And that something is simply the old confidence man had in himself, which led him to believe that he could always elicit human reactions from another man if he spoke to him in the language of a common humanity. We have seen men lie, degrade, kill, deport, torture—and each time it was not possible to persuade them not to do these things because they were sure of themselves.
>
> Before anything can be done, two questions must be put: "Do you, or do you not, directly or indirectly, want to be killed or assaulted? Do you or do you not, directly or indirectly, want to kill or assault?"
>
> For my part, I am fairly sure that I have made the choice. And, having chosen, I think that I must speak out, that I must state that I will never again be one of those, whoever they be, who compromise with murder.[4]

I THINK IT IS HUMAN / PETRAS ZELIONKA

The single biggest insight I got was the interview with the killer Petras Ze-lionka, who was involved in the killings in the *Einsatzgruppen*, when we questioned him about his motivation. One thing puzzled me from the first: How is it possible to shoot young children, how is that possible? We pushed and pushed, and eventually he said: "It's a kind of curiosity." I thought a lot about that in terms of young men killing, and I think that the motivation for some of the footage of the executions was this kind of curiosity. It's like a kind of pornography. I think that particularly men, especially at that age, are very much sensation-seekers, they are looking for different types of sensation.

What is terrifying is that I do not think this is a uniquely German thing, I think it is human; I think we are social animals and people adapt to the group they are in and to that group's norms.

In Germany, if you were not in one of the high risk groups—if you were not a socialist, if you were not a Jew, if you were not gay—you were relatively safe. The Nazis targeted only those specific groups, and the terrifying thing about human nature is that most people—if they are not in those groups— just turn the other way.

This story tells us of the deep dark side of what it is to be human. You can't explain this historical episode as just a load of madmen hypnotizing a nation. There is something in this story that tells us about the dangers of throwing away democracy, the power of the group and victimization.

Today I believe that it is possible for this to happen again at any minute. That is why I called the series "a warning from history."[5]

CRUELTY / L'ESTRANGE[6]

There are a sort of Men that take delight in the Spilling of Human Blood; and in the Death of those that never did them an injury, men who we cannot so properly call Angry as Brutal.

CRUELTY / HANS TOCH[7]

Pure forms of cruelty may remotely originate in resented injury, but can with frequent custom become functionally autonomous.

EVIL / PRIMO LEVI

Evil is contagious. [T]he inhuman being robs others of all human feeling. Evil procreates itself. . . . It multiplies, corrupts the conscience of others and surrounds itself with collaborators who abandon their camp because of fear or because of some form of temptation.[8]

3

Exaggerated Self-Defense, Exaggerated Power, and Dehumanization

PROJECTING RESPONSIBILITY ONTO OTHERS

FOUNDATIONS OF EVIL 1

PROJECTING ONTO OTHERS AND SACRIFICING THEM AS SCAPEGOATS

Projection is a universal human defense mechanism.

- Projecting responsibility onto others
- Manifestations of projection in everyday life

Projection is a universal defense mechanism. The Jews are the enemies of the entire human race, and we need to destroy them entirely—this was the claim of Nazis and, before them, of anti-Semites in Europe through many centuries.

Projection is a gross attribution—strange and ultimately irrational—that attributes to others the responsibility for some problem, threat, or disaster in life. "I didn't do it," "I didn't cause the problem," and "It's not my problem" are replaced with "They did it to me."

The maneuver is a familiar one to all of us from childhood. Children rush to protect themselves by projecting responsibility and blame onto others. This is also the basis for the biblical concept of the "scapegoat," which uses an animal sacrifice in order to atone for human sins. Concretely, there are many people who are concerned with animal rights who decry such practices, but an even larger concern is in order when responsibility is projected onto other human beings. Such projection results not only in the defamation and persecution of the individual but also potentially in the persecution of an entire group to which the individual belongs.

Individuals and groups must remain vigilant against the human tendency to project onto others. As noted earlier, Rudolph J. Rummel has shown that democracies usually succeed in thwarting mass extermination. They do so by maintaining "watchdog" institutions such as a legal system in which human life is relatively valued and protected, distributing government powers and maintaining checks and balances, heeding public opinion, respecting freedom of the press, and more.[1] Democratic institutions discourage the projection of responsibility onto others by debunking false accusations against blameless parties.

MANIFESTATIONS OF PROJECTION IN EVERYDAY LIFE

Manifestations of projection, such as behavior that ridicules, humiliates, and domineers, are common in our daily lives. Thus, in academia, as in all professions, we find a substantial number of people who are typically condescending and intoxicated by their own sense of self-importance and the power they wield. Other common examples in everyday life include

- Physicians who instill terror in patients and their families in the way they respond to questions about illnesses and proposed treatments
- Aggressive lawyers and many judges who, from the safety of the raised dais, do not hesitate to insult and humiliate people in the courtroom with scathing remarks
- Clerks and inspectors of city municipalities, customs agencies, tax authorities, and police departments who push others around and bully the people who are dependent on them

The above examples are intended not as a sweeping criticism of any profession but rather as a mirror in which to view some of the nasty behaviors that crop up in our lives in many situations. We all stand to benefit from a better understanding of the ways in which we project onto others in different contexts in our lives.

Another example of the widespread manifestation of projection in our everyday lives will be found in relationships with one's neighbors. There are, of course, many relationships between neighbors that are positive, but it is no secret that many neighbor relationships suffer from undue hostility, shouting, threats, and acts of revenge. Many neighbors walk by one another for years without even saying hello. Such patterns of rotten neighborly relationships are more common in some cultures than others, but there is no doubt that the relations of many people around the world with their neighbors are unduly hostile, and the tension runs quite high. Obviously at the root of such "unneighborly relations" lies the eternal mechanism of scapegoating, now with the role of the goat (which may have been well-suited for the role during the biblical period) being played by the neighbors.

Sometimes the scapegoat role is even assigned to the neighbors' children, as projected hatred has the tendency to be collective and may therefore be applied to all members of the family.

The following incident took place outside a lovely home in a good neighborhood in Jerusalem. A group of ten-year-old children were playing together in the yard of an apartment building when their ball bounced over a fence into one neighbor's garden. The children politely rang the neighbor's doorbell, only to have the man of the house open the door and berate them: "Get out of here! I'm not giving you your ball back, you brats." And then, directly addressing the son of his detested upstairs neighbors, he added with even greater intensity, "You're truly disturbed!" Actually, the boy was a wonderful child onto whom the neighbor had clearly projected his hatred of the parents.[2] The truly "disturbed" person in the story was the adult neighbor who projected his feelings with great intensity onto a group of innocent children.

Typically strangers in a community are subject to a long list of projections—some harmless and others quite serious—but first we should consider our relationships with our own family members and loved ones. Thus it is common sense that we should not harm our children by calling them derogatory names. Humiliating characterizations and nicknames obviously can cause children severe emotional hardship and may make it very difficult for them to reach their real potential in their future. Nonetheless, we often hear parents refer to their children angrily as "bad," "stupid," "insufferable," "idiot," or "jerk"—and much more. We also hear parents making threats and derogatory predictions, such as, "I'll leave you," "No one will want you," "You'll end up being crazy," "You'll be fat for the rest of your life," and "You'll be a failure in everything you do."

Danish physician Evelin Lindner, who studies the impact of humiliation in our lives, describes it as "the nuclear bomb of the emotions." Although the human tendency to humiliate is natural, she maintains people can train themselves to respect others and to refrain from humiliating them.[3] According to Barbara Coloroso, mockery and humiliating aggression stimulate and increase people's tendencies to harass and murder those who are perceived as the source of injury.[4]

From a psychological perspective, when we take an in-depth look at the subconscious emotional life of parents, we discover a troubling degree of jealousy, competition, and hostility in the heart of **every** parent toward **every** child. Some of this hostility is undoubtedly a response to aggravating characteristics and actions of the children themselves. However, psychological insight teaches us that parents naturally also hold extremely negative feelings toward their children that simply are not justified. Psychologists interested in the depths of the inner psyche regard such feelings as a natural part of human psychology, similar perhaps to our immune system's reaction to foreign bodies. In this case, on the most basic level, notwithstanding even truly great love for one's children, the parent also perceives the child as a foreign body with which he or she is in existential competition. On an unconscious level a competitive battle for survival of the fittest takes place between all living creatures—even with genuinely loved ones. For this reason, somewhere deep down, parents also have parts of themselves that somewhat want the worst for their children (but oh, it's a big secret).

British psychiatrist Donald Winnicott, a pediatrician who subsequently entered the fields of psychiatry and psychoanalysis, is considered to have been a very friendly and nice man, as well as an outstanding expert in his field. Winnicott established that *all* mothers must necessarily possess feelings of anger and hatred toward their children because every living being constitutes a burden and poses an existential threat to every other living being with whom it is connected in life.[5]

British psychologist Melanie Klein has shown that children must develop an experience of hostility toward their mothers as a "bad mother," in contrast to the "good mother," who also occupies a warm place in their heart. Such feelings enable children to separate from their mothers and to prepare themselves for the realities of life in which they must be able to distinguish between good and bad and contend with a multiplicity of situations. Woe unto those who are overly naive, do not know how to experience anger, and are always happy and satisfied because they have no conception of how to defend themselves against those who will really try to harm them in the course of their lives.[6]

Of course, deep down, most parents love and feel close to their children. In most parents, love is the dominant emotion. Nonetheless, a healthy parent feels *both* positive and negative feelings toward his or her children but can accommodate or contain the negative feelings and keep them to a minimum. Children, for the most part, also love their parents, but here too a fuller and more accurate account accommodates both types of feelings. In other words, at times children feel anger at, and even hatred for, even the most beloved parents.

Unfortunately, some parents' negative feelings in fact dominate their emotional lives, which results in the evolution of an openly hostile relationship between parent and child. However, this is not the norm. In most cases parents' negative feelings toward their children remain subconscious and are expressed symbolically and metaphorically—thus surfacing periodically in dreams and also manifesting in a variety of other subconscious feelings, as well as in some conscious experiences of dislike of and anger at a child. The psychological apparatus of the human subconscious, in both parents and children, is like a properly functioning optical reader. It is able to read messages correctly, quickly, and accurately, and healthy personalities are able to process and accommodate combinations of experiences of love and hate.

The very positive aspect of this complex structure is that children who develop an ability to withstand parental pressures and hostilities can subsequently develop into more distinct individuals and assume an increasingly independent identity. Children who are unable to do this often remain overly attached to their parents. If the processing of both positive and negative feelings proceeds with love and sensitivity, the negative feelings do not take over the relationship, and the possible negative impact is contained. It is healthy for children and parents to develop mixed feelings toward one another (including anger and rejection). This enables them to separate from one another and to live out their lives in the face of the various dangers and separations each will encounter.

Indeed, sooner or later children undergoing healthy development must acquire an ability to honestly criticize their parents. Healthy children must be able to identify their parents' true flaws, get angry, understand, and also forgive a great deal. Ultimately it is best that children are able to show their mothers and fathers love and gratitude for their upbringing and develop the capacity to care for their parents loyally and sympathetically later in life. The overall process is an integral part of becoming good and healthy people.

Not all psychologists agree with the above perspective. Many today prefer a behavioral psychology which refrains (sometimes with ideological adamancy) from digging under the outer shell to see inner feelings. Nonetheless, numerous psychological therapists—including Donald Winnicott—accept the process described above. As we have seen, Winnicott taught us that healthy people are capable of accommodating feelings of love and hate simultaneously. Intriguingly, he also taught that thorough, deeper psychological therapy requires a corrective experience that addresses therapists' own angers and hatred of their patients—alongside their love for and sincere desire to help them. Similarly, the patient is encouraged and freed to experience and express anger and hatred as well as love for the therapist.

The film *The King's Speech* offers a compelling portrayal of such a mutual expression of anger between the king of England and his speech therapist. Ultimately, the characters prove capable of accommodating both positive and negative feelings for one another, resulting in a sense of mutual trust and a closer relationship—and facilitating considerable healing. The patient comes to understand his contradictory feelings of affection and anger toward his therapist and to realize that he himself can be the object of criticism and anger as well as love. According to Winnicott, such corrective experiences in therapy teach patients how to accommodate contradictory feelings toward the people with whom they are close—to both love and be angry at them.[7]

The exploration of parent-child relationships also enables us to learn something about the everyday "battlefields" and "cemeteries" of marriage.[8] As we know, most marriages today end in failure.[9] A primary reason for this depressing state of affairs is the fact that, on a psychological level, spouses have a natural need to project their shortcomings onto one another. In this way, married life can be thought of as a union of the basic projections of each spouse, creating a situation requiring "treatment" of each spouse by the other to enable each of them to grow. In practice, however, this often does not happen. Many couples do not find a way to "treat" their projections and tap the energy of their clashes to free greater growth. (Many couples try quite sincerely but do not figure out how to "manage," or pace and unfold, the natural "therapy" they are trying to generate in their relationship).

Of course, some reactions to the tensions and conflicts of married life very much stem from objective anger, which is typically easier for couples to contend with through reasonable negotiation. The critical problem tends to be couples' inability to overcome primitive urges to project onto one another. Many married people lose control of their anger toward their spouse, although they may hear a muffled internal voice warning them that they are being unreasonable, but so many of us are incapable of stopping the outpouring. Metaphorically, all too many marriages are plagued by their own small-scale blood libels.[10] The reassuring feeling of having someone to blame other than ourselves intensifies and, for a time, prevents us from seeing our own true weaknesses. Instead of being honest with ourselves and with each other by acknowledging our negative actions, we attack our spouse.

Ultimately this book aims to help readers understand the psychology of out-and-out genocide, but I also want to reveal the very "building blocks" of genocidal hate and destructiveness in our common daily lives. Such understanding can advance our understanding of fearful genocide, even as it can also contribute to much saner conduct in our everyday personal lives.

We have surveyed a number of human behaviors and reviewed a number of cultural patterns at play in our everyday lives, including humiliating and disrespectful treatment by some professionals and service providers, hostile relations between neighbors, and unhealthy parent-child relationships and marriages. Similarly, this discussion can be expanded into many other realms, such as behavior while driving, shameful and violent conduct on the part of sports fans, and the aggression displayed by some travelers around the world. In all cases we are learning how projection plays a large role in preventing us from achieving the tranquility we so desperately yearn for and, at its magnified worst, results in the deaths of other human beings.

Conclusion 1

People who wish to avoid harming others must learn to identify their own personal style of projection. Do we condescend, accuse, attack, ridicule, or humiliate others? These hurtful behaviors, which we use to frame someone else as a scapegoat, are all manifestations of our own weaknesses and our deepest anxieties.

■ See Independent Study 2 ■

THE ADVANTAGES AND DISADVANTAGES OF POWER: FOR GOOD AND BAD

FOUNDATIONS OF EVIL 2

THE HUMAN NEED FOR POWER AND THE DANGERS INHERENT IN ADDICTION TO POWER

Syndromes of aggression, arrogance, humiliation, tyranny, and the persecution of others.

- ■ Striving for excessive power
- ■ The justification of power
- ■ The intoxication of power
- ■ Changes in personal character and the moral self resulting from positions of power

HEALTHY POWER

People need high degrees of positive, healthy power in a variety of forms to enable them to function, be productive, cope with and meet challenges, and succeed in life's many tests, such as overcoming illnesses, facing one's real enemies, and "going for the gold" in the many different competitions we face in our everyday lives.

A person devoid of power is just that—powerless. It is no coincidence that in serious mental illnesses we often find a high incidence of passivity, weakness, excessive dependence, and an inability to exercise appropriate personal power for coping with life. We also find a high correlation between passivity and sexual disorders and an inability to love. To put it simply, passive people end up losing in love, in the workplace, and in life in general.

Still, we must also remember that some passive individuals regard themselves as quite strong and may even make an outward appearance of being powerful, when internally they are not. We can only truly assess a healthy level of power versus inner passivity by looking honestly at one's true self-confidence and at one's ability to contend courageously and effectively with difficulties in life.

Healthy power imbues its possessors with a sense of energy. It enables us to look others squarely in the eye, speak in a strong voice, and function under pressure. It also gives us a sense of humor. It is completely different from the human quest for power aimed at contending with our own personal fears by exploiting others and controlling their behavior.

STRIVING FOR EXCESSIVE POWER

Quite different from the self-respect that healthy power gives its owner is the other side of the coin: that is, the disorder and destruction of human lives caused by the exercise of excessive power. Excessive power finds expression in domination, perpetration of injustices, destructiveness in interpersonal struggles such as in severe rivalries between competitors, violence within families, endless battles between different national and religious groups, and, of course, the mass murder of hundreds of millions of people by perpetrators of genocide.

An intriguing and somewhat tragic paradox lies in the fact that as a result of their sensitivity to the dangers inherent in the unhealthy use of power, some people take the "high road" of excessively "good" behavior to avoid all confrontation, and they ultimately end up overly passive and weak. Several mental health clinicians have noted that a high percentage of schizophrenics are thoughtful, gentle people who initially had no desire to cause harm to anyone. At some point in their lives, however, they became filled with pent-up anger and hostility (as we all occasionally experience) and seemingly chose to become crazy rather than risk becoming violent. To avoid giving in to their internal destructive thoughts and feelings, out of their fears that they might end up actually doing something destructively violent, these gentle, sensitive individuals opted to take their leave of the world of the "sane" in order to avoid giving in to their internal destructive thoughts and feelings.[11]

Between 1966 and 1970, I directed an interdisciplinary research group on the psychology of aggression and nonviolence. Within this framework we enjoyed a memorable presentation by Robert Clark, a psychiatrist from the Quaker community, a peace-loving Christian group that emphasizes the importance of living at peace with oneself and with others. At the time, Dr. Clark was in charge of the acute psychiatric ward at Friends Hospital in Philadelphia.

Quakerism rejects anger and hatred and requires people to act in moderation and with restraint. In his lecture, Clark described a typical Quaker patient arriving at the hospital in a state of psychological breakdown resulting from a buildup of anger toward a particular person that he could not express due to this prohibition. After the anger exceeded a certain threshold and the patient began to fear that the floodgates would open and that he was on the verge of losing control and possibly becoming violent, he broke down. In effect he preferred to break down into mental illness, Clark explained, than to commit an act of violence. Although in most cases there really is no danger of real violence, people who are incapable of distinguishing between violent *emotions* and violent *actions* are liable to fear that their feelings will automatically be translated into actions—or that feelings and actions are equivalent from the start.[12]

A key principle in psychology is that violent thoughts and desires are neither identical to nor as significant as violent actions. Psychologically and morally we can allow ourselves to be angry on the inside, and to a certain extent we can allow ourselves to express our anger toward others verbally in an appropriate manner. However, we may not strike, injure, or harass others in actual physical violence. Although this is a principle that can be learned, many fail to do so. The Quakers are one case in point. For Dr. Clark's patients, the experience of internal anger was insufficient and did not provide the necessary release, and they worried they might lose control of their actions. These religious men and women believed they were about to cross the line into prohibited territory and therefore developed a mental illness to forestall violent outbursts.

Managing the power within us is no simple task for any of us, even when unrelated to the possibility of violent outbursts. Too many people are on an unhealthy quest for excessive power in order to rise above and dominate others. Such people are what we refer to in simple everyday language as "aggressive." The quest for excessive power is characterized by an emphasis on achieving a position of power and control over others and differs from the use of power for the actualization and achievement of desirable aims. We all see excessive aggression manifested in many areas of our lives, and each example emits foul odors of self-interest, lack of consideration for others, and readiness to exploit others for personal gain.

Aggressive people give off an air of arrogance and conceit. They make visible efforts to exert control over their surroundings and over others. They are the masters, supervisors, teachers, and doctors who exercise their control in excessive displays of power that humiliate and weaken others. Such control seekers often accompany their displays of power with abusive and degrading expressions of verbal insult.

Within the family context, it is not difficult for an adult or child to recognize excessive aggression on the part of a spouse or parent. Today, there are also many cases of aggressive children who usurp control from their parents and intimidate them. In modern-day Western families, in many instances the excessive control once exercised by husbands and fathers has been transferred into the hands of wives and mothers. Today women often are the pillars of their families and hold much of the true power, while the role of the father often has taken on secondary importance. Among other indications, see the fact that most divorces today are initiated by women; not that long ago in the Western world, the opposite was true. Both styles have one thing in common: a lack of power on the part of one of the spouses and the absence of fundamental equality between the two. And just as men for years refused to acknowledge their abuse of women, many women today do not acknowledge their control over their husbands.

Some aggressive individuals are able to conceal their aggressiveness by not externalizing it and instead make themselves appear gentle and friendly. Behind closed doors, however, they are really tyrants who do not hesitate to control and diminish others. This explains why some spouses and parents appear to be pleasant people but actually convey to their spouse or children the emotional message that they dare not try to attain anything approaching their status, success, or power. For example, one man was praised for his loyalty and attentiveness to his wife during years in which she had grown weak and fallen into a deep depression. The truth of the matter, however, was that he welcomed her weakness because it made him stronger in comparison. Deep down, the woman and her children knew that the father was actually inflating his sense of self as the all-powerful savior of his helpless wife.

In our professional lives, aggressive and devious people often rise through the ranks to positions of obvious prominence, as no one questions their apparent powerfulness. However, when called upon to confirm the authority and promotion of others, such aggressive leaders are liable to seek to undermine them, humiliate them, and prevent their promotion—unless they are certain that the person in question will enhance their own power. For example, a well-known professor promised a younger colleague his complete support for promotion to the rank of professor. However, when the time came, behind the closed doors of the committee discussing the younger candidate's promotion, the older professor rejected his colleague's candidacy summarily. In subsequent interactions, he continued the charade and unequivocally assured his younger colleague that he had supported him at every step of the way. Only after the young lecturer's application for professor status was rejected did he learn who was actually responsible (although such proceedings are supposed to remain confidential, it is almost always possible to discover the identity of the person who prevented a promotion).

As noted, in most cases aggressive people are usually relatively transparent and display clear manifestations of their superiority, superciliousness, arrogance, domination, humiliation, and tyranny.[13]

- A sense of superiority entails seeing oneself as "more equal" than others. People with such a sense think they know all there is to know about everything and regard themselves as more important than they actually are.

- Supercilious displays of power refer to the manner in which people with a bloated sense of superiority order others to serve them in a demeaning and demanding manner. An example of someone exhibiting this quality is the biblical Joseph, who placed himself above his brothers and earned their disdain and retaliation.

- Domination entails an assertion of authority and a desire to make decisions for others. Domineering people believe they know "everything," including what everyone else "needs" to do and how everything "must" be done. They achieve domination not through a positive leadership that accommodates and strengthens others but through a drive to be the sole decider and recognized ruler.

- The drive to humiliate reflects aggression transformed into a desire and need to ridicule and belittle others. By definition, a sense of superiority, supercilious displays of power, and domination relegate others to a position of ridicule and embarrassment in themselves. Now, however, we are speaking of humiliation as an ever more directly intended goal. A notable number of unhappy marriages are hotbeds of such humiliation of one spouse by the other. In some institutions, societies, and cultures, humiliation plays a very prevalent role in everyday aspects of life and in the structuring of organizations.

- Tyranny involves a power to rule others crudely, with no cover-up. In a medical department or institution, the instructions of tyrants must be followed; in the army, their orders (even those that are manifestly unlawful) are supreme (even though obeying orders in a military context is necessary, this is true only up to a certain point); in the business world, they determine final policy; in couples and families, they "wear the pants" and go about deciding things in ways that display and expand their undisputed superiority. Although decisions by more enlightened tyrants may be rendered relatively graciously, nonetheless they are made with an undisputed authority that is sensed by all involved.

As a rule aggressive people seek to amass more and more resources that make them stronger and enable them to control others. In fact, control of others will become their most important goal, although their power seeking may also manifest itself in other more "acceptable" ambitions, such as financial or professional success, attainment of social influence or status, physical strength, and a host of other seemingly legitimate purposes. Some individuals engaged in the aggressive quest for power are unaware that they are doing harm to anyone. Others, in contrast, actually seek to do harm in order to display their supremacy more effectively and in some cases to express an element of sadism in their character. In both situations, they trample others.

For aggressive people, the end justifies the means, and it is of no consequence to them if they achieve their goals at others' expense.

THE JUSTIFICATION OF POWER

Those who adopt an aggressive mode of behavior will almost always find some way to justify their conduct. Their supreme status is conferred by one god or another, or by the people who naturally and affectionately select them in "elections" in which there are no other candidates, or by authorized institutions that recognize their exceptional abilities. In their own eyes, they are worthy, chosen, and undoubtedly deserving of the power they wield.

In many instances aggressive leaders issue orders solely to prove their control over others. According to legend, Napoleon ordered a regiment of soldiers to march over a cliff to their deaths merely to prove his power. Tyrants exercise their power without reservation, and they themselves have no doubts and certainly do not invite contradictory opinions. As a doctoral student in clinical psychology during the era of lobotomies (a surgical procedure involving removal of part of the brain's frontal lobe, common for a period in the twentieth century), I witnessed a professor of psychiatry deciding which patients would undergo the procedure without having conducted any meaningful investigation or discussion with the staff members who were officially responsible for making the decision (a dynamic very effectively depicted in the film *One Flew over the Cuckoo's Nest*).[14] Even if staff members harbored doubts or objections, they did not dare to raise them. I have taken part in many meetings within the mental health systems, in Israel and the United States, in which everything was decided by a professor or director, while other staff members sat silently—concerned primarily with their own professional security. In an institution run on an authoritarian basis, contradictory ideas— even those based on information already published in the medical literature— are neither raised nor discussed, and staff members' genuine inner objections to decisions regarding specific patients go unmentioned.

As we have seen, an accepted premise in power systems is that those who have achieved power must be worthy of being leaders—as if power in and of itself justifies leadership. This is an important underpinning of order in society, as the threat of social disorder indeed demands that there be a leader. The status of "leader" tends to justify any and all actions. This in turn provides people with a sense of security that issues are being managed properly and effectively. More power to the leader who imposes order!

In a well-known study on the authoritarian personality, Theodor Adorno and colleagues explained the relationship between the veneration of power and the conception that because we all live in dangerous surroundings, someone must always be subjugated for us to feel safer.[15] The power hungry make a clear distinction between those who are "one of us" and those who are not. From their perspective, the aim of power is to put those who are "not us" in their place so they cannot threaten our strength.

Example from Everyday Life

A physician refuses to inform a patient about his condition and maintains that the patient would not be able to understand the explanation, even if it were given. As far as the physician is concerned, he or she is the expert with the knowledge and is responsible for making all the decisions. (In several cultures this style, which used to be very common, has been reduced in recent years, but it still lurks and appears often enough.)

Example from the Holocaust and Other Cases of Genocide

The Nazis justified the extermination of the Jews as a contribution to German culture and to humanity as a whole based on the claim that the human race would be "healthier" without the "evil" and "malignancy" of the Jewish people.

THE INTOXICATING NATURE OF POWER

The perception that one has the power to control and harass others in an arbitrary manner and impose on them unnecessary demands is intoxicating and addictive. For those who experience it in this way, the exercise of control and authoritarianism is not only enticing but stimulates an insatiable hunger for more and more power.

People who hold positions of power are strongly advised to make conscious ethical decisions to exercise their leadership for the advancement of legitimate goals and the interests of the people they are serving, to subordinate their own experiences of power to the pursuit of ethical goals, and to keep their hunger for additional power in check, lest they grow intoxicated by it. For many holders of positions of power, a failure to focus their leadership on achieving worthwhile ethical goals and to devote their power to reaching those goals will result in an increasing intoxication with all aspects of their power. And then when this occurs, their existing sense of power over others grows insufficient; they come to desire more and more, increasingly abusing and humiliating others and constantly testing the limits of their power. Power addicts need more and more power to feel alive and to prove that they wield power. Like with any addiction, the process results in a loss of capacity for moderation and progressively increasing losses of control. The abuse and humiliation of others delights power addicts. It imbues them with a sense of satisfaction and allows them to laugh at others from their perceived position of superiority.

Examples from Everyday Life

A classic example of the intoxicating effect of power is reflected in the behavior of the student-prison guards in social psychologist Philip Zimbardo's well-known prison simulation study, which aimed to demonstrate the aggressive tendencies of "normal students."[16] At Stanford University, Zimbardo created a simulated jail and assigned students to be either prisoners or jailers. Before very long at all, the jailers became so abusive to their fellow students who were the prisoners that Zimbardo felt constrained to stop the experiment.

Examples also abound outside the laboratory. Consider an apartment owner who asserts his power over the building by causing a delay in a renovation planned by the rest of his neighbors. Another example is a workplace supervisor who makes decisions at odds with the opinions of the rest of the staff simply to prove that he or she is the boss.

Examples from the Holocaust and Other Cases of Genocide

Photos from the Holocaust show Nazis shaving off Jews' beards and earlocks and forcing them to clean the streets. These tormentors can frequently be seen laughing at and taking pleasure in the scenes of humiliation.

Photographs taken in Kenya in 2006 of individuals from one tribe slaughtering members of another reflect a similar dynamic.

▪ See Independent Study 3 ▪

CHANGES IN PERSONAL CHARACTER AND THE MORAL SELF RESULTING FROM POSITIONS OF POWER

The exercise of power and control often causes people to undergo changes in their personal characters and morality that are so significant that they can only be described as constituting a metamorphosis. Power intoxicates those who possess it and seemingly transforms them into "someone else." An intoxication with power imbues people with pride and an obsessive drive to acquire more and more. It also stimulates their potential inner sadism and brutality.

Example from Everyday Life

A senior professor is appointed to serve as the dean of graduate studies at a well-respected university. Immediately following his appointment, he informs his former colleagues from the department in which he has taught for many years that henceforth in all communications—even personal exchanges with old friends—he should be addressed as "Honorable Dean."

Examples from the Holocaust and Other Cases of Genocide

- Who were the prison guards and murderers in the Holocaust? To a certain extent they were "ordinary people" blinded by the newfound power. For example, who would have expected Norwegian prison guards to treat their own countrymen with intense brutality? A study of the guards serving in the Nazi detention camps in Norway found that they were not necessarily sadists but rather rank-and-file Norwegian citizens intoxicated by their own power to the point of addiction.[17]
- Christopher Browning shows that German policemen who executed Jews were also ordinary men following the orders of their superiors (including orders to kill civilians!), who ultimately derived satisfaction and pleasure from determining who would live and who would die.[18]

On the basis of his extensive statistical study of the subject, Rummel concluded that the primary factor in the prevalence of genocide is intoxication with power and that it finds much clearer and more exaggerated manifestation in fascist regimes than in democratic ones.[19] A British theatrical production, which was also performed in Israel, illustrates the process by which a man appointed to a position of authority is intoxicated with power. The protagonist is an academician from prewar Germany who has a close relationship with his friend, a Jewish psychiatrist. Upon Hitler's rise to power, the man is issued a uniform and a position and turns into a menacing and destructive enemy. Note the conceptual twist in the name of the play, *Good*.[20]

In Zimbardo's study, we saw how "ordinary people" react when assigned tasks as jailers guarding prisoners. Zimbardo had selected young, normal student subjects with no known sadistic tendencies and divided them into two groups: "prisoners" and "guards." The prisoners were put in "prison." Within days the guards who were charged with maintaining discipline and order became extremely brutal and started humiliating and hurting the prisoners.

A fascinating story is told by Christina Wallach, whom Zimbardo later married. Wallach describes how she had a chance encounter with one of the student subjects outside the laboratory during which she was struck by his charm and pleasant demeanor. Later, when she observed him through a two-way mirror in the lab, she discovered that he was one of the guards who "excelled" at brutal treatment of the prisoners. She was shocked that although the student-guard was an extremely nice person under the earlier normal social circumstances, his job appeared to have exaggerated his arrogance and brutality to frightening proportions. In other words, he became intoxicated by his job.[21] In light of her observation, it was Wallach who pleaded with Zimbardo to halt the experiment, which he did. (Wallach and Zimbardo were engaged to be married at the time. Wallach writes with candor that she was afraid that her advice could rupture their relationship. I love giving couples this example of genuineness when I teach about healthy marriages.) Although discontinued soon after it began, Zimbardo's prison experiment became a well-known illustration of the brutality that can emerge in "ordinary" people granted power over others.

Christina Wallach's story appeared in a recent book on new developments since Stanley Milgram's renowned experiment assessing the willingness of "ordinary" people to follow orders to perform monstrous deeds. In this study, initially conducted at a university, Milgram's subjects were instructed to administer electrical shocks to subjects who gave wrong answers to questions, with a shock intensity that appeared to increase with every incorrect response. In fact, the respondents were not actually receiving electrical shocks but rather pretended as if they had been. The real subjects were those directed to give what appeared to be increasingly severe and even life-threatening shocks. These subjects had no reason to suspect that the respondents were not receiving the shocks; nor did screams of pain motivate the subjects sufficiently to stop flipping the switches.

For many psychologists, the Zimbardo and Milgram experiments represent the most dramatic and important psychological experiments of the twentieth century.[22]

Conclusion 2

Exaggerated use of undue power is a primary source of evil perpetrated by human beings against other human beings—in our private lives and in our group relationships. In order to avoid harming others, people must learn to identify the extent of their drive for power, as well as the ways in which they use it, once acquired. Most important is the ability to stop the addictive processes of enjoying power, because power is naturally intoxicating, and in a culture that promotes power, it is even more so.

■ **See Independent Study 4** ■

DEHUMANIZATION

FOUNDATIONS OF EVIL 3

DEFENDING ONE'S TERRITORY
AND PERSONAL INTERESTS BY
DEHUMANIZING OTHERS

Some people are classified as strangers, as "not one of us," and are therefore not entitled to the rights we regard as fundamental for human beings.

- Dehumanization and categorization of others as objects or as repulsive things
- "Thinging" and categorization
- Attributing demonic powers to enemies, particularly those classified as "not human"

"You're an ape!" yells a three-year-old boy at his friend or at his parent. He then freezes, frightened by the audacity of his own words, but at the same time begins to laugh with a sense of victory. It feels good to describe others as something we regard as miserable and inferior. It feels good to insult and mock others and to confront them with what we regard as their lesser status.

Where does the need to insult others come from? As far as we know, it is innate, and in our development, all of us must learn how to avoid the automatic use of derogatory expressions that degrade others. We need to learn how to overcome this tendency inside of us and to interact with others on the basis of true equality.

I believe that primitive and "fascist" thinking is characteristic of the early stage of human cognitive development, whereas thinking that is mature, scientific (based on empirical evaluation as opposed to prejudices and ideologies), and democratic (oriented toward goals of equality and nonviolence) requires additional personal development and mastery of our primitive tendency to disparage others.[23]

Dehumanization entails the characterization of other human beings as inferior and devoid of value to the point of denying their fundamental humanity. Classifying others as not truly human implies that they are not entitled to the moral and legal rights we regard as fundamental to all people. Objects of dehumanization may be associated with national, religious, or racial groups; they may belong to a certain gender; they may be residents of a specific region, or supporters of a particular political platform, or people who maintain a certain lifestyle (such as intellectuals or farmers), or be classified according to some other differentiating criteria—no matter how illogical, random, or foolish.[24]

Dehumanization is the process through which "they"—be they Jews, blacks, Muslims, Chinese, or others—become characterized as "rats," "cockroaches," "germs," "lepers," "cancers," or any designation that portrays members of target groups as nonhuman. **Dehumanization denies the humanity of another.** This alone is a reason that we can already see that the list of genocide victims throughout history is almost endless and that the list of potential victims in the future is truly infinite.

Metaphors of dehumanization are often formulated in biological terms. On the one hand, they assert the biological supremacy of human beings over other animals, particularly animals that humans find especially repugnant. Depicting members of a particular group as animals metaphorically grants us the right to hunt them, trap them, domesticate them for work or as pets, kill them, and, of course, in some cases devour them. We are superior, and their fates lie in our hands.

Other times such metaphors are formulated in terms of serious illness. Groups targeted for vilification and persecution are portrayed as dangerous infectious agents and as biological enemies of the human race, deserving of eradication. On this basis, the victims are not eligible for protection by the rules and principles designed to protect other human beings from unwarranted harm and aggression.

The language of dehumanization is not only biological. It also makes use of many different kinds of terminologies. Some are taken from the world of religion (they are "infidels who reject god") or the realm of economic, sexual, or military competition (they "lust" for control, are "devoid of morals," and are "determined to do us harm"). The most visible outcome of dehumanization is the inevitable result that negatively designated groups become the targets of discrimination, persecution, and other unfortunate phenomena that they are seen as "deserving"—too many times including annihilation.

Dehumanization is a language:

- If they are animals and not humans, then they should be killed.
- If they are pests or insects, then they should be exterminated.
- If they spread disease, they must be eradicated before they can infect us humans.
- If they are economic parasites or enemies of religion, if they are threatening to take our women, or if they pose a political danger or a military threat in the region, they must be countered with appropriate solutions such as persecution, oppression, imprisonment, and massacre (chosen according to the preferences and values built into each culture that responds to the threat).

Examples from Everyday Life
- "What does a Polack say when?"
- "Romanians have been thieves for generations."
- "Blacks are ruthless savages."

The world is full of examples of racist language that assigns crude, negative attributes to different national and racial groups, often initially in jest but subsequently in all seriousness. These lay the foundation for widespread insulting and discriminatory behavior. The endless list of examples includes comments frequently made by Israeli Jews about Arabs (including Arab citizens of Israel), or the traditional negative descriptions of Jews within anti-Semitic discourses in European history and of course in the Nazi culture, and in widespread derogation of contemporary Islam—the latter is overwhelmingly widespread in our world today. In our workplaces too, we find individuals imbued with a sense of superiority talking about other workers as inferior.

Examples from the Holocaust and Other Cases of Genocide

- In 1994 in Rwanda, in just one hundred days, Hutus murdered approximately eight hundred thousand Tutsis as government radio stations issued daily calls for their slaughter, referring to them as insects and not human beings.[25]
- Under the leadership of Pol Pot, the ruling Khmer Rouge political movement in Cambodia referred to prisoners as slaves. "'You are pigs!' the soldiers shouted at them. 'We have undergone much suffering. Now you are at our command, and you will suffer.' One soldier told a prisoner that it would be better for his mother to die instead of a cow, because 'cows provide us with a lot, they do not eat rice, and they are worth much more than you pigs.'"[26]

"THINGING" AND CATEGORIZATION

A group of people can be discredited in the eyes of others and relegated to a lower status in the social hierarchy even without the use of derogatory terms likening them to animals or diseases or denying their humanity. For example, the managers of a factory might decide to stop employing blacks, Jews, or Hispanics. Other places of employment will designate lower-level positions for women and pay them less than they pay men for doing the same job.

American psychologist George Bach studied a group of husbands sentenced to life imprisonment for killing their wives. As noted, an important part of personality development is learning to accommodate negative emotions toward another and to manage emotional and metaphorical aggression appropriately. This principle also emerged clearly from Bach's study: when the murderers became extremely angry at their wives, they were unable to feel their anger and to release it emotionally. Instead they expressed themselves in violence. Bach also observed that at a certain point, the murderers ceased seeing their wives as human beings and began relating to them instead as "things" that they had the right to organize and arrange as they desired. He called this process of categorization "thinging."[27] When genocidal serial killers gaze upon their countless victims, they see "things," not people.

In the contexts of war and collective trauma, medical response teams apply a selection process known as "triage," which aims at distinguishing between patients requiring maximum investment and those in whom less effort should be invested. The factor guiding the triage system is the patient's chance of survival. Another principle typically applied by medical authorities is the prioritization of younger patients, with the potential for more years of life, over the elderly. In this way, we see that categorization can also fulfill humanitarian and ethical goals and not just the ideology aims of a bureaucratic government or other powerful body. However uncomfortable it makes us, especially older people, triage conducted in accordance with objective medical criteria can reflect an element of humanity, whereas the process of "thinging"—for instance, by governments, of different ethnicities, religions, and so on—considers neither people nor their needs but rather prioritizes the goals of the regime.

For many years in Israel, public offices of the Ministry of the Interior, the Vehicle Licensing Bureau, and even some hospitals were managed with attitudes toward citizens ranging from indifference to callousness. Today many of these practices have been eradicated, and most government offices and the health-care system receive the public much more courteously and efficiently. The phenomenon, however, has not disappeared entirely and can still be observed in complex security contexts, such as when armed Israeli soldiers are required to check civilians at checkpoints. The existential threat faced by the soldiers, combined with their position of power, leads some to treat Arab residents (both Palestinians from the territories and Arab citizens of Israel) in a degrading and aggressive manner.

Who among us has not suffered the terrible feeling resulting from disparaging, controlling, offensive, and impolite treatment at the hands of others?

Examples from Everyday Life

- A corrupt clerk in a government office indefinitely delays the installation of a telephone line for an ordinary citizen until he receives a bribe. After the citizen pays, the telephone line is installed immediately. This occurred frequently in Israel during the 1960s and early 1970s.
- A busy public health-care system schedules appointments for examinations and surgeries on a first-come-first-served basis, often forcing citizens to wait months for treatment, even when such delays might increase the risk of death.

- The Motor Vehicle Licensing Bureau in Israel, which issues driver's licenses, would keep members of the public waiting for hours on end with apparent indifference.
- The Unification Church, a religious movement better known as the "Moonies," performs mass marriage ceremonies for thousands of couples simultaneously. Immediately afterward, the spouses are sent off in different directions for a specified period before they are permitted to be together. In actuality, the wedding serves to honor the church, which is to be the most important, and in effect the ultimate, institution in the lives of its members.
- An airline does not arrange the earliest possible alternative flight for a passenger whose flight was cancelled due to inclement weather or technical problems.

Examples from the Holocaust and Other Cases of Genocide
- The Nazis tattooed identification numbers on many of their victims.
- In the 1970s the Cambodians kept photographs and records documenting the prisoners at the central prison at Tuol Sleng, from which only a small number of inmates emerged alive.[28]
- In the 1930s, when Japan invaded Manchuria, Dr. Shirō Ishii of imperial Japan conducted brutal experiments on Chinese prisoners in occupied China and recorded the results—for scientific purposes, as it were—without relating to his subjects as human beings who were sick, suffering, or dying. Like Josef Mengele's surgical procedures in Nazi concentration camps, Ishii's operations were performed with great brutality and without the use of any anesthesia or pain-prevention measures.[29]

"Thinging" and categorization relegate human beings to the status of objects serving the needs of others, depriving them of their identities as human beings whose fundamental human rights must be protected.

ATTRIBUTING DEMONIC POWERS TO ENEMIES, PARTICULARLY THOSE CLASSIFIED AS "NOT HUMAN"

As seen in the above examples of dehumanization and "thinging," the "things" or "nonhumans" are frequently portrayed as possessing great powers and as liable to harm or kill those labeling them as inferior. In this way the people considered unworthy and "not human" are simultaneously attributed superhuman powers. Although the two characterizations—of inferiority and undue power—clearly reflect a contradictory internal logic, it is a contradiction of which the minds of racists take no notice. On the contrary, now they have two reasons to despise members of the targeted group:

1. They are so different from us and so unsightly and revolting in our eyes (dehumanization).
2. They endanger our existence and possess the power to annihilate us (demonization).

This is how the Nazis described the Jews.

Chanan Rapaport and I dedicated years to developing a Genocide Early Warning System. In the process we identified early processes that escalate to the commission of genocide. Of all the processes, we found the combined dehumanization of designated victims and attribution of demonic superpowers to them to be particularly lethal, and most cases of genocide involved both.[30]

This combination presents a clear contradiction: on the one hand, the objects are portrayed as **inferior** to the point of not belonging to the human race; at on the other hand, they are characterized as possessing **supreme** destructive powers. The contradiction embodied in this combination produces a dialectical energy that is channeled into violence in the name of "self-defense against a dangerous enemy." It justifies, as it were, the destruction of an object that is both repellent and extremely dangerous to the dominant society. How can one not feel justified in eradicating such an enemy?

Conclusion 3

People who wish to avoid harming others must ask themselves two questions: (1) Are there people or groups whom I regard as inferior or nonhuman? (2) Are there groups of people whom I regard as possessing superpowers that could potentially destroy me and my loved ones? The conceptual linkage between dehumanization and the attribution of demonic powers to others lays the groundwork for the murder of those perceived as foreign and dangerous and therefore deserving of elimination.

▪ **See Independent Study 5** ▪

THE DEMONIZATION OF THE MURDERERS / CHAIM SCHATZKER

Our conceptual helplessness in the face of this phenomenon has sometimes led to the demonization of the perpetrators and executioners of the Holocaust operations, similar to the Middle Ages' conception of Satan as the source of all evil; an entity which man fears, rejects, hates, and constantly fights, but which remains beyond his comprehension and perception.

Since one cannot draw an analogy between Satan and man, any demonization is in the nature of a fixation of evil on an external object instead of a search for it in the soul of man. One must understand the origins of evil and the atmosphere in which it thrives and acts so as to frustrate any such phenomenon in the future.[31]

THE SANITY OF THE INSANE / THOMAS MERTON

One of the most disturbing facts that came out in the Eichmann trial was that a psychiatrist examined him and pronounced him perfectly sane. I do not doubt it at all, and that is precisely why I find it disturbing. We rely on the sane people of the world to preserve it from barbarism, madness, and destruction. And now it begins to dawn on us that it is precisely the sane ones who are the most dangerous. It is the sane ones, the well-adapted ones, who can, without qualms and without nausea, aim the missile and press the buttons that will initiate the great festival of destruction that they, the sane ones, have prepared.

We can no longer assume that because a man is sane he is therefore in his "right mind." The whole concept of sanity in a society where spiritual values have lost their meaning is itself meaningless. If he [modern man] were a little less sane, a little more doubtful, a little more aware of his absurdities and contradictions, perhaps there might be a possibility of his survival.[32]

"Just Like Everyone Else"

Conformity and the Lure of the Golden Calf

OBEDIENCE AND AUTHORITY

FOUNDATIONS OF EVIL 4

DOING WHAT IS EXPECTED OF ME, BEING LIKE EVERYONE ELSE

In many ways, the principles underlying what we are calling the foundations of evil can, in and of themselves, be extremely positive. For instance, it is generally constructive for society when individuals carry out the instructions of official institutions or engage in normative collective behavior. However, these same constructive behaviors can also serve as justifications for actions that are destructive to human life. Several democracies have defined "following orders," even those issued by the government and army, as illegal if natural understanding, under "natural law," clearly tells one the order itself is illegal. *For example, burning civilians trapped in a barn or killing unarmed male, female, and child agricultural workers is obviously illegal.*

- Obedience and the rule of authority
- Conformity
- Bureaucratization
- "Small-mindedness": a reduced sense of responsibility

Obedience is a disciplined and at times blind following of orders. The rule of authority refers not to the following of orders, per se, but to the role of the commander, the manager, the leader, or the responsible public authority. If the concept of obedience captures the act of doing blindly what one is told by whomever, the concept of the rule of authority focuses on the blind compliance and loyalty given to public authorities—a prominent element of the Nazis' emphasis on the leadership of the Führer and his officers.[1]

It is human nature to want to be accepted by others, and most individuals try to avoid standing out as significantly different. Individuals who diverge from standard norms are liable to face difficulties in life. The fact that all those around them are behaving in accordance with prevalent codes and principles is also likely to cause self-doubt in those who are "different." Furthermore, communities and societies simply cannot function without widely accepted codes of behavior. On this basis we teach our children to cross the street when the light is green and not when it is red; or we expect pilots of aircraft to follow safety regulations that require a systematic check of all flight systems before takeoff. A functioning society requires a significant number of laws and agreed-upon procedures in a wide variety of areas, in realms as diverse as immigration, childbirth, home construction, and religious practice, among many others.

Unfortunately, systems meant to establish and shape social order often become obstacles to good living. Most seriously and ironically, laws and proclamations issued in the name of public order sometimes go on to promote a popular participation in the destruction of life.

▪ See Independent Study 6 ▪

Most of us agree with expressions such as "Respect human life," "Do unto others as you would have others do unto you," "Love thy neighbor as thyself," and "Thou shalt not murder." In reality, however, both history and psychobiology demonstrate unequivocally that many people—perhaps most—are willing to participate in or cooperate with social processes that can even lead toward the possible murder of others. More tragically, an extremely large number of people will willingly take an active part in such killing. For example, consider events in Nazi Germany, China, Stalinist Russia, Yugoslavia, and Rwanda. Murderous regimes never encounter a shortage of murderers!

The tendencies to "do what is expected of us" and "try to be like everyone else" simultaneously reflect both positive and negative qualities. Under some circumstances, the principle of blind obedience in following orders is important and necessary. In military operations, emergency situations, and sensitive working environments, willingness to obey a trustworthy leader usually enhances prospects for success and often saves lives. However, even in such situations, it is still important that people exercise their discretion and remain able to modify, criticize, or oppose a leader issuing an erroneous command. For example, studies show that about 40 percent of airline accidents could have been prevented had the copilot refrained from following an erroneous instruction given by the pilot![2]

In some situations people are ordered to commit actions that are understood to violate ethical standards and, in some cases, the law of the country and/or international law. In many democracies orders to kill unarmed civilians are manifestly unlawful. In Israel, this principle finds decisive expression in legislation enacted in the wake of the genocidal massacre at Kfar Qasim, where forty-nine innocent and unarmed Arab men, women, and children were killed while returning home from work shortly after the beginning of a curfew, which the Israel Defense Forces (IDF) in that area (but not in others) had decided to enforce earlier that day, unbeknownst to the villagers. It was one regional IDF commander who ordered his local officers to enforce the curfew strictly. He used language clearly implying that they should mow down those in violation indiscriminately and mercilessly. Aside from this one tragic exception, all the other commanders who received the same order recognized that their superior officer had gone too far and did not follow it. They understood that it was their task to enforce the curfew without harming innocent villagers returning home from work with no knowledge of the curfew. It was one commander who demonstrated his "complete obedience" by following the order and commanding his soldiers to shoot the unarmed civilians. The soldiers in turn followed his order, which of course also was manifestly unlawful.[3]

We also sometimes encounter situations in our everyday lives in which we are expected to do clearly wrong things. For instance, a man returns home from work, and his wife demands that he beat one of their children for behaving in an obstinate and insolent manner during the day. Would it be right for the father to carry out his wife's demand? In a study of parental collusion in destructive behavior toward a child, Pnina Blitz[4] found that in 16 percent of the cases, the "second" parent took part in undue destructive behavior initiated by the other, and in 54 percent of the cases, the "second" parent stood by and failed to react—in accordance with the classic definition of the term "bystander," a concept we will explore shortly as another possible way of functioning when evil is being perpetrated against others.

CONFORMITY

Conformity refers to the desire to behave in the same manner as other people, which often means acting in accordance with the normative majority of one's community or society. True conformists follow the actions of others blindly, even when this means doing terrible things.

Conformity does not necessarily mean blind obedience to an order or unconditional submission to authority, although they often go together. Conformity in itself also poses a risk of cowardly, blind, and submissive behavior. The individual interprets the fact that most people are acting in a certain manner as a dictate that he or she should act likewise. "Average" or ordinary people typically relinquish their right to an opinion or a choice. They give in to a latent fear of being different and, as a result, unaccepted by their group or society.

From a psychological and sociological perspective, it is certainly preferable for a person to be basically normative, to fit into his or her community and behave in a socially acceptable manner. In individual psychology, marked divergence from societal norms often indicates an unwillingness or inability to interact cooperatively with others. Markedly different people may be strange or disturbed; they may suffer from negative or narcissistic personality disorders; they may even be psychotically mentally ill. In contrast, someone who behaves solely in accordance with the prevalent normative model of society is, on the face of things, quite devoid of "personality," independence, and moral fiber. He may have surrendered or failed to develop an ability to innovate, shape, create, and develop his own ideas.

Any comparison of conformity and nonconformity needs to consider their meaning for society and for the individual. On the one hand, a substantial degree of conformity is clearly required of all members of any organized society; on the other hand, it is advantageous for a society to be endowed with a significant degree of innovation and creativity and with a leadership that encourages pursuit of new and enriching concepts. Thus, the importance of this dynamic can be seen more clearly when we look at the likely fate of an army that blocks all innovative thinking. An American military commander once said that, as he saw it, in the Israeli army new ideas often come from "below," whereas in the armies of many other countries, new ideas can only come from "above."

To a great extent, conformity is beneficial to the individual and the community alike. So is personal independence, however, which produces the innovations society needs by enabling people to evaluate issues using their own honest thinking and sense of ethics, unfettered by social norms. Without personal independence, how could we possibly resist the emergence of a lethal fascist society? Without cultural heroes who refuse to become fascists, we would all simply grow accustomed to, get drawn into, and participate in the normative destructiveness of a society that has turned fascist.

Finding the appropriate balance between conformity and individual freedom is a difficult challenge in a nontotalitarian, nonlethal society in which many different groups demand adherence to their respective norms. For example, in Israeli neighborhoods with large Jewish religious populations, pressure is exerted on the local secular population to observe the Jewish Sabbath in public. But the nonreligious population has rights as well. The struggles that ensue cannot be left simply to majority choices but require the overall guidelines of a democracy that protects both majority desires and individual freedoms. In France, a struggle has developed over the Islamic religious requirement that devout Muslim women wear veils to school and a democratic principle that members of different religious groups not be differentiated from one other in a manner that results in significant separation among citizens. Must society surrender to the conformity that prevails within individual religious groups? And how far can a society go in demanding that people not demonstrate the individual symbols of their religious identity?

To a certain degree, obedience and conformity are also necessary for learning professions and forms of artistic expression that require total dedication. For example, serious students of music, pilots, and surgeons must undergo very intensive training. Without trainees' considerable obedience and conformity in such areas, society would lag behind in important and precious fields and face a shortage of artists and professional experts. The true question appears to be where and when not to "follow orders" and where and when not to act as the majority of others act.

This question does not have one absolute correct answer. Obedience and conformity serve important purposes in producing a foundation of skills and expertise in areas requiring precision, accuracy, and significant practice. Nonetheless, we should try not to be obedient and conformist to a point of conflict with our own authentic individuality. The discipline needed to achieve professional excellence should not be allowed to negate the creativity required for cultivating innovative artists and inventors that are so important for society. Even more importantly, we must never succumb to blind obedience or acceptance of a role in the rank and file of a society that is patently destructive of human life.

If you have a sense of "philosophical humor," we can formulate on this basis the following paradoxical principle: above all, we are in need of obedience to a universal moral ethic that forbids us from harming and killing others, except in clear situations of self-defense against someone intent on killing us. *Absolute conformity to this rule is expected.*

Habib Malik, a Christian Arab intellectual who was president of the Council of Christian Colleges and Universities in the United States, advanced the position that moral values are, in essence, universal. The human mind and the conscience, he maintains, will respond, always and everywhere, to the call of moral universals and natural laws, regardless of local context. He acknowledges that the Islamic world's perception of universal values is flawed, but insists that universal values nonetheless reverberate strongly in the hearts of Muslims and in overall Islamic culture.[5]

BUREAUCRATIZATION

Bureaucratization refers to the manner in which managers, officials, and clerks within administrative systems direct people to act obediently in accordance with instructions and prescribed procedures or risk punishment and the loss of their rights to the bureaucracy's services.

Bureaucracies inherently require a great deal of obedience and conformity. In essence they rest on the premise that the system itself takes action against those who do not follow its instructions and requirements, even when thinking people judge these unnecessary or illogical or when they threaten people's health and security. Below are some examples of past and contemporary abuses in Israel:

- A hospital sets an insensitive policy that all those in need of treatment must report to the hospital at the same time. As a result, patients are forced to wait in the hospital for hours on end before receiving treatment.
- The embassy of one large country (hint: that has fifty stars on its flag), which one would expect to be especially courteous and considerate, requires foreign citizens in need of visitor visas to stand in line outside the embassy for hours, regardless of the weather, before seeing an embassy official.
- An authorized importer charges inflated prices for spare parts, and customers have no choice but to pay.

There is no doubt that bureaucracy plays a central role in many systems that violate human rights and carry out discrimination, illegal arrests, persecution, population transfers, and genocide. From the perspective of the perpetrators, bureaucratic structures provide them with the power to rule people. Moreover, when we take into consideration the intoxicating effects of power, we understand that bureaucracies, by their very nature and even without evil intent, invite increasing levels of authoritarian treatment of other human beings. Many bureaucratic clerks take real pleasure in playing the role of master—the person who decides the fate of others. Really good bureaucrats must make a personal decision *not* to derive satisfaction from the powers of their position and instead to work for the best interests of the people they serve. How many bureaucracies train and supervise their staffs to focus genuinely on the needs and interests of people?

Examples from Everyday Life

Bureaucracy plays an important role in maintaining public safety and quality of life, but it can often be damaging.

- A clerk of the Interior Ministry in Israel who receives new immigrants to the country with an emotionless or angry expression is literally damaging the emotional experience of the new members of the society with his indifference to or humiliation of them. In effect he is sabotaging the immigrant absorption process, and the damage can affect people's lives long into the future.
- Hospital receptionists who register new patients with empathy and a pleasant demeanor and wish them a full recovery are making a very important

contribution to their healing process. From this perspective, the reception-
ist is actually functioning as a member of the hospital's medical staff!

Examples from the Holocaust and Other Cases of Genocide
Bureaucrats played a major role in the Holocaust:

- Clerks typed the names of prisoners into lists and assigned a serial number
  to each to be tattooed on the bodies of the prisoners.
- Railroad employees prepared "tickets" and trains for the transport of victims to extermination camps. In some cases, the railway authority required
  a military or government department to pay for the transports.
- Truck drivers continued their regular work delivering food and equipment
  to concentration camps.
- Certified physicians carried out "selections," determining who would be
  killed immediately and who would be allowed to live for an undetermined
  period.
- Physicians conducted cruel, lethal experiments on human beings.
- Secretaries typed letters requesting "quantities" of subjects for experiments
  or conveyed price quotations for furnaces to burn the bodies of those who
  had been murdered, promising "meticulous, excellent service."
- Scientists and other employees worked in factories that produced deadly gas.

▪ See Independent Study 7 ▪

"SMALL-MINDEDNESS": A REDUCED SENSE OF RESPONSIBILITY
The Hebrew phrase *rosh katan* (translated literally as "small head") is an
Israeli expression used to refer to people's small-minded and blind participation in a system and execution of the actions it prescribes—doing no more
than asked and no less. The phrase also contains an element of denial of
responsibility, implying that the person chooses not to understand the significance of his or her actions. For example,

- A physician for the Nazis who took part in a selection maintains to himself—and later, after the war, perhaps also to a court of law—that he merely

assessed who was fit for work and had no idea that those he found unfit would be killed.

- A locomotive engineer maintains that he merely operated the train and was completely unaware of the conditions in its cars and what would happen on the other side of the barbed wire fence after the train reached its destination.
- A secretary who typed letters argues that she did so automatically, neither reading them nor understanding the information they contained.

A psychologist from one South American country worked for the police force there, treating policemen just as a psychologist treats any of his patients, aiming to ensure their psychological welfare and alleviate the pressures on them in the workplace and in their lives. But years later, after becoming a US citizen, he admitted that while he had worked as a therapist on the upper floor of the building, he was fully aware that on the lower floors, policemen were torturing and executing prisoners as ordered by their officers (over the course of several years in Guatemala, Chile, and Argentina, thousands of people simply "disappeared"[6]). The psychologist recounted that during this period of his employment, he completely ignored and behaved as if he were totally unaware of what was transpiring on the lower floors. According to him, he had no other choice.

The phrase "small-mindedness" graphically captures the limiting of one's sense of responsibility, as if a person is unaware of and thus not accountable for the true implications of his or her actions.

In cases of families in which incest is committed with a child, health-care professionals often debate whether the other parent who is not a perpetrator (typically the mother) is aware, even if only subconsciously, of what is happening. Even if a mother is not explicitly aware that a father is secretly having a sexual relationship with their daughter, she is still quite likely to have a sense that something seriously problematic is taking place. Personally I believe strongly that the other parent always senses, in fact knows, what is going on, but such knowledge often is left in the subconscious. Consciously, the parent really does not know. This is the psychological process at work in small-mindedness.

Conclusion 4

People who wish not to do harm to others must consider carefully the instructions they receive, regardless of their source. This includes military commanders, government leaders, clergymen—anyone. If any doubt exists regarding the legality or morality of an order, unquestioning obedience is simply unacceptable. We must not conform blindly to our surroundings— even in our places of employment. In all areas of our lives, we need to remain aware of and responsible for our own actions. We must not be "small-minded"—we need to be morally "large-minded." Despite any understandable desires we have to behave as expected by those who wield authority over us, we all need to be morally responsible for what we do or allow to be done to others.

• See Independent Study 8 •

"GOING WITH THE FLOW"

FOUNDATIONS OF EVIL 5

"GOING WITH THE FLOW"

"Going with the flow" involves continuing to do what we find ourselves doing, regardless of the reason, without reassessing or correcting our course of action.

- Passivity
- Habituality
- Blind participation in a process
- The power of suggestion
- Retroactive justification of past acts

Many people not only do what they are told to do and copy the behavior of those around them, but also continue to do what they have already started doing, without evaluating or seeing the significance of their actions.

Because they lack the flexibility necessary to change, they can find themselves caught up inextricably in lifestyles that are unworthy, unhealthy, and in some cases immoral.

"Going with the flow" represents an additional layer of the human behaviors that we have described in which people simply "follow orders" and do what others around them are doing without evaluating the ethical and moral implications. It simply does not occur to most people to ask questions such as, Is this right? Do I really agree with this course of action? Do I really want to do what they expect of me? Too many people continue to do that which they are used to doing, adapting themselves to their surroundings and adopting the prevailing fashion. In short, human beings live in a world of habit in which much of what takes place stems from the functioning of bureaucracy, acceptance of authority, mimicking of fashion, adherence to routine, and a desire to conform.

There is no question that people who attempt to mount resistance to the prescribed ways face formidable difficulties because societal systems are adept at punishing those who complain. Many people simply have no idea how to wage such struggles, and it never occurs to them to try to make a difference. Nonetheless, everywhere in the world, a core of individuals live their lives authentically, according to their own internal experiences, needs, and respect for others. In other words, they experience their actions toward themselves and toward others in a real way. A person who exercises critical thinking, as well as authentic moral judgment, in making personal decisions about the rights and wrongs of action in a given situation is a person to be respected.

PASSIVITY

Passivity may be defined as a quality that combines an absence of active experiencing, a lack of active energy, and a failure to listen to one's emotions with a failure or inability to consider the possibilities of alternative responses. In other words, passivity is the acceptance of whatever happens, as if it were destined to be.

The following examples illustrate this dynamic: Many employees, in both low- and high-level positions, simply follow "what is done" at their places of work. For instance, many lecturers employed by the Israeli university system tend to take a long time to return graded papers to their students because this is "accepted" behavior in the country. (I saw one PhD student wait a whole year before his exalted professor returned his thesis.) Most married couples tend to adapt to the behavior of the dominant member of the couple, and in most cases so do their children. There is no vision of a basic equality, of either gender equality in the marriage or a complementarity in shared parental roles where both parents are fundamentally equal.

On an individual level, passivity represents a person's weakness vis-à-vis him- or herself. In fact, it has been found that most psychiatric patients internally display profound passivity. Genuinely managing one's own affairs internally may not "show" fully in an exterior way, and any number of people who seem to be actively in charge of themselves may turn out to be very passive internally. True assertiveness is built from within. There are big differences between individuals who are really assertive and true leaders in their lives and others who may appear to be assertive but are actually controlled by their surroundings, emotions, routines, and habits.

Passivity plays a role in the psychology of genocide. When faced with events of historic magnitude, many people do not know how to act according to their conscience and simply remain passive. Under a murderous dictatorial regime, many people will submit to the tyrant and end up as victims or collaborators and may even actively persecute others. Many will agree to follow orders involving the sacrifice of human lives because this is what they were told to do.

Examples from the Holocaust and Other Cases of Genocide

- Many have argued that during the Holocaust the Jewish people "went like lambs to the slaughter." From a national and Zionist perspective, this depiction evoked in many Israelis a strong sense of shame, contradicting as it does Zionism's clear-cut primary goal of cultivating a strong Jewish people who will never again be passive victims. However, taking into consideration the prevailing conditions at the time, the consensus has been that, in the face of the Nazi murder machine, the retreat of the Jews into their own passivity was inevitable. People were physically and psychologically broken and devoid of any real means of resistance. In such situations we cannot stand back and judge people for their "passivity." We can only truly speak about passivity when people have other options, yet still stand idly by.
- The behavior of the silent majority of the German military and society, as well as of many other national groups conquered by the Nazis (Vichy France, to name just one),[7] can be understood—but not excused—as the

continuation of processes into which they had already been inducted. They were required to send Jews to death camps by train, so they sent them. "Ordinary" men were required to murder the Jewish population, so they did so. Physicians were required to carry out selections of those who would live and those who would die, so they complied.

HABITUALITY

Habituality means acting without thinking and without assessing and reassessing the desirability of a given action. It is also linked to the above-mentioned dynamic of reproducing and perpetuating the behaviors we see around us. People act out of habituality because they are accustomed to doing so or because "everyone is doing it."

Habitual actions are automatic, performed without thought or active choice. Even people who initially react with panic and fear to murders carried out by their governments and political organizations or harbor doubts regarding the massacre of unarmed civilians may soon become desensitized, experiencing a reduction or loss of sensitivity. This means that the action has become routine for them. Quite a few regimes, such as the military regime in Greece, used this principle to inculcate brutality in their prison or concentration camp guards. Slowly but surely, they exposed the guards to the brutal actions of their colleagues until they too were ready to make their "contribution." The Nazi regime trained death camp physicians in a similar way—especially those who initially experienced pangs of conscience on a professional or personal level but eventually grew accustomed to the routine of "selection."

Habituality is similar to obedience in that it involves people carrying out actions as instructed by a leader or dictated by a social norm or copying the actions of those around them. They join in the actions and then, as if to emulate themselves, continue what they have already been doing. When Stanley Milgram highlighted the obedience displayed by the subjects of his study, he also emphasized the fact that a significant number of subjects observed what the other participants in the experiment were doing and continued emulating their behavior—even when the other subjects asked them to stop.[8] Browning's study indicates that some individuals in Nazi Germany refused to carry out orders and were not punished for doing so, but most followed orders and allowed their brutal behavior to become routine.[9] (Indeed, the commander of the operations explored by Browning explicitly indicated that those who felt unable to take part were not obligated to do so and would not be punished if they chose not to.)

Like passivity, habituality involves performing an action without first evaluating its merits. The concept of habituality places emphasis on the element of habit and routine and on not truly wanting to know what is happening around us and what we ourselves are doing. It means "going with the flow" of actions already underway and behaviors that are already routinized, without making a conscious decision to do so.

A good number of regimes have succeeded in recruiting large numbers of individuals to take part in genocidal murders through a combination of issuing orders, offering enticements, overcoming individual opposition, and cleverly integrating individuals into ongoing operations of murder. Tragically, so many people can be guided relatively quickly and without much self-doubt into self-perpetuating, self-legitimizing routines of murderous action.

BLIND PARTICIPATION

Blind participation in a process should be understood as yet another behavioral layer that builds on the dynamics of conformity, small-mindedness, passivity, and habituality by adding an element of "blindness"—a lack of understanding of what is truly happening. The pronouncement of the majority is taken to be correct, and whatever ideas and policies society advances assertively and persuasively are magically endowed with legitimacy. According to this dynamic, people must go along with what everyone else is saying and doing: *If everyone else thinks so, then so do I. If the majority agrees, then who am I to think otherwise?* It is not even important to "know" (experience, see, take note of, or think about) what we are doing: the most important thing is to do what is acceptable and expected.

This is what is happening, and I find myself in the middle of it. I have very few doubts or questions, if any at all. I accept my fate and my role, and I take my part in it. We don't need to fight society. That's just how things are.

Social psychologist Solomon Asch set out to assess people's ability to withstand prevailing opinions and proved that most of us are influenced by the opinions around us to the point that we are willing to believe blatant nonsense as long as we believe it to be the opinion of the majority.[10]

Asch examined subjects in small four-person groups to which he showed a long line and a short line. There was no real question about the length of the lines, as any sensible person could plainly see which line was longer and which line was shorter. Asch, however, instructed three participants in each test group to assert that the shorter line was actually longer. The aim of the experiment was to assess the impact of this erroneous consensus on the fourth member of the group, and indeed most of the real subjects went along with the "mistaken" majority. This well-known experiment has been repeated many times with different types of groups and in different cultures, and the outcome has always been the same.

 ▪ See Independent Study 9 ▪

THE POWER OF SUGGESTION

Another psychological dynamic that causes people to accept and adopt the opinions and actions of the majority is the proven power of suggestion. People usually believe what others tell them, even when it consists of nonsense or lies. Not only the views of the majority but also the statements of other individuals, particularly representatives of respected social institutions, influence our behavior. Examples of types of behavior influenced in this manner include

- Fashion: People feel the need to wear specific types of clothing that are considered to be in style and to refrain from wearing things that have gone out of style.
- Language: People tend to adopt currently used slang and popular expressions, even when they are purposeless and actually hinder clear communication. One good example of this phenomenon is the widespread repetitive use of the word "like" in English, or the Hebrew equivalent "k'eelu."
- Financial matters: When it comes to financial investments, people typically act like sheep, entering into and pulling out of specific investments based largely or even solely on what they have heard about the actions of others.
- The opinions of others: Opinions held by the majority of a society are quickly accepted as necessarily representing the correct view. This is also true when it comes to popular support for specific political leaders and opinions regarding minority populations. Consider, for example, the following widespread rhetorical question and subsequent explanation: "Don't

you think the Jews [substitute Serbs, Albanians, Armenians, Tutsis, Catholics, or any other group on the endless list of those targeted for persecution around the world] have it coming to them? After all, it is no coincidence that so many people loathe them and want to kill them!"

It is impossible to know how many people truly believe such words of contempt, whether in Rwanda, Germany, or any other part of the world in which the populace has set out to persecute or kill members of national, ethnic, or religious groups living in their midst. However, as noted, there has never been a shortage of individuals willing to follow criminal instructions to harass, harm, or murder. Indeed, many people not only approve of exterminating others but are themselves available to do so with their own two hands.

RETROACTIVE JUSTIFICATION OF PAST ACTS
People also tend to justify their actions after the fact, thereby avoiding "cognitive dissonance," a term coined by psychologist Leon Festinger for the internal psychological tension stemming from a contradiction between what one has already done and new information that calls one's actions into question. Festinger's work sheds light on the human desire to avoid such tension. He demonstrated that people will do whatever it takes to make sure that they can see their actions as consistent with the views they hold, including completely disregarding the implications of new information.[11]

Overall, people go to tremendous lengths to justify their own actions. Time after time, we are all guilty of distorting things to justify our positions and our actions.

Conclusion 5

People who wish not to do harm must not take actions that affect others' lives without first carefully assessing the potential outcomes and making responsible, independent decisions regarding the rightness and wrongness of any course of action. We must reject passivity, habituality, blind participation, and uncritical acceptance of both the opinions of others and our own past actions as weaknesses that can lead us to emulate erroneous and misleading actions and to hurt others.

SEEING BUT REMAINING UNSEEN

FOUNDATIONS OF EVIL 6

SEEING ALL BUT REMAINING AS IF INVISIBLE

How do we protect ourselves when faced with the misfortunes of others, and how do some people even benefit from others' tribulations? When faced with the suffering of others, the easiest psychological course is simply to wipe our conscious awareness clean and refuse to see what is actually going on. A less absolute but nonetheless quite effective protective measure is to remain on the sidelines and watch what is happening, but to take care not to be seen oneself—to remain as if invisible.

- Those who benefit directly from the misfortune of others but behave as if they have done nothing wrong

- Bystanders

People who see but remain "invisible" observe what is going on but make as certain as possible that no one sees them. This tactic is typical of people who believe they could be in some sort of danger if others see that they can testify about what they have witnessed. Bystanders look on as evil befalls others. They blend into the background to go unnoticed, as if they have no identity. They suppress facial expressiveness, acting as if they have no personality.

"Invisible people" make themselves blind to their surroundings and to what is going on around them. Like air, like nothingness—they neither feel much nor draw much emotion toward them. When we witness things that are so upsetting that we want no knowledge of them, we distance ourselves from the events and transform ourselves into people who are seemingly not seeing anything that deserves to be remembered. In other words, we repress and deny what we already know—not as a malicious ploy but out of a true aversion to and fear of witnessing disturbing episodes such as torture and murder.

Children often imagine what it would be like to be able to see but to remain invisible and experience the freedom of omniscience without being personally threatened. Later in life, in times of danger, we may strive to return to this imaginary refuge.

Seeing but remaining unseen is a common dynamic in families. For example, children who witness abusive acts in their households, such as a parent's abuse of another family member, often intuit that they will be better off if no one else knows what they have seen. Indeed, most children block out the harmful acts committed within their families. Only as adults are many able to reconstruct a clearer perspective on many of the things they witnessed as children. Many parents also behave as if they are unaware of wrongdoing inflicted by their spouses on one of their children and take no action whatsoever.[12] During my career as a family therapist, I have encountered many children who were bystanders to abusive behaviors, who failed to see or react to what was happening. Although this is a completely natural reaction in such contexts, individuals who experience it ultimately suffer from an immense sense of guilt and regret—often far into adulthood. The experience of witnessing shocking acts of evil and observing the suffering of victims without intervening penetrates the very souls of decent people, generating feelings of guilt and a sense of moral "debt" that may take forever to quiet.

This dynamic has far-reaching consequences for society. All over the world, people are executed every day, both literally and metaphorically, as in mundane actions like the unfair firing of a colleague at work. The question that arises is whether we, the untouched survivors who escape this fate, are better off simply accepting things as they are. On a practical level, we oftentimes are, but that doesn't mean it's the right thing to do. In many situations we are better off not knowing and not intervening, and we repress what we see and hear. In this way, many people in close proximity to the sites of horrifying events, such as those who lived near concentration camps, remain as if unaware of what is actually taking place. Their objective is to avoid attracting attention and to spare themselves from becoming objects of those perpetrating the evil acts. When I visited the Auschwitz-Birkenau extermination camp, someone who grew up nearby told me that although his family and neighbors claimed to have been oblivious of what was going on inside the camp, they all knew, without a shadow of a doubt. Today, this man continues to try to pay off his debt by working as a visitors' guide at the camp. He speaks with a touching passion about the evils of Auschwitz.

We also face situations in our everyday lives—for example, at work and in other social contexts—in which an individual in a position of power, such as a business manager or owner, disparages or mistreats another person. In some cases, we know that if we speak out in defense of the victim, we might very well be made to suffer a decline in our own status. In such situations, should we respond? And if so, how?

Examples from Everyday Life

- A woman abuses one of her children, and no one in the family intervenes.
- An ill-tempered husband ridicules and beats his wife, or a domineering wife abuses her despondent husband. The children act as if they do not notice the abuse. They neither see nor are consciously aware of what is going on around them. It is simply the way things are.
- A young businessman is hired to manage a medical institution and increase profits. He has an active relationship with the institution's trustees, which becomes stronger than that of the institution's medical director. The new manager acquires increasing power and thus permits himself even to stray into the medical realm. One day, he demands the dismissal of a physician with whom he has come into conflict over administrative issues.

Examples from the Holocaust and Other Cases of Genocide

During events as violent and troubling as genocide, members of nonpersecuted national, ethnic, and religious groups understandably weigh the pros and cons of taking a stand. In such contexts, the easiest course is to neither see nor be seen.

- An extermination camp operates just a few kilometers from a residential area, but the residents themselves are "unaware" of what is happening inside.
- The army conquers a location, and special units working in conjunction with the military go into the field to assemble all those to be killed. (The *Einsatzgruppen* followed the German army into the field to organize the murder of Jews captured during the German invasion of the Soviet Union.)

The commanders of the occupying army celebrate their victory, prepare for their next military operation, and take no interest in the persecution and mass murders, as if they are none of their business.

- A physician in a regional hospital treats wounded soldiers and fails to take notice of the fact that no members of the groups designated to be victims of expulsion or murder have been admitted. The doctor proceeds with treating his patients as usual and asks no questions about what he does not see.

DIRECT BENEFICIARIES WHO ACT AS IF THEY HAVE DONE NOTHING WRONG

Many people benefit directly from the suffering of others. Some benefit directly from the misfortunes of victims of genocide by appropriating their property or their positions in society. Some beneficiaries do everything in their power to avoid drawing attention to their own personal interest. Instead of hastily pouncing on the spoils, they find it more prudent to let the spoils fall into their laps, as if out of nowhere, such as when a government authority declares the victims' homes available and perhaps even sets criteria for eligibility to take them over. A man who suddenly disappears can be replaced at work because someone has to fill his position. As far as such beneficiaries are concerned, they themselves took no part in the process; the spoils simply came into their possession.

An Example from Everyday Life

The father of a young boy is subject to nonstop criticisms by his wife, which the father is unable to stop. At the same time, the mother is maintaining a particularly loving relationship with their son, spending a great deal of time with him. She is kind to him and praises him extravagantly—and of course is "proving" that she is a better parent than her miserable husband. When grown, the son is unable to realize his full potential. He cannot love a woman, let alone maintain a romantic relationship, because he is eternally waiting for someone to worship him the way his mother did; in fact, he is more in love with his mother than he can ever be with another woman. In this way, the "benefits" of his mother's doting and his father's failure end up costing him dearly.

BYSTANDERS

Bystanders allow others to perpetrate evil and do not intervene.[13] They appear to be, and at times actually are, completely innocent of wrongdoing, and in some cases they are also truly unable to help. Nonetheless, it is always important to take note of their personal response: Did they take notice, form an opinion, and try to find ways to help? Or did they remain indifferent, unaware, and unconcerned?

From the perspective of a bystander, it is best not to become involved in the misfortunes of others. This stance has a seemingly practical dimension: in our unconscious there is a tendency to believe that if something bad happens to the other guy, there is a smaller probability it will happen to us. Our universal subconscious—that is, the cognitive apparatus operating within all of us—apparently is programmed with such a belief that something negative happening to someone else diminishes the chances of it happening to us.

This is the characteristic experience of a soldier whose friend is killed beside him in battle while he himself survives, and this experience forms the core of what used to be called "shell shock" and today is known as post-traumatic stress disorder (PTSD). The survivor experiences guilt for surviving and further guilt for experiencing a perfectly natural inner joy that he survived. How dare he when his friend is dead? The combination of these feelings causes confusion, restlessness, and tormenting depression.

Of course, in truth the reaction is completely illogical. When bullets are whizzing past your head and shells are exploding around you, the death of your friend actually indicates that you are quite likely to die next—the enemy is targeting the area that you are in. And if your neighbors have been infected by an epidemic running rampant in your area, this clearly puts you at greater, not lesser, risk of infection. You are really lucky if you survive, and nobody really knows why you had this good fortune and others did not. It is not that you have cheated and done something bad. But in such situations, it is not logic that determines our reactions. The superstitious thinking inherent in the functioning of the human psyche includes the belief that various destinies are "assigned to each of us" and that the death of someone in your midst decreases your chances of being among the victims.

Of course, in some contexts, this way of thinking may actually hold some truth. For example, if and when an enemy sets specific quotas—as Nazis did when they rounded up a specific number of victims in retaliatory killings against resistors—their deaths do in a sense serve to protect you. If a murderous destiny has passed you by and befallen others, your risk of dying may have been reduced not only on a superstitious level but practically speaking as well. However, you still have done nothing wrong, and it is only normal that you are inwardly happy. This does not mean you wished the others would die. The superstitious thinking still has no basis in reality.

Many believe that if large-scale killers such as Hitler and Stalin had managed to extend their time in power significantly, they would have targeted additional groups for genocidal persecution. Thus, historians tend to agree that Hitler would have expanded the "Final Solution" to include the Slavic peoples. The Nazis had already murdered more than 1 million Slavic prisoners of war (many Soviet soldiers died in the same extermination camps and gas chambers as Jews).[14] Stalin is also believed to have been on the verge of initiating plans for the mass extermination of Soviet Jewry.

Bystanders cannot allow others to see that they are benefitting from their nonintervention. "Unseen" bystanders feel compelled to accept—and better yet not to "know"—what is happening, so as not to suffer the pangs of conscience. Their best possible course is to guard their seeming lack of knowledge of events around them.

The dramatic case of Kitty Genovese, who was murdered in 1964 on the grounds of her apartment building in New York City, provides a classic illustration of this dynamic. For a long time it was believed that despite her cries for help, none of her thirty-eight neighbors came to her assistance or even bothered to call the police, and the incident became a powerful symbol, certainly in American culture, for what is called "the bystander phenomenon."[15] It subsequently became clear that some neighbors did attempt to call for help and that the police department was derelict. Still, some neighbors certainly did nothing. An assistant superintendent for the building across the street had a clear view of the first stabbing and later told prosecutors that he had "thought about going downstairs to get my baseball bat" but took a nap instead. When asked by the prosecutor why he didn't help, he shrugged. A prosecutor later said, "It made me sick to my stomach dealing with this man."[16]

In one of his books, Holocaust survivor Elie Wiesel describes the march of victims to their death in a European city. Through his window curtains, a man observes the events taking place in the street outside. At one point, one

of the victims looks up and meets the eyes of the observer. In that unforgettable split second, explains Wiesel, the two are linked by the electrifying energy of one person's awareness of the fate of the other, including the victim's
own comprehension that he cannot expect the observer to help him or feel
sympathy for him.[17]

Sometimes, of course, there is no point in trying to aid victims. They are
beyond help. Such painful situations are a poignant reminder of the larger
questions: What limits do we place on endangering or even sacrificing our
own safety in order to save another person? To what extent does concern for
our own well-being justify refraining from trying to save someone else? If we
can't help that's one thing. If we can, it's another.

Psychologist John Darley conducted an experiment at the prestigious
Princeton Theological Seminary. First, students heard a lecture about the no-
bility and mercifulness of the Good Samaritan and about the decent qualities
Jesus requires of all good Christians. After the lecture, the students were sent
to a studio on campus to record a sample sermon on the "merciful Christian
and the savior." Some were told that they were late and needed to rush to the
studio; otherwise they would lose their reserved time and be unable to record.
Other students were told nothing. On the way to the studio, located on the
other side of the campus, the students encountered a man (actually an actor
hired by the researcher) lying on the path, writhing in pain and pleading
for help from passersby. Darley posed the following research question: How
many of the seminary students on their way to the studio to record a sermon
about helping others would stop to help a person in actual need?

The outcome was disappointing. In both groups, a large proportion of
students failed to help the man, and, as expected, that proportion was higher
among those who had been told that they were running late and risked losing
their recording time in the studio.[18]

On a collective level, these results shed light on the attitudes of groups,
governments, and the international community.

There are no easy answers. We are left to search our souls. What should we
consider desirable "normal" behavior when someone else is in distress? What
are "civilization's" guidelines for responding to others in need?[19] How far do
we go in trying to rescue victims of an ongoing genocide?

▪ See Independent Study 10 ▪

Conclusion 6

There are benefits to being a person who sees, but as if does not see, and carefully tries to remain as if unseen, but we must first of all remain principled caring people. People who wish not to do harm to others must not pretend that they do not see what is going on around them, and if possible, they must oppose acts of wrongdoing and harm to others. As Hillel the Elder, a revered rabbi, taught, "In a place where human beings are not good, you yourself must strive to be a good person."

Of course, there are difficult questions regarding the extent to which we should be willing to endanger ourselves and the price we should be willing to pay to help others. The answers to these questions have important implications for many different aspects of our professional, family, and political lives. Personally, I see no reason to take the risk of resisting a merciless, immoral tyrant such as Hitler *if* there is unlikely to be any real benefit to my resistance. However, if there is a chance that my daring efforts can in some way disrupt the actions of the murderous tyrant, then they are certainly in order, even to the point of my risking or sacrificing my own life.

DANCING AROUND THE GOLDEN CALF

FOUNDATIONS OF EVIL 7

THE INTOXICATING LURE OF THE GOLDEN CALF

Emotionally exciting group rituals draw participants into enthusiastic identification with the collective. The collective's ritual is intended to galvanize our instinctive drives, blur our sense of reality, and suppress rational critical thinking. The story of the biblical golden calf is a well-known prototype of this dynamic. More modern examples include Hitler's dramatic mass demonstrations at Nuremberg and the gatherings of murdering groups at crossroads in Rwanda.

- Participating in the collective
- Loss and acceptance of self-identity via the collective
- Orgiastic experience in a collective

It is not difficult to imagine the episode of the golden calf depicted in the Bible. We are familiar with many instances of orgiastic festivals and uninhibited parties that have taken place throughout the history. Some modern examples include the Woodstock music festival in New York State, a kind of continuous party that has been underway in Goa, India, for years, and the intoxicatingly erotic carnival that takes place in Brazil each year. Mass events that include the release of strong and intoxicating instinctive drives are not necessarily negative or immoral.

Gustave Le Bon describes graphic examples of unruly behavior during a mass phenomenon taken to the point of loss of control in his 1903 classic *The Crowd*, which is still relevant today.[20] For a more contemporary work on the subject, see Elias Canetti's gripping *Crowds and Power*.[21]

The question is the degree to which the release of instinctual drives leads to, facilitates, or enables the destruction of human life—in terms of bringing harm either to the participants themselves or to others.

Psychological theory teaches us that we experience subconsciously a primal or basic joy about life that *we are not dead*. A good deal of the energy of human joy draws from this primal substrate. Much of joy appears to relate to our struggle against death. Moreover, and unfortunately, this fervor also apparently causes people to rejoice at the misfortune of others. That is to say, at our root we prefer for something bad to happen to someone else than to ourselves. To sensitive people, this sounds horrible. Indeed, although such joy at the expense of others is universal to human nature, decent people feel terrible when they experience it. As we have seen, many cases of PTSD are primarily caused by the pangs of guilt experienced by the survivor who, deep down, is thankful that he survived and that someone else was killed instead of him. In these cases, the best treatment is to persuade survivors that their joy at the misfortune of others is not evil or contemptuous but rather natural, based on an animalistic logic that should bring no shame. Of course, a very real problem is that many people do rejoice openly at others' misfortune and seek to do harm in order to protect themselves and take for themselves the spoils of others' destruction. They seem to say, "Let's celebrate! Let's strike them down so that we can live!" (See "Sacrificing the Other" below).

The phenomenon of the "golden calf" involves

- Blind obedience to a leader or a collective, whether on an ideological level or in the form of blind participation in collective actions.

- A loss of limits, self-control, individual significance, the ability to be self-critical and exercise a healthy conscience; a release of wild, orgiastic urges that are perfectly natural and normal inward parts of us, but are now released without restraint; and the release of anger or brutality and sadism (in people with these tendencies). We must recognize that every crowd contains a percentage of people who wish to harm and kill others.
- The possibility of unleashing group ideological claims with the explosive force inherent in mass behavior, particularly when fueled by religious or historical ideologies and memories that arouse a strong desire for revenge.

When masses dance around the "golden calf," people must be reminded to be good human beings. This, however, is often extremely difficult to do when there is a storm of passion—and all the more so when so many others are letting themselves go wild.

PARTICIPATING IN THE COLLECTIVE

Humans, by nature, want to be part of a group and to fit in with the people around them. We tend to accept as normal the dominant behavior style of the majority of those around us. After all, it doesn't seem possible or likely that everyone else is mistaken. It is also human nature to desire the sense of warmth and spirit of cooperation that belonging to a group gives us.

At sporting events, when we cheer our team on along with thousands of other fans, we are filled with joy. The same dynamic is at play at political congresses, mass rallies and protests, and public prayers. As part of a crowd, we feel happy, validated, justified, safe—as if we are being guided to do the right things. Because we are acting together with a large group, we know more clearly what our goals are and why we are doing what we are doing.

The crowd puts an end to our fears, doubts, ambivalence, emptiness, confusion, insecurity, and helplessness. Suddenly, we are part of a powerful collective, a thundering "we" whose organized power is inspiring and enrapturing.

As a member of a group, I can suddenly accomplish what I can't do on my own. Tragically, this includes genocide. *As part of a group, I know I can destroy, conquer, torture, and kill.*

Examples from Everyday Life

The fundamental process is well known to us all: many things that individuals are unable to achieve on their own they can accomplish in cooperation with others. All sorts of projects, big and small, work better when carried out by teams—think of surgical and research teams or construction and astronaut crews. In the same vein, wrongdoing committed by groups is also accomplished more efficiently and effectively through cooperative effort, as evident in the work of bank robbers, power-hungry rebels, gangs of murderers and criminals—and genociders.

Examples from the Holocaust and Other Cases of Genocide

Unfortunately, convincing others to take part in acts of mass extermination is quite easy when people are called upon to participate as a group. In Rwanda in 1994, the state radio called on Hutus to take to the streets and make their way to junctions and intersections to kill Tutsis (as well as some Hutus identified as Tutsi sympathizers). The killers joined together to attack their victims, making the murders group acts. Whenever a new person joined a gang of murderers, veteran group members took care to induct him into executing brutal killing under a threat of killing him if he did not do so. Paradoxically, in the Holocaust the induction could be less brutal. Thus, there are reports of doctors reporting for duty at an extermination camp expressing hesitations regarding their roles, initially being assigned "marginal" tasks. In at least one instance, a doctor hesitant about carrying out the selections and the piping of Zyklon B gas into the gas chambers typically executed by doctors in his camp was charged with carrying out a medical study—under the direction of a learned Jewish professor no less! Once the doctor had internalized the camp atmosphere and become desensitized, he was ready to take his place beside his fellow physicians as a murderer. Needless to say, the Jewish professor was executed.

THE LOSS OF SELF-IDENTITY AND THE CREATION OF A NEW IDENTITY VIA THE COLLECTIVE

The experience of being part of a group and having the ability to do things that we cannot do on our own overrides many of our inhibitions and transforms us into different people—even to the point of changing our personalities. If one aims to protect and preserve life, such a change is a blessing. If one works to destroy life, it is, of course, a curse.

The process of identity change is not only interesting but also "magical," and under happier circumstances it harbors a creative potential. The person who was no longer exists, and a new person suddenly comes to life. The individual who undergoes a transformation of identity may be pleased by the experience: "Look at me! I'm flying! I'm diving! I'm succeeding!" However, if he finds the activities in which he now engages inwardly embarrassing or confusing and suffers regret or guilt, the change in identity can provoke concern and anxiety: "That cannot be me! I can't even recognize myself! Something has taken hold of me! I suddenly find myself doing things that I don't want to do!"

The field of psychiatry is familiar with many different forms of identity loss (some with fancy Latin names)[22] that are classified on a continuum: from mild, passing phenomena, such as when people (especially children) leave a movie theater and imagine that they are the character with whom they most identified; to more problematic phenomena, such as when a priest dances wildly with sexy young women in a bar in a nearby town and truly has no memory of his own identity; to even more extreme phenomena, such as when people think they are Jesus, Napoleon, Hitler, or other historic figures.

When private individuals experience such serious phenomena in their everyday lives, the people around them take notice and notify the mental health authorities. However, when a collective identity loss takes place in the squares of Berlin or the streets of Kigali, Rwanda, contemporary "civilization" treats it as perfectly normal. This, however, is an illusion. Adopting a goal of cold-blooded murder should only be thought of as insane. And even if *all* members of a society have lost their minds and adopt insane behavior, then their collective identity must be understood as insane. In civilized culture we need to be able to say when a collective has gone mad. In fact, psychiatry has classified some collective actions as insane and indicative of mental illness—for example, when a group of nuns in southern France went to a bridge above a river to celebrate a religious holiday, fell into a collective trance, and danced with such intensity that the bridge collapsed, killing most of those involved. However, the field of psychiatry has not yet dared to identify as insane collective support for a tyrant or a commander who is calling for the murder of civilians.

The experience of identity-loss and identity-transformation can be understood as progressing along a continuum from conscious to subconscious. For example, one soldier can describe his newly acquired ability to withstand the pressures of wartime as stemming from his identification with his fellow fighters. When he is with his comrades, he explains, a sense of capability, at times even of heroism, replaces his fear. Another soldier may describe a more magical transformation based on an almost dreamlike experience of suddenly finding himself automatically following all orders, just as he was trained to do.

American soldiers in the Vietnam War sometimes carried out brutal killings, in villages such as My Lai, mercilessly slaughtering unarmed men, women, and children. Although these massacres understandably also stemmed from fear of traps that in many cases were set in the past by bomb-carrying Vietnamese children and old people, a variety of other factors motivated the soldiers' actions. Some were carrying out the orders of their commanders. Others were following the example of their fellow soldiers. And still others had mental breakdowns caused by the deaths of their comrades, by overwhelming fear, and/or by the revelry of spilling blood and running murderously amok. The common denominator is that collective experiences can loosen many an inhibition and override many an ethical guideline, setting off a big bang of impulse-driven behaviors.

Example from Everyday Life

In the following story, the collective is the Catholic Church. The story deals with the actions of a nineteen-year-old Catholic woman whose deep identification with her religious group resulted in loss of her identity and its replacement with the identity of no less than a murderer. The young woman had become pregnant out of wedlock and deeply feared the reaction of her family, her peers, and indeed her own conscience. She was so terrified that she felt the need to hide her pregnancy and managed to deny it completely even to herself. Due to her youth and build, she was able to prevent her body from showing clear external signs of pregnancy. When the time came, she gave birth in her locked room in a virtual sleepwalking state—completely dislocated from reality—in what psychiatry terms a "hysterical dissociative trance." After giving birth she cut the umbilical cord, strangled the baby, placed its body in a garbage bag, and put the bag in a trash can outside. Comprehensive psychological and psychiatric assessments ordered by the court confirmed that the young woman undoubtedly was not consciously aware of her actions. She was clearly fleeing her "sin" of sexual relations outside marriage and the disgrace of a childbirth out of wedlock. On the basis of the psychological findings, the court refrained from punishing her for murder or manslaughter and instead sentenced her to mandatory psychological treatment.

Examples from the Holocaust and Other Cases of Genocide

There are different observations and theories about the impact murdering Jews during the Holocaust had on the soldiers who did the killing themselves. For example, when the Nazis invaded Russia at the onset of the "Final Solution" and began mass executions of Jews, such as the massacres in the ravines of Babi Yar, some German soldiers reportedly suffered great anxiety and needed to get drunk in order to carry out their orders. The mass killings were too much for them. They were unable to identify completely with the task assigned to them. At a later time in the war, after the extermination operations had become more routine and assumed more organized and orderly forms, many murderers killed in a more routine manner. Historian Christopher Browning recounts that some clearly derived pleasure from the killing, but most "simply" did what they were told.[23] According to this description, most of the perpetrators managed to accept their own murderous actions and to wrap themselves in a sense of legitimate participation in their collective. (As we have seen, some soldiers who did hold on to their scruples were permitted, upon their own request, not to take part in the murders, and they suffered no punitive action as a result.)

ORGIASTIC EXPERIENCE IN A COLLECTIVE

▪ See Independent Study 11 ▪

The deeper our involvement in a group and the more it sweeps us up emotionally, the greater our enthusiasm intensifies. For example,

- A crowd cheers for a famous athlete after an impressive play in a game.
- Political delegates applaud their party's candidate (see US presidential nomination conventions).
- A huge crowd in Rome fills a beautiful square and cheers wildly for Italian dictator Benito Mussolini, who salutes from the balcony.
- Crowds fill the square at Nuremberg in Hitler's honor and scream wildly about extermination of the Jewish devil "for the benefit of civilization."
- During the Cultural Revolution in Maoist China, in village after village the discovery of the "traitors" among them is celebrated, and over time many millions are killed all over China.

Each of the above examples reflects the dynamic of getting swept up in a collective frenzy. A guttural voice comes up from one's stomach, a primitive "libidinal" (instinctual) joy fills the heart, and a sense of relief and distraction from responsibility dulls many of the senses.

It is important to understand that in the rapture of such gatherings, substance or content is of secondary importance. Most people follow their leader and the majority without truly considering their positions. During the excitement of an athletic event, a public celebration of an Indian guru, or an orgy of racism, hatred, and mobilization for murder, the common denominator is an altered state of being and a loss of self and conscience. In such situations people's individual judgment does not function. Only a minority remains able and willing to exercise independent judgment and act in accordance with the dictates of conscience. These individuals know without a shadow of a doubt that they will not join in calls for discrimination and murder. But only a few manage to maintain their "souls" during emotionally charged hells like a genocidal orgy.

Moreover, a sizable majority of people actually demonstrate a basic willingness to hate an object designated by leaders and society as deserving of discriminatory and inhuman treatment (see the section on dehumanization). Victimized groups vary from historical context to historical context, with so many examples—including Jews, blacks, whites, Chinese, Indians, Communists, Chechens, Tamils, Buddhists, and Catholics. Indeed the list is virtually *endless and all-encompassing.* Among so many groups who have suffered persecution, many "don't know" or find it difficult to recognize that many *other* groups have suffered as well. They have no idea that so many have suffered fates no less devastating than their own, and in no small number of cases they actively resist having such information brought up alongside their own terrible histories. Untimely, death is the decisive common denominator that is the constant for all victims.

The more we learn about the emotional processes leading to mass ecstasy, the more aware we can be of how people come to murder different target populations classified as "requiring extermination." Persecution, projection, and murder are instinctive aspects inherent to human nature and are not difficult to stimulate, particularly by means of mass emotional and orgiastic incitement. Mass ecstasy is hypnotic and exciting and stirs up primal passions deep within us. The individual seems to separate from his normal self and is carried slowly but surely by a wave of energy to a dramatic, orgiastic experience.

How many of us are capable of stopping such an experience? How many of us even want to stop such an experience? Too few—to be sure.

▪ See Independent Study 12 ▪

Conclusion 7

People who are involved and identify with an emotionally inspiring group and wish not to do harm must be careful to maintain their ability to judge whether a group is moving in the direction of actions that will hurt others. They must prepare themselves to resist the group's policies and actions in that eventuality and plan how they will stand in opposition.

OSKAR GRÖNING: THE GUARD FROM AUSCHWITZ WHO CRIED OVER A BIRD

For two years, SS officer Oskar Gröning served in the Auschwitz concentration camp. He counted the money of dead Jews and stood guard as incoming freight trains unloaded their wretched human cargo. He says he didn't commit any crimes. For the past sixty years Gröning has been searching for a word other than "guilt."

What did you feel when the Jews were taken to the gas chamber?

"I have to say—Nothing. Because the horrific wasn't obvious. When you know that killing is going on, you also know that people are dying. The horrors only dawned on me when I heard the screams."

Would it be correct to say that you became accustomed to Auschwitz?

"More and more I settled in over time. Or perhaps I can put it better: I became a part of the local community. Part of living in Auschwitz was perfectly normal. There was a vegetable shop where you could also buy soup bones. It was like a small city. I had my unit, and gas chambers were irrelevant in that unit. There were two sides to life in Auschwitz, and the two were more or less separate."

He loves birds. One was recently nesting in his mailbox. One day it was dead. Someone had shot the bird with an air gun.

"I could have wept," says Oskar Gröning.[24]

THEY KILLED FREELY PER MAO'S ORDERS / JUNG CHANG AND JON HALLIDAY[25]

The Communists under Mao slaughtered people freely—as much as their hearts desired. They labeled every landowner a tyrant. They searched for victims wherever they had the opportunity.

Mao became enamored with one particular weapon, the *suo-biao*, a sharp, twin-edged knife with a long handle like a lance: "It makes all landed tyrants tremble at the sight of it. The officers of the revolution must make sure that every young and middle-aged male has one, and there should be no limits on its use."[26]

Mao issued order after order berating provincial cadres for being too soft and demanded more dead people and massive killings. In January 1951, for example, he criticized one province for being "much too lenient and not killing enough."[27]

In March 1927, Mao wrote a report in which he said that he felt "a kind of ecstasy never experienced before." His description of brutal killings oozed excitement and flowed with an adrenaline rush. "It is wonderful! It is wonderful!" he exulted.[28]

5

SS Footsteps

Putting on the Uniforms of Camp Guards and Sacrificing Others

ABUSING POSITIONS OF AUTHORITY

FOUNDATIONS OF EVIL 8

JAILERS LORDING IT OVER PRISONERS, EXCESSIVE AUTHORITARIANISM, AND KEEPING PEOPLE "IN THEIR PLACE"

People in positions of authority have the potential to quickly become authoritarian, debasing people over whom they have power and even murdering those under their control. Even members of the helping professions, such as doctors and social workers, at times are overtaken by latent urges to harm their patients.

- Abusing positions of authority
- The dialectics of helping and destroying

The young child in all of us wants to believe that a policeman in uniform will assist us when we are in need. As a rule we believe that people holding public-service positions will provide us with good advice and help in times of trouble. Potentially, physicians, who are by definition committed to saving lives, rank above all others, but we understand that the job of all professionals—lawyers, accountants, and teachers, as well as clerks in government agencies, airlines, and railways—is to serve and assist the public. This is a core meaning of being a professional—the goal and obligation is to enable people to live better and healthier lives.

But so often things go wrong. It turns out that something ugly happens to many people who are authorized to make decisions and organize the lives of others. The something can be minor, but it can also reach major, life-changing proportions. People who are supposed to serve the public may develop a sense of undue importance. A sense of superiority will fill many who are empowered to decide the fates of others—to authorize and promote or reject and disqualify. Often it is possible to see their elation in their eyes as they exercise their power. The body language of those who wield power often enough reflects arrogance and ridicule toward the dependent and "inferior" people who need their help.

Philip Zimbardo's prison experiment, discussed previously, established that under the right conditions, we will find in most groups, composed of seemingly good and "normal" people—including academics—a significant number of power-hungry, evil, and cruel individuals.[1]

Furthermore, fascist regimes generally have no difficulty appointing government ministers, officials, and clerks or staffing teams of functionaries who are ready and willing to implement their policies. Although there are certainly some exceptions, most people holding positions of authority within such regimes are willing to oppress members even of their own national group. Indeed, all nations have a sufficient number of inhabitants who are willing to execute their own countrymen on the orders of the regime. On this basis, the Nazis were able to appoint locals to implement their plans in all the countries they occupied. For example, on a British-ruled island off the coast of Britain, British citizens did as they were instructed and expelled the island's few Jews to Germany.[2] As mentioned elsewhere, the same was also true in Norway, where locals exhibited immense brutality when appointed as prison guards in a Nazi concentration camp.[3] These and countless other instances repeatedly confirm the findings of the Zimbardo experiment.

Rudolph J. Rummel reached the unequivocal conclusion that the primary force fueling all genocides is the quest for power. In the words of the English thinker Lord Acton, "All power tends to corrupt and absolute power corrupts absolutely."

Examples from Everyday Life

- At all levels of an education system, students know how to identify intuitively which teachers disrespect and humiliate students and use their authority to insult students' dignity.
- A professor of social sciences typically advises master's and doctoral students on the methodology and statistical data analysis to use in their research. However, when the time comes for the students to defend their dissertations, the same professor viciously attacks them for using the very methods he himself recommended.

In one instance another professor who served as the senior advisor for one of these students openly criticized his colleague's unbridled and irrational attacks on the student in her dissertation defense. "How can you attack the student for working precisely according to the methods you yourself prescribed to her?" he asked. "I sat in the original meeting with you and her, and I was there when you recommended the exact method of statistical analysis she applied." In response, the nasty professor shrugged his shoulders, using body language to express clear indifference, and even confirmed his colleague's assertions: "It's true that this is what I recommended at the time, but now I am choosing to be critical. It's my right to do as I please." He then insisted on giving a low grade to the student, who emerged from the experience shattered emotionally. When advised to appeal the decision to the dean, the student ruled out this course of action and said shakily that she would accept any grade she received as long as it would bring the torture to an end. The professor's brutal exercise of power came very close to breaking her.

Examples from the Holocaust and Other Cases of Genocide

- Taking the life of another person is, of course, the most destructive use of power there can be.
- During many genocides, the power to kill has been entrusted to low-level officials, ordinary policemen, and guards.
- In Cambodia, the Khmer Rouge assigned the power to kill to soldiers who served in the labor camps that later came to be known as the "killing fields"

(the movie of the same name publicized the horrifying truth about the Khmer Rouge, which slaughtered between 1 and 3 million people).[4] At the central prison at Tuol Sleng, the regime's killings were methodically documented with an "administrative excellence" reminiscent of the Nazis' meticulously organized extermination system. In the case of the Khmer Rouge, the documentation included a photograph of each prisoner taken prior to execution, a record of his or her personal identifying information, and the reasons "justifying" the murder. A photographer on staff at the prison recounted how he had been forced to photograph members of his own family, and both he and his doomed relatives knew that they dared not expose their relationship, as doing so would have risked the photographer's life.[5]

The situation of the prison photographer epitomizes many other situations when a person is commanded to help kill others and does as he is ordered in order to save his own life. Unhappily, many people not only do what they are told but enjoy exercising the power to take the lives of fellow human beings—despite the fact that simple logic and a natural sense of morality tell them that their actions are profound sins and crimes against humanity.

THE DIALECTICS OF HELPING AND DESTROYING

The human drive to harm and destroy finds especially poignant expression when doctors, nurses, and other health-care professionals display cruelty. In several infamous incidents—a number of them in England—physicians or nurses became serial killers of their own patients. Clearly these cases involve a small number of pathologically disturbed individuals. More troubling is the fact that when called on to serve fascist regimes, many doctors had no compunction about doing everything asked of them. In Nazi Germany, hundreds of doctors and nurses implemented Operation T4, the regime's first program of mass extermination designed to exterminate mentally handicapped children and the mentally ill. The murders were committed under the guise of "mercy killing."[6] Doctors and nurses were also recruited to implement Operation T4 in occupied France and elsewhere, not just in Germany.

During the years preceding World War II, various countries and a number of US states enacted legislation aimed at sterilizing tens of thousands of mentally handicapped individuals.[7] Although not the same as murder, sterilization is certainly cruel and, in a larger sense, quite lethal. The same philosophical foundations taken to the extreme by the Nazis in determining who did and did not possess the right to live were at work in democratic America in mandatory sterilization. The larger justification in both cases was to "improve" the human race. Of course, in Germany the concept was taken "all the way." The German intellectual elite[8] adopted the concept of a "life unworthy of living," and the Nazis transformed this philosophical assertion into a rationale for mass murder. The concept served as the basis for determining who was and was not "worthy" of life. Beginning with the mentally handicapped and the mentally ill, the killing then progressed to the Jews and another 14 million civilians murdered by the Nazis. Were the Nazis to have won the war, *millions* more would have been deemed unworthy to live.

Armenian scholar Vahakn Dadrian has also documented the role of Turkish physicians in the Armenian Genocide.[9] Earlier in this book we noted the actions of Dr. Shirō Ishii of Japan, who tortured and slaughtered thousands of Chinese civilians and prisoners of war using "treatment experiments" during the Japanese invasion of Manchuria in the 1930s[10]—very similarly to Germany's notorious Dr. Josef Mengele during the Holocaust.

American psychiatrist Robert Jay Lifton examined the medical work of doctors at Auschwitz—who, as we know, assisted with Mengele's "medical experiments"—and of doctors who were responsible for piping Zyklon B into the gas chambers as if it were a medical duty (aimed at curing the world of the widespread "Jewish epidemic"). Lifton sought to understand how physicians, whose basic profession and its oath were dedicated to the preservation of lives, could be complicit in such cold-blooded murders. Lifton offered as an explanation that the doctors were able to *split* their experiences into different categories and that the human mind is capable of acting according to totally contradictory ideas and values located by a person in separate, unconnected parts of the psyche. Lifton named the basic and apparently universal mechanism situated deep within human cognition "doubling."

At the core of the mind structure, a readiness to destroy and kill sits in dialectical contradiction and apposition to a core readiness to help, rescue, and heal others. Lifton uses the unforgettable metaphorical term "the healing-killing paradox" to refer to the glaring contradiction between doctors' efforts to preserve and destroy life.[11] Lifton posits that the physicians—whose professional responsibility was to save the lives of their patients and to cure and rehabilitate the ill, the handicapped, and those in need—were subconsciously subject to the universal dialectical tension between the instinct to kill and destroy and that to save and heal. The very weight of their defined conscious obligation to heal exacerbated the tension—in many areas of life we may see good and just people who bear a heavy burden of responsibility experience an anger at the load they are carrying that unleashes a desire to harm others. It is a natural way of protesting against the heavy pressures they are feeling, but of course it is morally as wrong as one can get.

If Lifton is right, his work provides us with a newly useful way of understanding the troubling enigma of how people are capable of doing great harm to others. This is not to say that Lifton has provided a complete explanation. We are still left with a challenging philosophical and scientific mystery of how, from an ethical perspective, people can allow themselves repeatedly to do intentional harm to other human beings. Lifton's analysis certainly does not justify or "normalize" the act of murder. His explanation, however, may shed light on a hitherto unknown structural dynamic of the human psyche and in that respect enables us to better understand (though not to justify!) how human beings—including so many of the "good people" among us—frequently choose the option of murder.

Lifton is also known for his psychological studies of the human quest for immortality. He studied the lengths people will go to in order to delude themselves into believing that they can somehow evade death and achieve immortality. We will explore this concept further during our discussion of sacrificing others. Lifton's contributions to the psychology of seeking immortality help us to understand more about how imposing death on others can bring benefits to oneself: if you die, my chances of living increase, says magical thinking in the human mind. Many thinkers have testified throughout the generations to the fact that life is a "twin," so to speak, of the absence of life, meaning death, and that life and death forever are linked in a powerful dialectic. Life naturally involves a process of preparing for the certain death that awaits every living thing. Something similar is true of the concept of healing. By its nature it suggests the possibility of not healing and, more poignantly, of causing death. Indeed, in our minds, every concept points simultaneously to its very opposite, if only by the natural processes of association. This aspect of human mind can be understood using simple logic and does not require us to search more deeply within our psyches.

As we all know from the thoughts and feelings that flow through our consciousness continuously, at times we all have vivid thoughts and urges to be destructive—toward ourselves or others or both. And while thought must certainly be understood as distinct from action, it is imperative to remain aware of the fact that deep within us, we all possess malevolent urges. Even in the face of life's beauty and even at times when we love life, we are periodically assaulted by lousy and even quite evil thoughts. This is a natural dynamic with which we must all come to terms and learn to contend.

Lifton's healing-killing paradox is but one of the numerous fundamental dialectical processes in the human psyche that many of us believe characterize our basic human nature. We are at once loving and hateful, gentle and rough, sensitive and unfeeling, generous and stingy. Indeed, the list of mutually contradictory qualities that exist within all of us is endless.[12] In the present context, Lifton's work helps us to better understand the decisions faced by every therapist and every human being, all the time, as to whether to preserve and sanctify human life or destroy it.

Examples from Everyday Life

- We noted earlier that in addition to their strong, mutual feelings of love, parents and children also experience hostile and malicious feelings toward one another.
- Khalil Gibran, a poet known for his touching verses about human love, depicts a woman and her daughter going to sleep at night with wishes of "Good night, my love" and" Good night, dear mother." However, each later awakens during the dark of night with feelings of derision and hatred for the other—the mother with intense jealousy of her daughter's youth and the daughter with revulsion for her mother's ugliness in aging.
- We also noted that British psychoanalyst Donald Winnicott maintains that all parents must also experience feelings of hatred toward their children. These feelings play a healthy role in enabling children to develop independently and to separate progressively from their parents. As we have seen, Winnicott also recommends that psychotherapists do therapy in a way that enables them to experience and even express their hatred of their patients—as well, of course, as helping patients to experience and express their anger at the therapist. In both cases, the goal is to accommodate this

emotion of hatred within broader and more encompassing experiences of love. In pathological conditions, hatred overpowers love and emerges as the dominant emotion.[13]

Control, destruction, and murder are the ultimate manifestations of human pathology. In emotionally healthy relationships, love is dominant and successfully contains the angers and hatreds that also arise.

Conclusion 8

People who wish not to do harm to others must be able to take responsibility for their inherent human tendencies toward authoritarian behavior—including a potential to derive pleasure from harming or killing others. Within each of us there is an authoritarian police officer awaiting an opportunity to emerge or a homicidal doctor standing alongside the caring and healing doctor. In the poetics of the Jewish high holidays, we must therefore ask ourselves not only who will live and who will die, but who among us will be responsible for killing, and who will uphold the ethic of caring for and protecting other human beings?

THE IMPACT OF IDEOLOGY

FOUNDATIONS OF EVIL 9

TOTAL DEDICATION TO THE DIVINE CALL OF IDEOLOGY

People's identification with and commitment to an ideology in effect take on divine or theological meaning and importance— whether or not the ideology is in fact linked to theology or a religious movement.

- Ideology and ideologization
- The acquisition of power through identification with an ideology
- Justifying the use of power in the name of ideology

Who among us has not felt more empowered—at whatever age—by identifying with some well-known logo or brand name, such as Adidas or Levi Strauss, however trivial this seems. It seems strange that identifying ourselves as if with some well-known mass movement, based on a trivial symbol on our clothing, can imbue us with a sense of greater power and an ability to withstand pressures more effectively than when we are "naked," wearing nothing but our own identity. Ridiculously, the logos on our gym shirts, jeans, and shoes give us a feeling of power we would not otherwise enjoy. This empowerment is a mirror of the profound weakness to which we human beings are subject and the degree to which we are susceptible to the power of suggestion.

But when a mass movement is based not on material objects but rather on a serious ideology aimed at redeeming man from his suffering, or restoring a historic past glory to believers and loyalists, or reinstating lost justice, the passion and dedication can be limitless. Proponents perceive the ideology as the remedy for all of life's inequities and believe that achieving their ideological goals will realign human affairs to be more just. In the name of a monumental cause, people are willing to give all they have, even their lives, not to mention to sacrifice the lives of nonbelievers, opponents, and rebels, which by definition are worth little and are certainly inconsequential when weighed against the potential "Garden of Eden" that fulfillment of the ideology stands to bring into the world. As noted, people can give "everything" for such a noble and sublime cause.

A common mistake historians make is trying to understand the influence of ideologies that have shaped major historic events primarily in terms of the concepts that the ideologies put forward. They fail to understand that the basic human need to embrace an ideology is so powerful that people are ready to believe in almost any idea. When viewed through a historical lens, enthusiasm for an ideology can be quite misleading, giving the false impression that the primary motivation of people really is the idea itself. Belief in Nazism was often a celebration of the opportunity to identify with power for its own sake and could have little to do with the ideas the system promoted.

Another focus of historians is the politics of efforts to disseminate an ideology. To what degree did the exponents of an ideology amass power, and what means did they use to disseminate their beliefs to the masses and to defeat opposing forces? Again, the prevailing tendency is to view the power struggles as competitions over ideas and ideological goals. However, in many cases victory is more a function of which opponent assembles the greater power. The true triumph is not necessarily of ideas but of the strategies and means of power used to promote them. Consider the influence of financial corruption in many elections and in many shady business deals or deals between lobbyists all over the world—including in democratic countries. This power dynamic is also evident in brutal treatment of political rivals, such as imprisonment (Burma), poisoning (Ukraine), and execution (Zimbabwe), among a very long list of further examples. Was Hitler initially victorious in Germany as a result of his politics, or, more simply, did he simply seize power by brutal means and establish himself as a dictator? The most pathetic and lethal error of democracies may very well be their blind faith in the democratic process, while others are busy using the democratic process to gather more and more power.

Historians do not always understand the powerful process of identification and its resulting personal empowerment of the faithful. Nor do they understand the manner in which the process of identification will function in conjunction with the concepts and aims of a movement that fervently promotes an ideology. The process of mobilizing mass identification for an ideology can be applied to a whole variety of issues, including utterly trivial ones, as reflected in the jesting ironic statement, "Support mental health, or we'll kill you!" This comment is meant to illustrate the irony of blind faith in any belief.

The recipe for effective dissemination of an ideology includes an option not only to promote and spread whatever worthy idea but to identify the idea as the commandment of a living god. Whose heart will not tremble? Who among us has fully overcome our childlike fear of—and yearning for—a divine redeemer who will guide us with his teachings and commandments and enable us to become one with an almighty god? How many of us are fully free of anxiety that if, God forbid, we violate God's commandments, we will suffer severe punishment—perhaps not only in our current lives but for all eternity?

At this point I would like to explain to readers who sincerely identify with religious faith that my intention is not to be critical of religion. When religion provides a framework that allows people to achieve a level of spiritual awareness that is dedicated to the sanctity of life—for both believers and nonbelievers—it is a gift. But I do want to criticize all ideologies—including recognized religious faiths—that lead their followers into disastrous, foolish obedience and acceptance of the authority of any and all religious leaders, regardless of what they stand for, when such religious leaders engage in calling upon their followers to persecute and kill others. I am under no obligation to respect religions that perpetrate violent witch hunts against unarmed, defenseless people, even if they are considered enemies. This includes Islamic clergymen who send their followers on missions of jihad (holy war) against the "infidels" in the name of Allah, as well as Christian clergymen who in the past sent their followers on crusades that caused the death of large numbers of Jews and Muslims. Although the Jewish fundamentalist movement that has emerged in Israel is not so widespread, it too produces murderers, such as Baruch Goldstein, a Jewish physician who massacred innocent Palestinians, ostensibly in the name of God.

The power of religion to control people and cause them to commit criminal acts against others contradicts an enlightened conceptualization of a god who is the creator and sustainer of all people and all life. One root of the problem lies in the attitudes of religious leaders who regard themselves not as spiritual leaders and heads of institutions of religious study but as representatives of the divine who require blind obedience. Public discussion tends not to address this issue, as if to do so, in and of itself, is antireligious and a defiance of God's will. So many people tend to turn to religious leaders slavishly for advice on issues that are wholly unrelated to religion or God. Sometimes such appeals are simply requests for supernatural intervention, as if clergymen are omniscient representatives of God with a power to determine fate. And thus a culture emerges of blind belief in ideology and abject obedience to the ideological system—for all that such subjugation of one's own authentic spirit is an inappropriate way to express genuine religious-spiritual faith.

Of course, some immoral and murderous ideological movements are not defined as religious but also develop into indisputable faiths. It has often been pointed out that Nazism became a "secular religion" to its followers. Communism is also an all-encompassing quasi-religious movement. In this way the leaders of ideological movements can coax their followers into perpetrating destructive acts, much as when religious leaders send fervent believers to murder "infidels."

Essentially, all ideologies make use of the archaic power of religious faith that is so familiar to almost all people from their childhoods. It is meant to allay a fundamental existential angst shared by all human beings. Deep down we all have a need for divinities that will save us from oblivion and nonexistence and from the ultimate death that awaits and frightens us all.

As we have said, many scholars regard Nazism as a secular religion[14] with "religious" principles that included blood, race, land, and nation. At least three Communist regimes (Soviet, Chinese, and Cambodian) adopted similarly quasi-religious forms. Interestingly, although all three of these regimes were Communist, they did not necessarily emulate one another. Rather, each underwent individual processes that developed ideologies that were like religions in their totality and absolutism. The common denominator is that their tyrannical and destructive natures resulted in the murders of enormous numbers of people who failed to demonstrate their "unconditional faith" in the regime.

The Japanese also believed in their king as a deity and in World War II went to war to conquer the Pacific as if on his behalf. More recently, Osama bin-Laden and al-Qaeda embarked on a campaign to defeat the infidel Jews and Americans who, from a Muslim point of view, "insult the one true god" and are therefore "unworthy of living." Moreover, the people instructed to kill the infidels often also are to pay a huge price (e.g., in suicide bombings). The Muslim view is that all good Muslims should gladly sacrifice themselves as martyrs in the service of Allah. People pay for such beliefs with their very lives!

The time has come for enlightened people, including enlightened believers, and institutions of higher education to conduct a frank academic discussion of these phenomena without fear of being branded as "antireligious." The "anti" prefix should be directed not against religious belief in general but against the blindness and evil of the destruction of human life. After all, every human being has a right to live!

IDEOLOGY AND IDEOLOGIZATION

Ideologization refers to the construction and elevation of a particular belief and its positioning as an ostensibly divine code demanding complete obedience from believers, including following orders to slaughter nonbelievers.

The fundamental principle underlying this book is the sanctity of human life. With no offense intended to religious individuals with traditional beliefs, we are resolutely opposed to any belief, ideology, religion, movement, regime, or notion that requires its followers to kill nonbelievers as an expression of commitment to their faith.

The professional world also provides us with too many examples of a metaphorical "wiping out" of nonbelievers. For example, in the professional world of therapeutic psychology, "professional assassination" is regularly carried out against the followers of what are perceived to be incorrect schools of thought (Freudians versus Jungians, behaviorists versus family systems therapists, narrative and postmodernist therapists versus existential therapists, and so on). We also periodically witness "intellectual assassinations" in the politics of the profession, whereby an argument may appear to revolve around a competition of ideas, but the true goal is clearly the eradication of a rival. It is shocking how much energy is spent attacking and negating the professional status of those who espouse points of view that differ from ours.

The stakes are obviously much higher in political situations involving outright killing. In all types of dictatorships, holding intellectual outlooks not authorized by the ruling regime makes people vulnerable to prosecution, imprisonment, torture, and other punitive measures, including execution. Recent examples include the murders of several journalists who opposed the regime of Vladimir Putin in Russia. Plenty of other examples will be found. China, for instance, despite its status as a military and economic superpower and a proud former host of the Olympic games, continues to use threats of police action and imprisonment to discourage people from asking "undesirable" questions about democracy, democratic protest, and historic events that are inconsistent with the Chinese government's official version of the past.

Ideologization is a universal dynamic reflecting our human need to equip ourselves with beliefs on which we can depend. When organized around a belief system, we feel safer and have far less anxiety than we would otherwise about the frightening existential truth that, of course, we face endless dangers of imminent death, including a variety of natural disasters (tsunamis, floods, and earthquakes, among others), car accidents, plane crashes, terrorist attacks, and life-threatening illnesses such as heart attack, stroke, and cancer—and all of these can happen even if we are young and healthy. *Whew.* It's enough to scare the bejesus out of any half-sensitive person.

Passionate belief in a principled idea, a driving purpose for one's life, and allegiance to a movement, leader, nationality, or religion alleviate, to a certain degree, the grim fears and tensions brought on by existential angst. Of course we should remember that overall, systems of belief typically do provide people and civilizations with many benefits and much progress. All people should be entitled to believe in whatever is important to them and to express their beliefs and celebrate their identities as they see fit. However, human beings should not be entitled to call for the destruction of others and certainly not to do harm to others in the name of their beliefs.

People who detach themselves from all meaningful beliefs and cease to identify with and promote any meaningful principles and goals are left empty and in a sense even cease to be themselves because they have no context in which to anchor themselves. Interestingly enough, some empty people are more prone to certain kinds of violence, but the larger point here is that nature abhors a vacuum, and many people are drawn hungrily to an ideological system that can fill them.

Intriguingly, there is also a benefit to detaching ourselves, to an extent, from our beliefs and goals. Some philosophers and psychologists maintain that all people *should* detach themselves from their values and personal orientations for a period in order to gain perspective on what life has to offer and to acquire an ability to affirm the meaning and value of their lives simply because they exist:

I exist and I should exist because I am alive, and I have no need to justify my existence with any actions. I am worthy of my existence, not because of my status, actions, or beliefs, but simply because I am alive and deserve to be alive. I am a wonderful living thing. I love life, and I deserve to be alive and to have life love me.

In my view, it is very desirable for people to have a purpose in their lives, but they should also be able to affirm and confirm their existence regularly with no special reason and with no special justification in mind. Both conceptions make sense and complement one another. Philosophically and psychologically the desirable goal is for us to take joy in what and who we are because we are and, at the same time, not to abstain from taking on roles and contributing to our societies. Fulfilling meaningful roles also has a great beauty and confirms us even as we cultivate an ability simply to live, relax, and enjoy "being."

The critical problematic side of ideologization is that it often sanctifies specific ideas and goals, and many believers are willing to kill nonbelievers and those with other beliefs and identities. This book categorically rejects any persecution of other human beings. It calls for sanctifying human life—both our own and others'. Our fundamental criterion for judging people must be to look at whether their actions contribute to the preservation and quality of human life or, alternatively, to murder and destruction of human life.

In my professional work as a psychologist, this principle serves as my major criterion for defining psychological health versus illness. As noted earlier, I recommend to my colleagues that they accept this principle as a permanent basis for the psychiatric definition of normalcy. In every case we should ask the following two questions:

- Is the person destructive to his or her own life?
- Is the person destructive to the lives of others?

The hypnotic power of ideology saves many people by filling their void and allaying fears and anxieties. However, so many belief systems draw people toward trivial and magical beliefs, and so many draw people to rigid fascist (totalitarian) movements. So many individuals are so weak, vulnerable, and spiritually empty that they will answer the call of any leaders who proclaim their beliefs with certainty and exude a seductive confidence. Consider the large numbers of people who applaud the grand gatherings of tyrants with orgiastic fervor. See the paucity of resistance to bureaucratic regimes that persecute people, both in large-scale genocides and in more limited acts of murder, such as those perpetrated in Chile (during the period of "disappearances" under Augusto Pinochet), Argentina (where the number of Jewish victims was disproportionately high compared to their presence in the general population), and Guatemala (where Indians were the preferred target). How many nations and peoples have actually risen up against leaders who have embarked on campaigns of mass murder against ethnic, national, religious, or other groups who were declared deserving of mass extermination?

The combination of a charismatic leader calling for widespread persecution and a broad-based ideological movement produces situations of the most lethal kind. It creates a synergy, a mutually reinforcing interaction between the influence of the leader and the influence of the collective process, making the goal of murder more attractive. However, either one of the two factors is sufficient for achieving broad participation in acts of persecution. Note how murderous regimes are characteristically adept at lying and concealing their greatest acts of atrocity and endowing them with positive mottos even about "the sanctity of life." North Korea makes public declarations praising its "beloved" tyrant as its people go hungry to the point of starving to death. During the French Revolution crowds cheered at public beheadings ostensibly carried out in the name of liberty (!), fraternity (!), and equality (!). And year after year,[15] in a mass outburst of violence, multitudes of Muslims visiting the holy city of Mecca cause the deaths of thousands of their own people—not at the instruction of a leader but as a result of the frenzy of the crowd. Under Mao's rule, citizens in China were deceived by their charismatic leader and carried out every noxious task they were assigned, even when this meant large loss of life. Mao, we must remember, murdered more than 36 million of his own people!

Lethal ideological processes have the potential to be immensely powerful. Their massive orgiastic excitement is extremely appealing, and it generally appears much more beneficial and safer to abide by and identify with societal norms. The combined influence of the leader and the collective is seductive and marshals the fervent support of armies, civilian populations, believers, and the many who are willing to act in accordance with a murderous ideology.

There has never been a shortage of people willing to implement the projects of ruthless tyrants. This was true for Hitler, Stalin, Mao, Pol Pot, the Hutu leaders in Rwanda, Slobodan Milošević (the Serb leader in the former Yugoslavia), and many other murderous despots. As we have seen, Stanley Milgram also found an ample supply of American people willing to apply dangerous electric shocks to others. *Obviously there is something lousy in the state of human beings.*

THE ACQUISITION OF POWER THROUGH IDENTIFICATION WITH AN IDEOLOGY

Identifying with an ideology fills individuals with a sense of security, power, and purpose in life. It neutralizes the sense of futility and the existential fears that hover over all of us and provides us with a sense of protection and strength. Identification with an ideology offers many aspects of power, including

- The pragmatic benefits of supporting the dominant political entity
- The safety and other advantages of not refraining from supporting a dominant political entity

- Symbols, uniforms, and other markings of belonging
- An immense sense of power from being part of the cheering crowd or, more metaphorically, from an elation that derives from feeling powerful and having control over one's life
- A sense of superiority stemming from associating with a dominant idea or movement in one's culture or country
- A seeming moral, and at times also legal, authorization to ridicule, persecute, and abuse others

All people who value life must ask themselves whether they possess the necessary strength to resist collective norms that encourage them to persecute others. Will they be able to resist orders to support a leader or join a movement that sees nothing wrong with brutal violence and murderous actions?

Ron Jones, a junior high school teacher, wanted to teach his students about Hitler's rise to power and the willingness of the German people to obey him blindly. Without prior explanation, Jones announced to his students that, beginning on a specific day, they would be required to salute him in a prescribed manner and answer him with a prescribed slogan each time he called out the name he gave the group. Jones also appointed some of the students as supervisors, placing them in charge of other students. Surprisingly quickly, his students formed a loyal and disciplined group. They identified with their teacher and admired him for the new, spirited atmosphere he had introduced to the classroom. Jones described one boy in particular, who had always stood out conspicuously as not fitting in with the other students, as now filled with exhilaration and a sense of purpose in serving his strong leader loyally. The disciplined framework that Jones introduced gave this student a sense of power and superiority that he had never before experienced and could not have achieved on his own.[16]

It should also be noted that some cultures, religions, organizations, and groups do make efforts to discourage their members from following orders that are patently fascist in nature. For example, we can expect most devout Unitarians, Baha'is, Quakers, and Jehovah's Witnesses to refrain from following manifestly unlawful orders to discriminate against, torture, or kill designated unarmed populations. During the Holocaust, Jehovah's Witnesses refused to follow Nazi orders; as a result, many were imprisoned in camps, and some were murdered.[17]

Judaism also has no historical tradition of seeking to dominate other nations, certainly not in order to convert their inhabitants to Judaism. Nonetheless, Judaism does possess a degree of this ideological-spiritual tradition of destructiveness. Consider for example the biblical commandment to smite Amalek. Contemporary Israel has its share of brutality, and not only in military contexts. Trafficking of women and the violent exploitation of foreign workers are two examples. There have also been instances of Jewish terrorism and the murder of innocent unarmed Arab civilians over the years.

All individuals must consider and determine the extent to which they will willingly make themselves strong at the expense of others.

IDEOLOGICAL JUSTIFICATION OF THE USE OF FORCE

I am not harming someone else. Rather, I am just carrying out the commands of my officer, organization, regime, ideology, or culture.

We have often heard soldiers and guards on trial for abusing their prisoners attempt to justify their actions, and reduce their likely sentences, by claiming that they were "just following orders."

In democracies courts almost always reject such claims. From a psychological perspective, however, these claims are not always fictitious. A large number of cases over the years have shown us that people who would not be capable or desirous of "hurting a fly" on their own can be influenced deeply by a collective with which they identify into harming and in some cases killing others. They are unable to separate themselves from their group of reference.

Ideologies and collectives are extremely powerful when they command their followers to murder others.

▪ See Independent Study 13 ▪

We need to ask the question, In what image was man created? The candid answer, which is reason for a lot of thought and should be a subject of much discussion in universities, is that to a great extent the human race is weak and immoral. If we want to ensure that we are going to be positive people who will protect the lives of others, we have to work on ourselves as human beings.

THE CRYSTALLIZATION OF A TOTALITARIAN NATIONAL
OR CULTURAL MORAL TRADITION

Every culture develops its own unique ideology and way of life. As already noted, religions differ from one another in their willingness to kill others in the name of their gods.[18] Political cultures evolve differently from one another, with some advocating power and conquest and others advocating a tranquil life for people to sit without fear "under their own vine and their own fig tree" (Micah 4:4). People are usually willing to behave in accordance with the rules laid down by the society in which they live, and every person has groups of reference with which they identify.

But people also have a power to *choose*. So a fascinating question to consider is whether people are capable of separating themselves from the collective to which they belong when it is taking measures aimed at exterminating another people. Who is responsible for teaching youth to take up the challenge of speaking out against the orders and norms of extermination? Should such appeals be thought of as sedition and deserving of punishment? In most situations, people conform to the behavior delineated by their culture, and among most peoples a majority—or at least a very large number—will readily take part in destructive actions against others if instructed to do so by their leader and culture. This being the case, can moral people who believe in the sanctity of human life make a difference? Can people who care help bring about change once a government or leader has started moving toward murderous policies?

This book's premise is that decent people should not obey orders and should refuse to join any collective process aimed at mass extermination.

Conclusion 9

People who wish not to do harm to others must be aware of the point at which identification with an ideology or belief may lead them to be parties to actions that are aggressive, brutal, and destructive. We must never remain loyal to a movement that perpetrates such destructive actions, even if initially it represented laudable aims and values that we share. On an individual level, it is best to moderate our enthusiasm for any ideology, even if it is extremely important to us, and take care not to become overly dependent on the power resulting from participation in a collective. We will be wise to develop strong foundations of self-respect on which we can draw no less than we can from identification with a movement or belief. This caution applies even to an ideology that is generally positive and committed to human life.

HUMAN SACRIFICE

The Ultimate Abuse: Sacrificing the Life of Another for the Benefit of One's Own Life

FOUNDATIONS OF EVIL 10

SACRIFICING THE "OTHER"

Willingness to sacrifice the life of another person draws to a large degree on supernatural or magical thinking and a sense and joy that the death of the other reduces our chances of dying. Magical thinking maintains that the other victim somehow serves to replace or represent us and thus exempts us from death. Moreover, the ability to sacrifice another demonstrates that we are capable of determining the fates of others, thus proving our divine nature, for after all, God himself is immortal. Sacrificing others seemingly establishes our ability to end the lives of others and to delay our own demise.

- Man's tireless quest for immortality

- Brutality and the desire to kill: emotional and imaginary release versus actual brutality in practice

- Unbridled projection culminating in the construction of death furnaces for designated victims

- Sacrificing the other: you be the victim instead of me!

In former times, many peoples sacrificed other human beings in the name of their gods. Many of these groups placed a special emphasis on the sacrifice of young children, who were thought of as purer and more likely to be received favorably by the gods. For example, the Aztecs and to a certain degree the Incas of South America practiced rituals of human sacrifice.

In contemporary times, the families of Muslim *shahids* ("martyrs") take pride in the actions of their dead loved ones and are grateful that they have brought them great honor.[19]

People are easily misled, and it is apparently not difficult to convince large numbers of individuals and national groups to adopt distorted ideas about sacrificing themselves and others. Today in our world we witness an overabundance of examples of the linkage between suicide and the sacrifice of others in terrorist attacks. Such links, we must remember, occur not only in Muslim circles but among other groups as well, such as the Tamils in Sri Lanka, who preceded the Muslims in their political use of suicide attacks.[20]

During a seminar in a family therapy training program I was conducting for practicing therapists with advanced academic degrees, I allowed myself to implement an exercise on the subject of sacrifice. The goal was to understand the primitive foundations of the psychological process that takes place in families that designate one member as the "unsuccessful" one, the "idiot," the "criminal," the "drunk," and so on. In most cases, the internal process takes place subconsciously, albeit in plain sight of everyone but without their conscious awareness that they are actually aiming to reinforce and exploit the disability of a designated family member. Many times projection onto the victim characterized as handicapped in some way is so dramatic that, as outsiders, we can almost see the workings of the process visible to the naked eye. Nonetheless, in most cases, it is unconscious: family members remain unaware of what they are doing even as those who regard the designated victim as psychologically disabled derive pleasure from the sacrifice, which imbues them with a sense of superiority. In this way, the "disabled," "sick," or "disturbed" individual is made to atone for the transgressions and shortcomings of the others.

The participants in the seminar found this exercise difficult, as it touched on painful issues from their own pasts. Some had felt unloved as children and regarded by their families as "not good enough"; others had, in the past or in the present, engaged in hostile behaviors toward members of their own family.

THE TIRELESS HUMAN QUEST FOR IMMORTALITY

We have good reason to believe that the major factor responsible for addictions in general, and addiction to sacrificing the lives of others in particular, is man's fear of death and desire for eternal life. In order to relieve ourselves of the terrifying threat of death, we transfer it to others.

However, not only do we not want to die now, we want *never* to die. We want to live forever.

You, get out of my way! I want to live, no matter what the cost! I swear to you, you won't get in my way! You'll die, and I'll live![21]

People will do almost anything to prolong their lives and rid themselves of the threat of death. They make charitable donations to commemorate their names, build tall buildings, invent and create, compose poems, perform plays, write books, have children, wave flags, wage war, and more.

According to Lifton's in-depth study of the psychology of the quest for immortality, the pursuit aims primarily to neutralize all possible dangers and risks of our own physical death.[22] However, the search for immortality broadens and transcends the prevention of physical death to encompass broader meanings, such as the eternal perpetuation of a person's name and identity (ensuring that he or she forever remains present in the minds of others). According to Lifton, people are so intent upon perpetuating themselves and protecting their own lives that they will do anything to push aside those standing in their way.

Once we grasp the lengths to which people will go to prevent their own death and disappearance from this world, we are better able to understand so many people's willingness to kill others. The primitive mind believes that we are justified in killing others in order to save our own lives. This very human type of projection is natural and widespread. It is so primal, in fact, that we can think of it, to a certain extent, as instinctive. However, we also know that although killing is a natural option for many people, it is not necessarily a predetermined outcome. We can also choose to sanctify life and commit ourselves to refraining from sacrificing others.

Michael Berenbaum, who had served, among many other positions, as the research director of the US Holocaust Memorial Museum in Washington, DC, wrote a review of a new presentation at the Yad Vashem museum some years ago. He emphasized[23] the importance of *understanding* the Holocaust:

> Yad Vashem must also present . . . the human story of the killers. This is essential. So convinced are we Jews that the killers were inhuman that we fail to confront the ultimate truth: They were human. Will visitors to the new Yad Vashem

museum understand the role and the significance of ideology, conformity, the desire not to appear different from those around us, and the murderers' struggle to silence their own conscience? Will they understand the murderers are part of our world and therefore a serious threat to us, or will they disassociate them from our world emptying them of any real significance for us?[24]

■ **See Independent Study 14** ■

BRUTALITY AND THE DESIRE TO KILL: EMOTIONAL AND IMAGINARY RELEASE VERSUS ACTUAL BRUTALITY IN PRACTICE

A great many "good," "moral," and "faithful" people deny having anything to learn from the present discussion because they are certain that they would never harm another person. Some may be right. Nonetheless, we hope to better enable people to transform the primitive projection inherent in us from birth into an explicit conscious as well as subconscious decision to maintain the sanctity of human life, our own and others', as a supreme and absolute principle. This, we believe, will ensure the presence of more good individuals whom we can rely on to refrain from harming others even when acts of killing prevail in the world. The more people of this type we have, the better!

Unfortunately, the actions of some of those walking along the path of the "moral" and the "righteous" are superficial and motivated by a desire to garner the approval of parents and others. They behave like "good boys and girls" largely in order to avoid being labeled as "bad," but when truly put to the test, they do not have a sufficient resistance to their own immoral impulses. If and when evil impulses gather in force, these individuals are not sufficiently protected. Such "good" people construct their internal world on a foundation of the denial of instincts and emotions that do exist within them, albeit to a large degree subconsciously.

The best protection is to have a clear understanding that violent *emotions* are natural and rational but that violent *actions* are completely illegitimate and forbidden. Imagining ourselves acting brutally toward others is completely natural. Even the sweetest and gentlest children have thoughts of torturing, killing, and murdering others while they play, not to mention when they feel that they have been wronged and long for revenge. The human mind is far from being all "good" in nature. Many of us are familiar with fleeting violent thoughts and emotions, if not during our waking hours then in our dreams.[25]

Psychological studies have found that many of the bona-fide criminals and murderers in our world very much fear experiencing their true emotions and are unable to discharge anger in imaginary representations of anger and killing. Many are unable to imagine taking out their anger on their victims, which denies them a viable outlet for their violent emotions. They are moved only by action itself, which means that they do what they do "in cold blood."

This leads us to the unanticipated conclusion that it may be better to encourage people to express their anger through their thoughts and imaginations. As noted, George Bach's study of convicted spouse killers found that most were unable to experience and express intense anger toward their victims, and he concluded that in many cases this inability ultimately resulted in a violent outburst of the worst kind—actual murder.[26]

Based on an in-depth analysis of the Nazi mass murderer Adolf Eichmann, psychiatrist Shlomo Kulscar and his wife, psychologist Shoshana Kulscar, concluded that Eichmann was unable to feel emotions of anger, hatred, or loathing. This maestro of infinite killing did not experience violent desires to harm others.[27] Most evidence indicates that the more unwilling or incapable an individual is of experiencing violent emotion and conjuring the violent thoughts that every toddler and healthy child imagines at one time or another, the greater his or her chances of joining the ranks of actual murderers.

Most evidence also indicates that people who are in touch with their feelings and express them to themselves through their emotions and imaginations are much less likely to commit harmful acts, even against people they truly hate. The noted psychiatrist Carl Whitaker, known to have been a good person with a strong love for humankind, said in public presentations that he always carried around a list of the people he most wished would drop dead. (People in his audiences would burst out in sympathetic laughter.)

Such use of imagination, however, has its limitations. First of all, it must always remain unequivocally clear that under no circumstances can violent thoughts be acted upon or lead to active planning of violence. It is also important to refrain from exercising our imaginations in this manner excessively. These kinds of aggressive imaginings aim to achieve a sense of release and an internal sense of power to cope with violent impulses and to prevent an intensification of feelings of bitterness, hatred, and aggression.[28] After all, psychological therapy strives to enable people not to act on all their internal impulses but rather to acknowledge them while becoming and remaining positive, friendly, and morally upstanding members of society.

I again emphasize that the main goal of this approach is to express emotion without carrying out violent action of any kind. Without a doubt, we need to impose limitations in our management of emotion. We dare never lose sight of the fundamental distinction between emotion and action. It is most important that even when taking vengeance in our imaginations, we refrain from being pulled to an emotional extreme and certainly that we refrain from any planning of actual destructive action. The emotional freedom in our imagination must remain a healthy discharge of angry feelings. Our aim is to strive for emotional release and to develop an ability to experience ourselves honestly in order to overcome anger, not be overcome by it.

Whenever possible, it is also beneficial for those using their imaginations as a tool for expressing anger and violent urges to seek to cultivate whatever might be attainable in real-life, positive relationships with the objects of their anger. I did this with one of my parents, whom I hated, and the happy result—for both of us—was that I felt so free in my inner anger that I could now love and respect this same parent for many fine qualities, and I could be a genuinely compassionate and helpful son in his old age. Of course, this is not always feasible or desirable, but it is good to know that when we achieve a healthy release of anger imaginatively, we renew options for focusing on and strengthening possible positive aspects of the relationship. At times the outcome can be the development of a relatively healthy or at least civil relationship with the person one hates, even when one continues to feel anger and hatred toward him or her. In the words of philosopher Lionel Rubinoff,

Imagination of Evil: But how does one commit violence? Not in fact! For to commit it in fact is to surrender to it. To enter it through the imagination, however, is to transcend it. The existential moment is therapeutic precisely because it is imaginative. Because it is imaginative, it permits the necessary psychic disturbance without which there can be no transcendence. Through the imagination, one can endure all manner of sin and corruption without becoming corrupt.

A man who has imaginatively lived through the demonic and barbaric dimen-
sions of his own nature is less likely to surrender himself to evil when circum-
stances arise which tempt him in that direction.[29]

Rubinoff nonetheless also understood that using our imaginations to tap into our violent urges can sometimes be pathological and pornographic and may result not in the prevention but the commission of violent acts. For this reason he called for the development of a psychology and sociology of evil in order to advance our understanding of the ability to integrate the imaginary and the evil within us into a positive lifestyle for preserving human life. Intriguingly Rubinoff quotes from a sixteenth-century document in turn quoted by the arch figure of Machiavelli: "I believe that the shortest way of getting to heaven is to learn the way to hell, in order to avoid it."[30]

In conclusion, no medicine can be taken in unlimited amounts. Here, too, dosage is critical, and brutal imagining should not be practiced in excess. The philosophical aim to which we commit the use of our imagination is critical: to release anger and achieve greater inner peace, not to nurture a murderer within us or to craft a plan to commit murder in real life. In psychotherapy, when I prescribe this exercise, I tell my patients that the moment we identify within ourselves increasing levels of hatred or a greater propensity for cruelty or brutality, we have to stop the exercise—like stopping a medicine when there are severe side effects—and acknowledge our trouble. Only then will we be able to resume a more level-headed imagining that will allow us to express feelings of anger but aim explicitly to become more peaceful people who absolutely refrain from causing physical harm to others and make conscientious efforts to find ways of maintaining reasonable relationships, even with those we hate.

UNBRIDLED PROJECTION AND THE CONSTRUCTION
OF DEATH FURNACES FOR DESIGNATED VICTIMS

We began this book, which strives to understand how people can commit serious crimes against human life, by attempting to understand the psychological mechanism of projection. In doing so we saw that by virtue of our inherent human nature, we are all capable of denial and blaming others for our own failings, transgressions, and shame.

"He did it."

"She started it!"

"I didn't take it from him!"

"I didn't touch him!"

We hear these common phrases from our children, and virtually all of us say very much the same sorts of things in our more adult language. For example, at the scene of a car accident, the driver responsible for the collision will often shout, almost like a child, "You came out of nowhere!" or better yet, "What are you doing driving on this road!?" (I myself heard this statement from a driver who crashed into the rear of my car.)

We have seen how projection is the root of an endless list of destructive social phenomena, including dehumanization, racism, discrimination, and persecution: "dirty Jew," "dirty Nigger," "damned Serb," "disgusting Chink," "Jesus-hater," "infidel against Muhammad," and "enemy of the great leader" represent just a small sampling of the countless projection-based terms of disparagement created by people to express and justify prejudices, racism, discrimination, and persecution. We need to recognize the wide and dangerous range of this phenomenon.

Serious projections can have very serious consequences, to the point of persecution and escalation into massacres. The far-reaching dynamic of projection can result in genocide. Projection has been the cornerstone of the most horrifying projects of genocidal extermination, culminating in the delivery of millions of people to their deaths all over the world, such as to the gas chambers and furnaces of Nazi Germany. Day after day and year after year, the psychological mechanism of projection fuels uncompromising mass murders devoid of all logic. The intoxication of projection becomes an insatiable addiction.

SACRIFICING THE "OTHER" TO SAVE OURSELVES: YOU BE THE VICTIM AND NOT ME!

You're dead!

I have decided on your death—whether in cold blood by my own hands (a kind of murder that is considered to require a high level of "courage") or by issuing an execution order for you (and keeping a greater distance between me and your bitter fate).

> *By pronouncing your death, I take on divine attributes, for, as we know, life and death are in God's hands. Your death will prove my divinity. And once I have proven that I am God, I will certainly live forever, for God cannot die, and I am God.*

The terrible subject of this book poses difficult dilemmas regarding how to translate into words and concepts the horrifying realities of life with which we are dealing. The fact is that every person must decide whether to work for death or for the preservation of life. Life and death are the ultimate facts of life, and they loom over us larger in their reality than any ability we have to examine them philosophically. Still, we have no choice but to delve as deeply as we can into the human psyche, especially the psyches of those who commit genocide, to try to understand how they function when committing such crimes.

The fact is that ever since ancient times we human beings have rejoiced in mass murders. Generations of us human killers have issued victorious cries over piles of bodies of slaughtered human beings: husbands and fathers, young men, women and mothers, young women who were meant to give life, teenagers in the burst of their adolescence, boys and girls engaged in study and childhood games, innocent babies and toddlers who only recently came into the world. People are capable of killing *anyone* in an endless variety of ways: through brutal torture, sadistic experiments undertaken in the guise of "scientific studies," distraction and indifference to the wounded, ill, and weak, unchecked attacks on civilians, or racist projects of "cleansing" the world of a people defined as unworthy of life.

I—we are the murdering gods.
I—we are the gods who take your life away, so that we can live on indefinitely.

In the eyes of philosopher Ernest Becker, the denial of death is the root of cruelty in general and the sacrifice of others' lives in particular.[31] Our need to delay our own impending death, he posits, often results in our causing the deaths of others.

In conclusion, the psychological process of sacrifice lies at the foundation of perpetrating evil against others. Sadly, it is basically natural, beginning with our entirely legitimate desire to live, even if others die, and quickly progressing to the conviction that it is preferable for others to die so that we may live. It is a mechanism at play in all our psyches, initially based on no ill intent whatsoever. Psychology teaches us that this dynamic influences all of us subconsciously—even good people who are sincerely committed to preserving life and who, in a moment of truth, may even display exceptional courage and give their lives to save others. Even these special people can find themselves rejoicing at their own survival in the face of others' deaths. As we have seen, some such good individuals will then be shocked at their emotions and suffer mental breakdowns, or what we know as "shell shock" or "posttraumatic stress disorder," resulting from their guilt at rejoicing over the deaths of others.

It should be remembered, however, that experiencing natural rejoicing at being alive and, by extension, unconscious joy over the deaths of others and not ourselves is by no means the same as our sacrificing someone in our place. Nor does our desire to live and unconscious celebration of others' bad fate mean that we are compelled to do any real harm to others. Not at all! Although the feeling is natural, we can nonetheless manage it in a way that prevents and protects us from actually taking harmful action.

Genuinely moral people know that they will never sacrifice another person for their own benefit, even if the possibility does cross their minds.

Conclusion 10

The life of your companion shall be almost as sacred and dear to you as your own. People who wish not to do harm to others must make sure not to convince themselves that they can expose others to hazardous situations in order to save their own lives. Entrapping and sacrificing others make up an age-old mental mechanism apparently imprinted on the universal human psyche. Until we—personally and as groups—are able to rise above this tendency, we remain vulnerable to the risk that we too will join much of the rest of humanity in sacrificing others in order to preserve and ostensibly prolong our own lives.

ARMENIAN NATIONAL COMMITTEE: *BOSTON GLOBE* AND *NEW YORK TIMES* CEASE DENYING THE ARMENIAN GENOCIDE

After a quarter of a century, the *Boston Globe* announced that it would end its policy of not referring to the Armenian Genocide as a genocide. Michael Larkin, a senior editor at the paper, conveyed this message to the Armenian National Committee of America in a letter dated July 8, 2003, noting that the editors of the newspapers had recently met with representatives of the Armenian community and Professor Israel Charny, Director of the Institute on the Holocaust and Genocide in Jerusalem. Soon after, the *New York Times* announced a similar change in its editorial policy.[32]

GENOCIDE-DENYING CHINA DEMANDS THAT JAPAN CEASE ITS DENIAL

The Cultural Revolution, a period during which China descended into madness, began in the mid-1960s. In its course, Liu Shaoqi, president of the People's Republic of China, was denounced as a capitalist traitor and severely beaten. He died "under tragic conditions," according to the delicate wording of a Chinese museum recently established to commemorate this dark chapter in Chinese history.

China recently began demanding that Japan acknowledge its brutality during the Japanese occupation of China between 1937 and 1945. However, when it comes to China's own Cultural Revolution, the archives remain closed and the holding of academic seminars and conferences on the subject is prohibited.[33]

6

"I Did Nothing Wrong"

Denial and Improper Management of Emotions

WHAT FUN IT IS TO DENY!

FOUNDATIONS OF EVIL 11

"THESE THINGS NEVER HAPPENED": DENIAL OF WRONGDOING TO OTHERS

They weren't murdered. Certainly not by me or by any of us. We didn't murder anyone.
  Don't you understand? These things never happened!

For an especially striking example of denial, see Turkey's denial of the Armenian Genocide, an attitude that persists today—a hundred years later.

- The denial of death
- The denial of past wrongdoing
- The denial of evil committed by us with our own hands

The statement "These things never happened" is an all-encompassing denial of evil that has in fact been committed.

Neither I nor my people harmed anyone.

There was no Holocaust. There were no gas chambers. And there were no huge crematoria for burning the bodies. At Auschwitz, they played symphony music for the entertainment of the prisoners.

In Armenia, there was no Turkish government plan to exterminate the Armenians. In fact, the opposite is true: the Armenians attacked us, and we are now unearthing the mass graves into which they threw our bodies during the genocide they committed. We are establishing monuments for those we lost.

There is no limit to the creative deceit human beings and nations consciously use to distort and rewrite history in order to deny solid historical facts. Deniers have no shame. There is no limit to the lies they tell. They will say and publish anything to promote their preferred false historical narrative and establish it as "fact." They do so without hesitation in government declarations, in newspapers, magazines, and Internet posts, in films, television and radio broadcasts, books, and ornamented albums, on monuments, and at international gatherings, mass rallies, academic events, and museums. There are no holds barred in genocide denial. Everything is possible. This is the case with regard to denials of the Jewish Holocaust, the Armenian Genocide, the genocides perpetrated by the Chinese government—in Tibet and within China itself, including the genocidal massacre of students at Tiananmen Square in Beijing—and endless other instances in a variety of countries.

Deniers appear to take a distinct and special pleasure in reversing the public image of a murderous event by claiming that the victims were actually the victimizers. This type of denial represents a particularly humiliating and derisive attack on the victims and constitutes a repeat victory over them. The Turks, for example, employ this tactic by establishing monuments, museums, and memorial days for those killed by the Armenians, through publications, and most recently by promising to expose Turkish mass graves in order to immortalize the "Armenian massacre of the Turks."

The Turks have invested many years in the complete denial of the murders they committed, not only against the Armenians but also against other non-Muslim groups during the same period, including the Christian Assyrians and Greeks and the pagan Yezidis. The common denominator of all these genocidal murders was the non-Muslim identity of the victims. Did the Armenians massacre Turks? Indeed some did, but to a small extent, and they were fighting back to defend themselves. The Turkish accusations might be compared to the Germans erecting monuments in memory of their fellow Germans killed by Jews during the Warsaw Ghetto Uprising. (No, the Germans have not done so; the Turks have.)

The process of denial can be summed up as follows: kill, deny, and run!

The methods of genocide denial are varied and quite fascinating, ranging from complete denial, to flagrant distortion of facts, to redefinition of the event as anything but genocide, to the use of political tactics that prevent people from telling the truth. A catalog of the many methods of denial can be found in the *Journal of Genocide Research.*[1]

Clearly, the claim "These things never happened" intends, first and foremost, to protect individuals likely to be accused of crimes in legal settings. But more largely it is a nonlegal tactic for use by a collective with a stake in distorting the historical record. Denial not only serves as a means for perpetrators to avoid punitive measures, but also fulfills the psychological needs of perpetrators not to see, or remember, or suffer pangs of conscience for their actions

On a national level, the denial process produces a distorted history and a collective commitment to a culture of lies. It leads to situations where members of the denying nation are no longer able to distinguish truth from falsehood. Denial can begin as a conscious strategic aim, but its repetition and adoption as an act and test of allegiance to a collective transform it into a mantra in the collective culture that remains with people for generations!

It is inconceivable that we (our people and our culture) could have done such a thing.

The accusations against us are nothing but a "blood libel."

The rank-and-file citizenry believe in, and cannot help but identify with, their nation and culture. And if public denial is all they hear year after year, they will naturally feel shocked and as though they are being falsely accused when presented with the historical facts that their people did in fact slaughter another group.

And what happens to the academic scholar who sits among his own people, teaching and researching within a respected university? Let us assume that by nature this scholar believes in himself, truly seeks historical truth, and would not agree to lie for the sake of any individual or institution. And let us also assume that he is already well established within academia and unlikely to suffer a reduction in status if he speaks his mind. Nonetheless, scholars such as he, too, encounter immense social and institutional pressures to "toe the party line." Under these conditions, might professors be sorely tempted, perhaps subconsciously, to justify and join in the propaganda of denial that dominates their national-political-academic world? Unfortunately, the answer is yes. And we have no end of distinguished professors who take leading roles in denials: the German professor who characterizes the Holocaust as no more than a repeat pattern of persecution in European history; the Jewish professor who insists that all other acts of mass killing other than the Holocaust are not "genocide"; the Turkish professor who claims that US Ambassador Henry Morgenthau Sr.'s famous autobiography and other documents such as the protocols of the Turkish(!) courts-martial are forgeries. All are cut from the same cloth.

A conference on Turkish-Armenian relations, held on the island of San Lazzaro near the city of Venice, hosted several courageous Turkish professors who did not deny the facts of the Armenian holocaust. One of them, however, maintained that it should not be classified as a genocide because there was no government intention to exterminate all members of the Armenian people because they were Armenian. My response to his assessment was as follows:

It seems to me that it is not easy to teach at a Turkish university and to struggle to establish the facts of the Turks' mass killing of the Armenians as you do. As an Israeli who often finds it hard to use the word "holocaust" to refer to any other event aside from the Jewish Holocaust, even though other scholars in Israel preceded me in using the term "Armenian holocaust," I understand how difficult it must be for you to use the word "genocide" in your country.

I would like to propose a solution for you: I will lend you the Hebrew word for genocide, *retzakh am*, and when you are in Turkey, I propose that you refer to the Armenian Genocide as *retzakh ha-am ha-Armeni*. This way you will be remaining loyal to the truth without annoying your colleagues and your government—if only because no one will understand you. In return, you can kindly lend me the Turkish word for "holocaust," and I will use it in Israel as another word for large-scale genocides such as the Armenian holocaust and the holocaust in Rwanda. This way, I too will be genuine, but without insulting Israeli sensitivities and without angering my many compatriots who are obligated to maintain a completely unique status for the Jewish Holocaust—few of them will understand my words in Turkish.

From the speaker's platform I saw that in response to my suggestion, half of those in attendance broke into laughter, particularly a number of Turkish scholars known for daring to recognize the Armenian Genocide, while the other half of the audience remained mirthless and did not respond—although a few appeared embarrassedly unsure of what to feel.

In a lecture delivered at the Hebrew University, a well-known scholar maintained that only the Jewish Holocaust could be thought of as genocide because only in the Jewish context do we find an explicit intention to completely exterminate all people with a Jewish identity. With this assertion this scholar adamantly negates all of the many genocides that have taken place throughout history, aside from the Jewish Holocaust.[2] (The lecturer earned sterling accolades from the presiding host professor, who himself was well-known for many years as a champion of the uniqueness of the Holocaust. In recent years he had begun to soften his positions to adopt a more comparative view of genocides, including the Holocaust, but he couldn't resist backing the extremism of his invited lecturer.)

How does the denial of genocide affect those who have survived the tragedy? Denial strikes at the most wounding and painful aspects of being a genocide survivor and a member of a victimized nation. *Not only did the perpetrators attempt to exterminate us, but now they are denying the facts of their actions.* There is no doubt that an important psychological goal of denial is to upset and further humiliate the victimized people.

A member of the US House of Representatives who is of Armenian origin attempted to enact a law requiring that schools in his state teach the subject of genocide. As a result he was taken to court by Turkish parties who argued that they had the right to teach the opinions and "findings" of those who deny the Armenian holocaust and dispute its evidence. An educator who specializes in genocide-focused educational projects was present in the courtroom and described to me later that, beyond having to respond to the legal battle, the Armenian legislator was deeply hurt by being put in the position of having to defend the historical fact. He himself had been raised by parents who were survivors and whose memories of murdered loved ones permeated their otherwise newly secure lives in the United States with deep sadness. The legislator now found himself having to deal face-to-face with the descendants of the murderers who claimed, "These things never happened."

I repeat that genocide denial is intended not only to protect the perpetrators and the international status and image of the national group who carried out the killing. It also intends to offend and humiliate the victimized people. *Here we are again having the pleasure of abusing you.*

Deniers are also engaged in arrogantly "taking history hostage" and, in effect, defying the entire world by asserting, "We are the masters of human history, and you are all our slaves who will be subject to our rewriting of history as we wish it to read."

In an important and very famous book on Holocaust denial, Deborah Lipstadt, a professor of Jewish studies and the Holocaust, accused British historian David Irving of Holocaust denial and the distortion of history. In turn, Irving sued her in London for libel. Along with many other Jews around the world, Lipstadt awaited the court's ruling with great trepidation, as in legendary tales of Jewish history when local rulers would determine the fate of a Jewish community through a debate between a Jewish leader and the local cleric or ruler. Happily, the London court hearing the case ruled decisively that Irving was in fact a Holocaust denier and a fierce anti-Semite.[3]

THE DENIAL OF DEATH

The denial of death, as Ernest Becker calls this psychological phenomenon in his Pulitzer Prize–winning book by that title, is widespread and extremely powerful. Many thinkers maintain that denial of death is "the mother of all denials." Above all, it obviously constitutes an escape from death as a fundamental, unchanging fact in all of our natural lives. Death, after all, is a truly frightening and intimidating subject. It is no secret that many people prefer not to acknowledge the fact that we will all die someday. They will do everything that enables them to close their eyes to the subject.

Some health-care systems also tend to evade death as a fact of life. Studies have shown how some doctors and nurses in perfectly reputable Western hospitals suppress their own anxieties by refraining from communicating with dying patients or speaking explicitly with their family members about their impending death. Indeed, much of Western society's response to death tends to be a hurried process of covering and concealing the body.

We have already referred to Robert Jay Lifton's studies of the tireless human quest for immortality. Despite a blatant lack of logic, the inevitable death we will all eventually face emerges as one of humankind's best-kept secrets, forever to be hidden from our everyday consciousness.

As noted, many thinkers have pointed to the denial of death as a universal defense mechanism. It is perhaps the most powerful defense mechanism in human psychology, so that from a probing philosophical perspective, the denial of genocide ultimately also reinforces this universal denial of our own future deaths.

These things never happened. There was no Holocaust, and there was no genocide. They didn't die at the hands of people who were trying to kill them. And just as we can deny the facts of their deaths, we can proclaim that we will not die either. We can rewrite reality, and above all we want to be immortal.

The denial of death also emerges as a basic dynamic that facilitates and reinforces people's ability to sacrifice the lives of others. As we have seen, the fundamental thought process becomes as follows:

You will die!

Not me!

You will die, whether directly by my hand or by my command. My power is divine power.

I determine life and death. Your death proves that I will live forever—as befits a god!

To a significant extent, committing genocide against others serves the purpose of denying our ultimate death.

THE DENIAL OF PAST WRONGDOING

The phrase "nothing happened" is an archetypical denial of the most basic kind, even more so than "These things never happened." After all, if nothing happened, then there is nothing at all to talk about.

No matter how difficult it is to conceal and ignore events and actions that have taken place in reality, in our everyday lives we human beings do a great deal of denying of the harms we really have done. Toddlers and children deny spilling the milk, breaking a toy, stealing candy, and so forth. Adults deny that money is missing, or that something valuable has disappeared from the house, or that someone of the opposite sex was sitting with them in the car. Lying denial is a useful tool for most of us as we go through life.

Of course, the more serious the subject, the more significant its denial becomes. Moreover, when denial has to do with events and actions by societies and governments, it has less to do with preventing personal discomfort or shame and becomes an institutional violation of its responsibility to the public and the international community. In respect of denial of genocides such as the Holocaust and the Armenian Genocide, denial must be understood not only as a malicious, dishonest rewriting of human history but as an attack against humanity's future, which will now no longer be based on a continuity of truthful history.

Who remembers that in Manchuria during the 1930s the Japanese conducted brutal experiments in a concentration camp that were very similar to those conducted by Dr. Josef Mengele just a few years later?[4] The world does not remember to a great extent because to this day Japan denies the genocidal actions it carried out in Manchuria. Denial can be quite effective. To this day Japan zealously works to prevent the exposure of any number of its failings—the massacres it perpetrated in Manchuria, the brutal murders of American prisoners of war during World War II, and the sexual slavery the Japanese army imposed on thousands of Korean women. (There have been bursts of acknowledgement in Japan, but inconsistently, and the basic collective is still in denial.)

And how many people are aware that Mao Tse-tung murdered many millions of Chinese? China demands that Japan acknowledge its actions but is unwilling to admit to its own atrocities under Mao, the ethnocide in Tibet, or the massacring of students in Tiananmen Square. Even today, when the media thoroughly document historical events with endless newspaper reports, radio broadcasts, television movies, and video and audio recordings by professionals and amateur photographers, we humans still tell shameless lies about the things we have done to harm others.

There are also denials of alleged commercial transactions by governments—including democratic countries—that fail to disclose their illegal trading, such as of arms or women. Did American president Ronald Reagan ship weapons to the Iranians? It appears that he did, but only some lesser figures were brought up on charges, and the issue of Reagan's role was never subject to public scrutiny because of Americans' blind support for their president. Did Israel sell weapons that eventually reached the Hutu murderers in Rwanda in 1994? Here too the answer appears to be affirmative. Did France, Germany, and England sell Iraq equipment to produce possible weapons of mass destruction—virtually at the same time that the United States was organizing an attack on Saddam Hussein on the grounds that he had such weapons? Again, the answer appears to be yes.

In a world of so many lies, it is not at all surprising that some people deny the Holocaust and other genocides.

THE DENIAL OF EVIL WE HAVE COMMITTED WITH OUR OWN HANDS

"I didn't do it!" is a healthy response made by younger children in all cultures. No, "healthy" is not a typo. Such a statement is not so terrible in respect to a lot of little things children do. Denial in moderation is a natural defense mechanism universally. However, in more serious matters—for example, when one child injures another child or repeatedly does things likely to endanger others—we need to insist that children too take responsibility for their actions. Denials by children provide important educational opportunities to teach them about integrity. We expect properly educated children to acknowledge and take responsibility for their actions and to pledge that they will not repeat them in the future. We regard continued denials of destructive behavior as a personality disorder. Clearly all of us—children, adults, and societies—need to achieve a meaningful degree of responsibility, truthfulness, and integrity.

Still, life experiences teach us that many adults, at all levels of society and in many different countries, are unable to acknowledge the truth about their own errors and failings.

How many erring doctors actually admit their mistakes?

How many lawyers who have lost a case acknowledge the mistakes they made?

How many parents of children who committed suicide, or became mentally ill, or adopted a negative lifestyle due to parental neglect or other parental failures will recognize their role in the child's difficulties?

How many people admit to failing to offer a sibling or friend adequate help at a time of need?

The ability to acknowledge mistakes, foolishness, failure, or incompetence in an important area of life is not inherent to many people or most cultures. It is therefore no surprise that many groups and nations deny evil actions they have committed. Collective denial is, first and foremost, an extension of the denial that is so prevalent in our everyday lives, beginning during childhood and continuing in the more adult denials that are common in different realms of life. Many collective denials are understood and even tolerated as extensions of familiar childish denials.

Many who, consciously or unconsciously, are happy to see the struggles and misfortune of other people support collective denials of racism, persecution, and genocide. Sadly, it is another universal tendency not only to be interested in what happens to others but to be relieved that others are in trouble, and this pleasure also applies to situations in which we see others on the receiving end of racist persecution—hence the pleasure many people other than the perpetrators take in anti-Semitic acts.

I have written in the professional literature that many people who themselves took no part in genocidal actions should be considered "innocent deniers."[5] Unfortunately, too many people in all national groups and cultures around the world are willing to take part in such denials for a variety of reasons. Many people are willing to join in denials of genocide, whether of Jews, Armenians, or other groups, because by doing so they can slide or sneak in to join the explicit deniers who consciously or unconsciously accept, justify, support, or even go so far as to celebrate the extermination of victimized peoples. Put simply, "innocent deniers" are, even if unknowingly, joining in on the satisfactions of denials. They express justifications of the genocide ranging from a lack of concern for the fate of others to blatant justifications of the harm done to victim populations. Even among the Jewish people, who have learned firsthand about the realities of genocidal actions, too many demonstrate a considerable lack of concern for others and take no interest in the genocides of other groups.

As noted, denial not only serves to evade punishment or demands for compensation. It protects one's pride and dignity, which for many people requires concealing their flaws and weaknesses. On the collective level, the process becomes something more grotesque and horrifying, as entire peoples and their governing and cultural institutions dedicate themselves to the lies of denials. In his great novel *1984*, George Orwell describes a regime that censors and dictates a false reality to its citizens.[6] In Orwell's world, people are arrested and caused to disappear forever because of thoughts deemed objectionable by the ruling regime. At the time the book was published, people living in democratic countries deplored such practices. However, over the years, we have come to accept considerable rewriting of history by many governments, including democracies, as well as by major organizations and companies like Google and Yahoo, when they surrender to and cooperate with regimes that promote and insist on false history.

Thus we have seen that the Chinese government refuses to acknowledge its murder of large numbers of Chinese youth who engaged in protests against the regime in Tiananmen Square in 1989. How many people know that the Chinese Communist Party general secretary at the time, Zhao Ziyang, did call for his regime to refrain from killing the protesters but himself was placed under house arrest for the rest of his life? Totalitarian regimes make no exceptions even for prime ministers. Other people who spoke the truth about the massacre also went to prison (at the time human rights sources estimated approximately ten thousand were incarcerated). Today, China is developing a thriving, open capitalist economy and expanding its ties with the international capitalist market—on condition that no one involved mentions things like Tiananmen Square or the brutal regime of Chairman Mao, which killed millions of Chinese by starvation, torture, and execution. Even today, people in China who tell the truth about these events go to prison.

An extremely widespread type of denial is the refusal of governments to acknowledge their part in starting wars. For example, the two Japanese museums commemorating the nuclear bombings of Hiroshima and Nagasaki make no mention of the fact that Japan attacked the United States with the intention of seizing control of the entire Pacific region.

In recent years the United States has become better about acknowledging some of its own acts of genocide, such as its treatment of the Native American tribes. At the same time, it continues to conceal other genocidal events in which it took part or to which it was a partner—such as the Indonesian genocide of 1965 and 1966[7] or the CIA-assisted murders perpetrated by Augusto Pinochet in Chile.[8] The list of such denials by governments and cultures is truly endless.

In conclusion, many cases of denial, on both the individual and collective levels, are meant to further pragmatic interests in avoiding punitive actions or otherwise accepting responsibility. Ultimately, however, many instances of denial also stem from the desire to defend petty concerns and fears of revealing shortcomings, weaknesses, and errors—whether individually or collectively.

Conclusion 11

People who wish not to do harm to others need to develop an ability not to deny their own errors and evil deeds. All people find it difficult to admit that their past decisions or actions were wrong or unjustified and that they have to behave differently. Who is truly a hero? True heroes are those who can acknowledge their mistakes and change their ways.

We must also not deny the injustices and evil actions committed by our own nation, or in the name of our religion, or through any other collective framework to which we belong. Instead, we need to develop the ability to acknowledge and accept responsibility for our mistakes and the injustices they have caused.

Is this an absolute principle applicable in all situations? I prefer to avoid the self-righteousness of aiming at absolute integrity, but I do want to advance our ability to acknowledge our personal and collective errors to the greatest extent possible. In the long run, such genuineness and integrity will safeguard both individuals and nations.

INNOCENCE AND THE FLAWED MANAGEMENT
OF PSYCHOLOGICAL PROCESSES

FOUNDATIONS OF EVIL 12

INNOCENCE AND FLAWED MANAGEMENT OF EMOTIONS

Many destructive acts are not results of harmful intent but rather manifestations of poor emotional management and self-control and an inability to think ahead, or of a flawed philosophy of life— the basic values by which we assess and guide our actions for the benefit of ourselves and others.

- Extremism—pushing the limits
- Completing the gestalt
- Testing limits
- The pleasure of taking risks
- The folly of nihilism

Some natural elements of human behavior lead people to commit destructive acts by virtue of the inherent structure and natural process of the behavior itself rather than because of any conscious decision to harm someone. One example is the human need to "go all the way." The processes of going all the way can draw people far past their original aims and aspirations. Instead of reaching the goal they set for themselves at the outset, they may find themselves causing harm—to themselves and to others—that they never intended but now fail to stop themselves from inflicting. Drug use, for example, initially a source of pleasure, often leads to a personal downfall when it gets out of control, at which point pleasure seeking takes on an unexpected destructive character.

In order to understand human behavior, we need to understand the array of mechanisms with which people respond to life. Every species has a different range of natural responses in their instinctual repertoire. The human psyche appears to possess a number of mechanisms that push us toward extremes and behaviors that become destructive, not as a result of any explicit desire to destroy but due to the extremist structure of our response mechanism.[9]

It seems that we also possess psychological mechanisms that attract us to destruction of life as a result of our inability to be satisfied with what we have and our constant need for *more*. These mechanisms lead us to harm life—not out of an explicit desire to be destructive but rather because we allow the extremisms to move into their destructive range. Thus, on an individual level, a successful person unable to limit or restrain his or her ambition will suffer from excessive stress stemming from too much desire and the need to achieve too much.[10] So too collectives—groups, movements, and nationalities—often go too far in their efforts at self-defense. In the process of defending themselves against a perceived enemy, they may strike out aggressively at another group or nation, but the conflict that develops may then trigger a more explicitly adventurist war that can result in the weakening and ultimate defeat of the people who went too far in their originally legitimate quest to protect themselves.

All this suggests that people often do not choose to kill others; rather their natural behavior patterns motivate them to become destructive without their having actually adopted a contemptible goal of murder.

From a moral perspective, those who truly believe that a commitment to ethical behavior—beginning with the commandment "Thou Shalt not Kill"—

is a paramount obligation to all human life cannot justify killing others. And yet we see that even well-meaning, good people many times participate in doing harm to life. Even democratic countries commit some massacres and genocides. This means that all of us must teach ourselves to monitor our behaviors honestly and critically, lest we go too far and act too unethically. If some psychological mechanism or another draws individuals or groups into excessive behavior, they need to stop themselves. People attracted to harming others must restrain themselves, overcome the compulsive urges raging within them, and redirect them to less lethal outcomes. If we speak in the terms of Stanley Milgram's classic experiment, people need to know that strong electric shocks really can be lethal and that nothing in any way can justify obeying the experimenter's instructions and applying such dangerous shocks to others.

I again stress that our attempts here to understand acts of evil are not meant to justify or excuse them. Even if genocidal murderers initially commit such acts without prior malicious intent and are drawn into a situation where they find themselves murdering victims "like everyone else" is doing, they are no less responsible for their serious actions.

I strive to understand the mechanisms resulting in genocide but never to justify them. I dedicate my analysis to enabling us to develop new tools with which to change our behaviors for the better.

THE EXTREMISM OF "PUSHING THE LIMITS"
Human beings have a tendency to push their limits by continuously focusing increasing energies on a task, such as in an endless variety of physical activities, including running, biking, swimming, and so forth. We continuously aspire to reach new goals that surpass our previous records and to increase the pace and duration of many of our activities.

In the context of recreational activities such as sports and even romance, this drive for "more"—within limits—generally presents no problems and can be fun. The trouble is that oftentimes intensive energy expenditures also result in powerful "explosions." For example, be it in playing sports or shoveling snow or racing a car, a person pushing himself past the limits of his capabilities can collapse and quite possibly die, and a person focusing an explosive level of energy on his or her immediate self-interests can destroy vital aspects of life and relationships and/or do harm to others.

"Pushing the limits" is a characteristic dynamic of fascism. It initially can imbue people with positive feelings of excitement and hope for a glorious future, but this enthusiasm almost always fades, and it becomes tragically evident that the fascist agenda leads down a long road to a hell paved with suffering and death.[11]

It is surprising and even strange to see the extent to which people typically are drawn into testing their ability to "go all the way," that is, to push their limits to attain every possible maximum and to achieve prominence by surpassing others. We see this not only in serious athletic competitions and major feats of engineering but also in much less significant achievements and even in the totally nonsensical, such as competitions over who can give the most kisses in one day or who can eat the most hot dogs or pies in a given amount of time.

Today we understand better that the human psychological mechanisms responsible for the mass extermination of others may also be prompting such desires to set new records, and this "push for more" also plays a role in preventing perpetrators from stopping their actions. Many Rwandans were likely intoxicated by the collective action and the desire to prove their killing skills to their friends—a motivation in its own right that bore little relation to the goal of eradicating Tutsis itself. In addition to the aspiration to set new records and push the limits, another "normal" mechanism is probably also at play here: a tendency not to stop whatever it is that one is doing. In the killing fields of Cambodia and at the central prison at Tuol Sleng, the killers reportedly functioned according to routines of killing that, once begun, "simply" could not be stopped. It has also been argued that the mechanism of "pushing the limits" may have played a key role in shaping the Nazis' fervor to continue exterminating the Jews until the bitter end of the Nazi empire, even when they were on the verge of defeat: many Nazi guards and soldiers continued blindly pursuing this goal during the final death marches even as the soldiers of the Allied powers—the United States, England, and the Soviet Union—closed in on them.

The mechanism of pushing the limits may be built into the basic structure of the human psyche to fulfill perfectly healthy needs to investigate and attempt all possible options. If something is possible, human beings tend to give it a try. But a great many natural things are not good for us and have to be controlled and redirected.

One school of Holocaust history maintains that the Holocaust, as a process, developed in phases and that even Hitler, for all his ravings, did not plan the "Final Solution" in its entirety ahead of time. The Nazis embarked on brutally persecuting the Jews and imprisoning them in ghettos; then, given the absence of significant resistance from the Jews themselves or from the populations in occupied countries and the "civilized" world at large, the Nazis progressed more and more to going all the way and aiming at total extermination of the Jewish people.[12] There should be no confusion: a clear-cut ideological goal of killing the Jews was certainly at the core of the process, but human psychological dynamics, including a tendency to take things to their extreme, also shaped the manner of its implementation.

Unfortunately, the process of going all the way and pushing limits progresses relatively quickly. That is to say, from the moment one group beats another into submission and relegates its members to the status of prisoners, the occupying group can rapidly develop an orientation that permits not only abuses but also executions without a need for legal proceedings. Such readiness to commit atrocities can also emerge all too readily between different ethnicities within the same national group, as with the Hutu majority's mass murder of large numbers of the Tutsi minority in Rwanda in 1994, and even among fellow members of the same ethnic, national, or other identity, as in the genocide in Cambodia.

The major cause of genocidal evils is a society's definition of the "other." In cases of genocide perpetrated by the state against a group of its own citizens, the country's government, military establishment, or religious authorities often define and construct the victim based on an arbitrary political designation. This definition in effect authorizes one part of the population to go all the way in exterminating the "other" part, whose members are now classified as "enemies of the people."

A prime example of this dynamic is the genocide that took place in Cambodia. As far as we know, no one has claimed that the Khmer Rouge ever planned or intended to carry out genocidal mass murder of the scope that it actually did, killing approximately 2 million people, or one-third of the population. The initial aim of the movement was to overpower and break the opposition of those regarded as enemies. However, as it progressed, the abusive treatment of victims assumed the form of murders that reached such horrifying dimensions. As noted, the majority of victims were other Cambodians who were not even of a different ethnic or religious grouping. In Cambodia the role of the "other" was largely assigned to millions of members of the very same Cambodian people so that the Khmer Rouge murderers had an endless supply of fellow Cambodians on whom to carry out their executions. It has been said that people wearing glasses or otherwise exuding intelligence were consistently marked for victimization. Bespectacled people were identified as dangerous!

One Muslim group, the Cham, were singled out for execution, as were Buddhist priests to an extent that, in the early years of genocide studies, many scholars seized on the murders of these named groups to justify calling the killings in Cambodia "genocide," while ridiculous definitional purities inhibited them from seeing the overall program of killing so many millions of one's own people as genocide. The same thing was true for many scholars who grappled with Stalin's murders of Soviet citizens. We human beings really get stuck on our ideas and definitions.

COMPLETING THE GESTALT

One form of "going all the way" is known as "completing the gestalt." German psychologists developed the concept of the "gestalt" during the nineteenth century. The German word *gestalt* means "form," and the concept refers to the natural human need for forms to be completed.

Who among us has not experienced an internal compulsion to complete a task or a series of actions we have already begun? We can become quite nervous and irritated when prevented from doing so. Unfortunately, this mechanism also applies to the execution of malicious actions toward others. Once we have started a job, we tend to want to complete it.[13]

This may be another reason why it is nearly impossible to find perpetrators of genocide who express regret for their actions. We have seen that once a certain amount of blood has been shed, participants become prisoners of an overpowering thirst for more blood and are transformed into serial killers. This is obviously a powerful dynamic in its own right, but the simpler explanation, at least in earlier stages of the genocidal process, is that the human desire to complete the gestalt also pushes genociders to finish what they have started.

When we go all the way, we set off an energetic process—that is to say, an urge in our nervous system to complete the action already taking place. We have a strong need to complete the gestalt or structure of the process or action underway. Underlying the process is a combination of physiological and psychological urges. The act of completion is calming, whereas non-completion is irritating and unnerving. The Turkish executed part of the Armenian population, the Nazis executed part of the Jewish population, the Serbs executed part of the Bosnian population, and the Cambodians executed other Cambodians. In all of these cases, the perpetrators went on and on, as if always predisposed to finish the job—to bring the process underway to its fullest completion.

The mechanism of completing the gestalt functions in conjunction with mechanisms of going all the way and pushing the limits; together they generate an inherent desire to continue actions to their quantitative maximum or their maximum intensity. The specific mechanism driving us to complete the gestalt is an aesthetic need to complete an action that has already been started, to achieve closure and a seemingly whole shape—all of which sounds perfectly nice until one sees it applied to hellish destructiveness.

TESTING THE LIMITS

Another mechanism that motivates people to continue a course of action already underway stems from simple cognitive curiosity about what will happen if they intensify or expand a reaction or process.[14] We have all experienced such curiosity about many different types of behaviors, including consuming questionable kinds of foods and beverages, pushing harder in an athletic activity, intensifying an emotional response, or refusing to comply with instructions and orders. We wonder, How far can I go? Can I get away with it? Once people begin such "sinful" behaviors, they are liable to continue and intensify them, pushing and pushing—until they hit a limit.

Example from Everyday Life

A woman who is regularly verbally abused by her husband becomes increasingly introverted and closed up within her pain and anguish. She fails to set any limits for her husband to make clear to him that he is not permitted to hurt her. Under such circumstances, the abusing husband is most likely to continue abusing his wife and to intensify the scope of his abuse.

Examples from the Holocaust and Other Cases of Genocide

During the Holocaust, it was as if the Germans proceeded step-by-step, asking themselves a series of questions at each step of the way:

- What will happen if we send the Jews to concentration camps?
- What will happen if we starve the Jews in the ghettos more?
- What will happen if we pipe gas from automobile engines into truckloads of Jews?

The murderous deeds of the hate-filled Nazis continued to expand in scope. Although a fundamental hatred of Jews clearly guided the overall direction of their plans, they were also influenced by an untiring curiosity regarding the limits of their own capabilities. To what extent could they intensify their actions? How many Jews could they actually kill?

Let's kill more and more of them. What fun, and what pleasure.

THE PLEASURE OF TAKING RISKS

People have a tendency to increase continually the dangers and risks to which they expose themselves—as if they are tempting fate. What point will I be able to reach? How far can I go in increasing this behavior? Human beings enjoy tempting fate and testing the limits of their capabilities and the limits of what is and is not permitted. People like to take risks and to feel the drama of a struggle for life.[15]

Examples include

- Acrobats walking on tightropes high above the ground
- Swimmers holding their breath as long as possible—some are even seriously injured
- Test-pilots flying a new aircraft
- Mountain-climbers ascending to increasingly higher altitudes and challenging their ability to survive—despite the fact that a fair number of climbers do die during high-altitude climbing in weather conditions they can't endure

What pleasure exactly do people derive from taking such risks?

Psychologists tell us that some people are inveterate thrill-seekers. They are almost or actually addicted to thrill seeking. And many others of us like to take some risks, which can have an exciting and addictive emotional intensity. There is an existential adventure in finding out whether we can make it. In a larger sense, the mortal lives of all of us unfold as an adventure and test.

Now let us take a moment to think about the combined impact of the several different mechanisms we have been discussing (listed in no particular order):

> The pleasure of risk taking + completing the gestalt + going all the way + testing the limits

The combined effects can be powerful, and they apply not only to good deeds but also to committing evil actions. The "hero" spurred on by such combined dynamics might be someone capable of developing a deadly bomb and dropping it on a civilian population, a doctor capable of investigating methods for killing greater and greater numbers of an enemy population, or a person who supervises a program of mass rape and impregnation of female members of an enemy population. The results are huge disasters to life—which is what genocides are.

In conclusion, the human psyche includes a large number of natural response mechanisms that can lead to extreme behaviors that test the limits of human capability in our universe. Until man succeeds in learning—and teaching—the sanctity of human life and developing the social and personal tools required to stop human beings from taking the lives of others, humanity will continue to degenerate into genocide, time and time again.

THE FOLLY OF NIHILISM

At some level, somewhere not far removed from our consciousness but nonetheless deep within us in a place we do not typically access in our everyday lives, we are all rushing toward our own deaths.

- Death is a fact of life from the moment we are born. Even during our younger years, when we are still growing, we are actually already on the way to our "end." As we get older, the signs of aging and decline appear at an increasingly rapid pace. If that's the case, why not spice up our lives with some adventure? After all, we only live once.

- Whether out of fear or a healthy curiosity, we all want to know more about our own impending death. We do not want to die, but we know that death will inevitably overtake us sooner or later. So why not learn more about it?
- Often enough we bring ourselves closer to death as a result of our own desperate efforts to find new ways of preventing it and attaining immortality. These efforts to delay the bitter end, however, often blow up in our faces (as when we work too hard in order to "succeed in life" and wear ourselves out or put together a lethal weapon for self-defense that blows up in our own face).
- If we are going to die anyway, why delude ourselves by delaying it? It's the next station in any case, and it beckons us to come forward toward it.
- Suicidal tendencies naturally increase during the darker and more painful periods of our lives.

We eye our future death and tempt the ultimate end that awaits us in many different ways. We all engage in seemingly normal behaviors in our everyday lives that actually increase our chances of premature death. For sure we risk our lives on the roads, too many of us still smoke cigarettes, many of us gain too much weight to the point of obesity, there are plenty of alcoholics and drug addicts, and an amazing number of us also sign up quite explicitly to carry out suicide bombings. Of course, the list goes on and on.

Why do we do these things?

Just because is the first answer. That's how we humans are.

According to Sigmund Freud, human beings simultaneously possess two coinciding and contradictory drives: a drive for life, love, instinctual pleasure, and creativity, which together constitute *eros*; and a death drive—which I suggest we regard first of all as a curious, investigating approach to death and then as a darker force of seeking our death—which Freud referred as *thanatos*.[16]

Freud was correct. But is it an open-and-shut case that all people want to die that much? Common sense says the opposite is true. And yet, for all the reasons discussed above, people are not aware that they are also engaged in a subconscious edging toward the most frightening fate of all. Our curiosity, tempting of fate, and risk taking all bring us closer to possible death, even as there is no doubt that most people's conscious and decisive desire is to live! In addition, there is a more ominous yet also natural flow of unconscious wishes in all of us to get it over with, rest, surrender, and die.

We should take note that notwithstanding Freud's acknowledged eminence in the field, many therapists have expressed doubts about his understanding of the subconscious human movement toward death. Today, so many psychotherapists are engaged in "positive" psychology and prefer not to delve deeply, if at all, into evil and the destruction of human life, either as "pathologies" or as natural elements of the human psyche that exist alongside the good and alive in human beings. With the exception of the existential therapeutic approach, Freud's analysis did not result in a substantial development of treatment methods to help people gain control of their ignorance or premature or hazardous behaviors owing to stupidity, excessive risk-taking, arrogance, tempting of fate, and the like.

As a scholar of genocide, I do think that Freud's pioneering concept of *thanatos* can contribute to our construction of explanations for the horrible phenomenon of mass killing. Apparently some leaders in our world have adopted a nihilistic philosophy of life that rejects its sanctity and have decided that if we will all eventually meet our deaths anyway, we might as well do so sooner than later. For them there is no moral deterrent to accelerating the arrival of death—for other human beings and in truth quite likely for themselves too. I believe that if we delve deep into the psyches of quite a few murderous tyrants throughout history, we may discover that this outlook played an important role in shaping their horrendous actions. As already noted, there is also no shortage of quite "ordinary" people who are willing to carry out suicide attacks. Among the various factors that make them willing to volunteer for such tasks, the race toward death would seem to play an important role[17]—for they are more than tempting fate.

Even without the help of Freudian concepts, many thinkers have reached frightening and pessimistic conclusions regarding the future of the human race.[18] Clearly, we have a great deal of work ahead of us to save our future, but we must first work on ourselves and on learning how to refrain from harming and killing both ourselves and others.

Examples from Everyday Life

Man's desire to "end it all" and to wreak havoc on himself and those around him takes many different forms. Terrorist and wartime suicide attacks are typically motivated by a national-political ideology that appears to provide a justification of some kind, but much more than ideology is involved. In fact, such attacks are sometimes carried out without any underlying political ideology, as in the case of the students who murdered their classmates and committed suicide at Columbine High School in the United States (similar attacks have been carried out at a number of other schools, located in different parts of the world as well), or the Egyptian pilot who committed suicide by intentionally crashing a 747 full of passengers in a fit of anger.

Example from the Holocaust

As the Allied armies approached the extermination camps, the Nazis marched tens of thousands of prisoners to their deaths. Why? After all, the war was nearing its end, and it was clear that the Nazis were not going to win and that many of them would probably be killed. What explains this passion for murder? Why did they refuse to cease their evil efforts even at that final hour? Were they overcome by some sort of fervor? Why?

Conclusion 12

People who wish not to do harm to others must examine their own emotional responses and style of reacting in real life to understand why they behave in extreme ways. For example, in clear-cut cases of self-defense, the most extreme action possible is the taking of human life. Will I do this? Under what circumstances? We need to carefully consider our emotions and intentions and not react with automatic justifications. Most importantly, we must always avoid endangering human life and direct ourselves to take actions that preserve and improve it—for ourselves and others.

AFTER AUSCHWITZ / VARTAN OSKANIAN

After Auschwitz, we are all Jews, we are all Gypsies, we are all unfit, deviant and undesirable, for someone, somewhere. After Auschwitz, the conscience of man cannot remain the same. Man's inhumanity to men, to women, to children, and to the elderly, is no longer a concept in search of a name, an image, a description. Auschwitz lends its malefic aura to all the Auschwitzes of history, our collective history, both before and after.[19]

AFTER AUSCHWITZ / GERHARD SCHROEDER

I feel ashamed in the face of German history. We Germans remain silent, unable to speak, when we stand face to face with the atrocities that took place on German soil and in the name of the German people. The Nazi government was founded and operated by human hands and minds.[20]

AFTER AUSCHWITZ / MICHAEL MELCHIOR

Not to engage the subject of the Holocaust or to minimize its significance also reflects a certain degree of denial.

There is nothing more Jewish than being universalist, and there is nothing more universalist than being Jewish.[21]

UNIVERSAL LESSONS / BENYAMIN NEUBERGER

I have just returned from Rwanda, where the genocide of the Tutsi people was carried out a dozen years ago—about 1 million people were murdered in three months. I stood at the Murumbi site and I learned that in this place, 54,000 Tutsi were murdered in cold blood. There are only four known survivors. One of them stood there before me and told me about babies who were flung live into pits which were covered with dirt. I saw skeletons, and clothes taken from those who were murdered. I could not help but recall my visit to the Nazi death camps in Poland. However, we have been taught that it is forbidden to compare.

In Nyanga, I visited the ruins of a church into which, in those terrible days of April 1994, 2,000 Tutsi were forced. They were abandoned by a Hutu priest, who handed them over to the Interahamwe militia, who murdered all of them. Again I recalled synagogues that were set on fire by the Nazis, with their Jews inside, but I had to fight this memory, because after all, it is forbidden to compare.

The time has come to say that the approach that negates comparison does not stand the test of reason. After all, anyone who says that it is forbidden to compare says this after he has made the comparison. Comparison does not mean that everything is identical—but rather that there is a similarity, and there could also be a difference.

Teaching of the Holocaust in a way that presents only Jewish uniqueness leads to a conviction that the Jewish people will always dwell alone, that gentiles must not be considered, that all of them are Amalek, and therefore universal morality and international law are of no importance.

We should instill awareness of the Holocaust that leads to conclusions about the need for a Jewish state and an army, but also universal lessons about respect for every human being and every people and opposition to all discrimination, racism and oppression. Such an awareness can be instilled by means of teaching the Holocaust alongside the study of other cases of genocide.[22]

Summing Up

Who Are We and What Will Become of Us?

Toward Our Individual and Collective Futures

THE MORAL IMPERATIVE OF PREVENTION OF MAJOR ILLNESS ALSO APPLIES TO GENOCIDE, THE WORLD'S NUMBER ONE CAUSE OF DEATH

Professor Elihu Richter is a member of the Hebrew University's School of Public Health and Community Medicine at the Hadassah Medical Center in Jerusalem, where he has established a Genocide Prevention Program. In his capacity, he has treated patients suffering the effects of environmental and public health mishaps, including poisoning, illnesses, and epidemics resulting from pollutants such as lead and asbestos, substandard sanitary conditions, air pollution, and the like. Richter concludes, however, that the world's number one cause of unnatural death is genocide. Although social psychologist Marc Pilisuk[1] of the University of California first reached this conclusion in the 1970s, Pilisuk's assessment did not gain popular acceptance, and the medical world took few preventative measures against this killer.

One of the most important principles in public medicine is the prevention of disease and epidemics: it is the true purpose of the medical profession. In medicine, this principle is known as the precautionary principle.[2] While we are obligated to treat people infected with illnesses and survivors of disasters, we bear an even greater obligation, if possible, to prevent lethal developments, particularly those with a potential to become disasters that endanger larger and larger portions of the population.

If up until now the prevention of genocide appeared to be largely a political or political-legal issue, along comes Richter, a physician who maintains that it is also the business of the medical profession. In light of the extremely high cost of failing, he argues, we must work to prevent genocide just as we work to prevent other epidemics. Thus, many thinkers believe that democratic countries espousing the principle of freedom of speech must also prohibit incitement and hate speech and certainly public calls for the extermination of a particular group—ethnic, religious, political, national, or any other. The precautionary approach, Richter argues justifiably, shifts the emphasis from searching for *proofs of events* that constitute genocide to real-time efforts to *prevent the killing* before it begins. Such calls to murder warrant public censure and possibly punishment as criminal acts. Intervention should begin at as early a stage as possible to prevent massacres or at least minimize the extent of harm.

The medicine-based precautionary principle is a welcome development in genocide studies and joins other models from different fields, such as social psychology, political science, international relations, and law. All these models share the common aim of detecting processes that could result in genocide as early as possible, while they are still developing, in order to mobilize other nations and the international community to intervene and prevent the destruction.[3] The medical approach reinforces and expands the goal by including the outbreak of genocidal murders in the larger medical category of dangerous epidemics. They are just as perilous.

Admittedly, in some cases the international community has identified evolving genocidal processes but failed entirely to take the necessary measures to prevent them. One poignant example is the case of Darfur-Sudan. The United States, the Organization of African Unity, and the United Nations have all failed to take effective action against the genocide in Sudan, despite the belief of professionals that realistic possibilities existed of at least of reducing the number of dead by establishing no-fly zones in civilian areas, implementing an arms embargo, and dispatching international forces to defend the targeted population. The precautionary approach must be allowed to set the tone of international actions and antigenocide efforts. Clearly, the nations of the world must take all possible measures to prevent genocidal events prior to their occurrence.

The precautionary approach also complements the concept of early-warning processes or early indicators of genocide. I have personally been engaged for many years in the study of early-warning signs of genocide.[4] During the same years, a Methodist minister, the late Franklin Littell, was also hard at work on the subject of early warning.[5] (Over the years Littell emerged as a leader in the field of Holocaust commemoration, with an emphasis on the Christian theological significances of the Holocaust.) More recently, a growing number of scholars have conducted further research on the subject of early-warning signs, influenced not only by the Holocaust but by other cases of genocide as well. Prominent among such scholars are Helen Fein,[6] Barbara Harff,[7] and Gregory Stanton.[8] Stanton, a former president of the International Association of Genocide Scholars, is founder and president of Genocide Watch, an organization that closely follows indications of impending outbreaks of genocide. Stanton appears to have done a better job than anyone else in summarizing the step-by-step processes leading to genocide in a short and simple table. The eight processes he identifies are as follows:

- Classification
- Symbolization
- Dehumanization
- Organization
- Polarization
- Preparation
- Extermination
- Denial

A NEW PRINCIPLE IN INTERNATIONAL LAW: THE OBLIGATION TO PRESERVE HUMAN LIFE—THE RESPONSIBILITY TO PROTECT (R2P)

As I have noted, along with the continuing and very real dangers of new instances of genocide in our world, we are also witnessing a new awareness of the evil of genocide and the emergence of efforts to prevent it. A number of legal institutions have been set up to contend with genocide, such as the tribunals established by the United Nations to prosecute the perpetrators of genocide in Rwanda and the former Yugoslavia, and the International Criminal Court in The Hague.

The international media are also paying increased attention to instances of present-day genocides in real time, which reduces the possibilities of concealment. In comparison to the situation that existed until only recently—when there was a lack of public knowledge about and awareness of major genocides, such as even the Holocaust, or the killings of millions in Maoist China, or the Cambodian Genocide, which some said took place behind a "bamboo curtain"—much of the factual news about ongoing genocidal killing now gets out promptly and reaches far and wide in our world.

In 2006, the UN Security Council passed a landmark resolution obligating governments to protect human life (UN Security Council Resolution 1674). Former Australian foreign minister Gareth Evans, working alongside Mohamed Sahnoun, a Muslim special advisor to the director-general of the United Nations, spearheaded this legislative initiative, known as the Responsibility to Protect (R2P).[9] Former UN secretary-general Kofi Anan and current UN secretary-general Ban Ki Moon also subsequently joined the initiative as staunch supporters.[10] The resolution was revolutionary because the long-prevailing principle dominating international law for many years negated the right of states to interfere with the decisions of other sovereign states. As a result of R2P, state sovereignty is no longer absolute.

R2P stipulates that states have the right to interfere in the affairs of other states that do not provide their inhabitants with security and protection! The right to life is now a paramount principle that supersedes all legislation and policies of states carrying out programs of human extermination.

Of course, this legislation contains various limitations, and as one might expect, no lack of politicians are seeking ways to neutralize or negate the new principle. Altogether, today's superpowers and the international community basically continue to delay or fail to undertake actions required to save human lives. Nonetheless, the resolution stands out as an important step forward both in human thinking and legislation.[11]

In the intellectual and academic worlds, we see an increasing number of studies that address the factors leading to genocide and the process by which it develops. This body of work includes many new books by scholars like psychologist Steven Baum on the psychology of genocide,[12] anthropologist Alexander Hinton on the anthropology of genocide,[13] and criminologist Alex Alvarez on genocidal actions as criminal offenses of genocide.[14] Theologian and rabbi Steven Jacobs writes about the role of religions in sanctioning and designing genocides, while simultaneously preaching the commandment "Thou shalt not kill" and the importance of compassion.[15] David Hamburg, president emeritus of the Carnegie Corporation, describes different mechanisms currently developing in the international arena that offer hope for the possibility of preventing genocides in the future.[16]

A number of dictionaries and encyclopedias of genocide have also been published in recent years, the most recent being the excellent *Dictionary of Genocide*, edited by Samuel Totten and Paul Bartrop.[17] We are also witnessing the introduction of university courses on the subject of genocide, such as "The Pain of Knowledge," a course offered by the Open University of Israel as part of its Democracy Studies program—which has attracted a record number of students (twelve hundred in 2012!). An increasing number of academic programs around the world explicitly grant degrees in both Holocaust and genocide studies. Among them, the PhD program offered by Clark University in the United States stands out: even in its early years it is already shaping a new and promising generation of professionals in the emerging field of genocide prevention.[18]

And yet genocide continues to run rampant in the contemporary world, as demonstrated by the recent and ongoing genocide perpetrated in Darfur-Sudan and the larger region. Eric Reeves,[19] an English professor at Smith College, has shed powerful new light on the events in the Sudan. Zoologist Konard Lorenz[20] has concluded that the human species is, in fact, exceptional in that it devours its own kind. According to Lorenz, in nature species tend to direct brutality toward species other than their own—although intraspecies brutality also exists under conditions of excessive population and territorial conflict. However, Lorenz posits that human brutality is so widespread and so clearly unrelated to territorial struggles that it may actually represent a full-blown bona fide genetic mutation. My opinion is that the human exception is anchored in or based largely on our brain's unfortunate psychological ability to classify "others" as "nonhumans"—although, of course, regarding strangers as potential enemies in itself is a natural and beneficial quality, but it needs to be exercised in moderation and carefully.

In a discussion of the psychology of perpetrators, bystanders, and rescuers in the context of genocide, Steven Baum writes,

> An old Cherokee tale tells of a grandfather teaching life principles to his grandson. The wise old Cherokee said, "Son, on the inside of every person a battle is raging between two wolves.
>
> "One wolf is evil. It is angry, jealous, unforgiving, proud, and lazy.

"The other wolf is good. It is filled with love, kindness, humility, and self-control. These two wolves are constantly fighting," the grandfather said.

The little boy thought about it, and said, "Grandfather, which wolf is going to win?"

The grandfather smiled and said, "Whichever one you feed."[21]

THE HOLOCAUST MEMORIAL MUSEUM IN WASHINGTON, DC

The museum is far more than a memorial to the Jewish genocide. It stands as a testament, and perhaps as a challenge, to the central issue of any democratic society: the responsibility of individuals in a free society and a nation dedicated to the core American values—indeed, the core human values—of **individual dignity, social justice, and human rights.**[22]

COULD I COMMIT GENOCIDE?

So we come to the conclusion of this book, and in the heart of every reader there will be some element of a reply to the key question, Could I commit genocide? *Could I—*

- When the government or army mobilizes volunteers to kill civilians?
- When I am in an army company that is ordered to kill civilians?
- When my society organizes mass killing of civilians and threatens to kill me if I do not join in?
- When I am subject to enormous group pressure to join others in killing, but there is no threat to my life or safety?
- When I am crazy with grief and anger over injuries to and the deaths of my family, friends, fellow countrymen, army buddies, or coreligionists?
- When I am an engineer or businessman given a lucrative business opportunity to build machinery for mass killing and disposal of bodies?
- When I am a doctor assigned to medical killing of whomever—the weak and mentally ill, members of a given religion or ethnicity, people faithful to a certain ideology, whatever . . . ?
- When I am assigned to be a concentration camp guard and need to keep the prisoners fearing me and obeying my orders?
- When I am a secretary or clerk assigned to arrange the logistics of mass killing (e.g., trains for transport, requisitioning poison gas)?
- When everyone around me is doing it?

Even those of us who do not answer these questions explicitly and/or inform ourselves consciously of where we stand nonetheless do have answers taking shape inside us.

I acknowledge to the reader that the questions are horrible and that the dilemmas in many situations are agonizing. But they are very real, having been posed over and over in history. The conditions leading to genocide can appear in our lives too, just as they have for millions before us, so better to be prepared—at least somewhat.

This book invites each of us to prepare to be as human as possible under terrifying conditions.

I appreciate so much what Pope Francis said (addressing a Joint Session of the US Congress in October 2015):

> Every life is sacred, every human being is endowed with an inalienable dignity.
> . . . Our efforts must aim at restoring hope, righting wrongs, maintaining commitments and thus promoting the well-being of individuals and of peoples.[23]

The painful truth nonetheless is that our normal human equipment includes the desire and urge to kill. In simple words, instinctually we want both to live and to die, and we want others both to live and to die. The dialectical parts are not necessarily equal in our minds, and they most certainly undergo transformation in the course of our life experiences, especially as expressions of the choices we make. They are, however, intrinsic to the human condition.

Clearly our many different cultures place variable emphases on each of these sides of normal human experiencing. An al-Qaeda spokesman reportedly said after 9/11, "We love death as much as you love life, so we will win!"[24] This frightening but true-to-life concept has become something of a mantra among Islamic terrorists around the world, such as Hamas toward Israel,[25] ISIS in Iraq and Syria, and others elsewhere.[26]

Moreover we have seen over and over again in the flow of this book a wide variety of dynamics and situational structures (such as different political regimes, different systems of organization of society, and different leaders) that can literally pull many of us who had no intention whatsoever of doing harm to others into becoming full-blown perpetrators or enablers of genocide, as if it is beyond our will and even beyond our knowledge of what we are doing when we do it. Hannah Arendt says in a very widely cited quote, "The sad truth is that most evil is done by people who never make up their minds to be good or evil."[27]

The disgusting, incredible ease with which huge parts of human civilization will launch massive campaigns of death, over and over again, in era after era, in one area of the world after another, is overwhelming proof that much of the machinery for human experiencing is directed toward approving, conforming to, and delighting in killing masses of other people. The proof is everywhere: Americans killing native Indians; Australians killing Aboriginals; Germans killing Jews and Roma (Gypsies); Serbs killing Moslem Bosnians; Rwandans, Cambodians, Russians, and Chinese each killing millions of their own peoples (even when there is no prior identity difference between the perpetrators and the victims); Muslims—in too many places—killing fellow Muslims, e.g., Sunnis killing Shi'ites and others.

The choice to love life and eschew killing requires a spiritual core (from whatever source, secular or religious), conviction, courage, and self-discipline—because the other side of our human nature doesn't simply go away, even when we do make a genuine and firm choice not to perpetrate evil. Thus Dumbledore, Harry Potter's mentor, teaches him, "Voldemort! The Evil Presence and Bearer of Death, who killed dear Harry Potter's mother and father, always lurks, waiting to pounce on each of us."[28] (This is one reason millions of us love the stories and many other tales and legends that pit good against evil.)

And just as every person, consciously or unconsciously, must choose whether to participate in an epidemic of killing, groups, organizations, nations, and societies also have to choose. We see how on a college campus one fraternity fosters a tradition of hazing and cruelty, while another excels in its emphasis on respect and dignity; we see different hospitals, one offering its services indifferently or even callously, while another takes pride in offering respectful care; we see police forces that are quick to brutality and violence, whereas others carefully monitor uses of violence and help people to feel safe and protected. In all of these instances the preferred values can be embedded in the culture of the organization for long stretches of time until bold new leadership policies introduce sweeping change—for better or for worse.

Obviously there is a relationship between individual and group choices. It will be much easier for an individual to opt for safeguarding and promoting life in a culture that has chosen a life-protecting direction. Yet we need to know that in these cultures too, people who choose violence and destruction can and do arise, as do those who seek to reroute their culture's affirmation of life as a whole toward a quest for power and killing. And it is infinitely harder for individuals to affirm life in organizations and societies that have adopted policies of overpowering and wantonly killing their defined enemies. Yet, even in the worst of societies, there are individuals and groups—a village or region or religious group of whatever denomination—who choose to be what we have come to call "Righteous People" who risk their lives to save others. So,

Where am I?
Could I commit genocide?

Each reader who dares can ask themselves.
I, the author, wish you good choices.

Independent Study

Learning Exercises about How
We Cause Harm and Protect Life

The following exercises are *not* meant to assess knowledge or understanding of the subject matter discussed in this book. Rather, these experiences are intended to encourage self-observation and honest insight into our own human psyches, examining how much we make ourselves aware of genocide and other types of evil, and how available we are—perhaps—to take orders blindly and participate in groups and societies that are perpetrating evil.

You are invited to complete these exercises. You have a right to decide that you will not. Please note that your decisions about whether to do so, and where and with whom you may share what you learn about yourself, are entirely up to you. These exercises may be emotionally difficult and may provoke disturbing thoughts and feelings. Each reader is responsible for making a personal decision about how to proceed, whether to explore the exercises, and how deeply—if at all.

INDEPENDENT STUDY 1
EXAMINING OUR WILL TO LIVE OR DIE AND OUR WISHES
TOWARD OTHERS

Warning: The following two exercises are disturbing and may cause psychological discomfort to those not prepared to confront the depths of their feelings about their own ultimate deaths and about mass deaths of others. Readers are advised to determine for themselves whether or not they are prepared to explore these issues. The purpose and justification of this exercise lie in the terrible fact that tens of millions of human beings have died horrible deaths at the hands of other human beings, and this exercise is meant to advance what many believe to be the true aim of culture and education, the cultivation and preservation of the sanctity of human life.

Exercise 1.1
An Exercise about Our Will to Live

Close your eyes.
Imagine a pendulum swinging back and forth between two extremes: your desire to live (on the right) and your desire to die (on the left).
Imagine in your mind's eye the movement of the pendulum.
To what extent do you wish to live?
To what extent do you wish to die?
Notice the fluctuations of the pendulum.

Note: The results of this exercise will change frequently throughout the course of your life, from period to period, day to day, and even hour to hour. We can all benefit from learning more about the contexts and how much, deep in our hearts, we experience wishes not to live. For example, to what extent do we feel a need to escape from the stresses in our lives and reach a "restful place"?

In connection with our goal of gaining an understanding of the psychology of genocide, this exercise teaches us about a darker and less familiar side of the inner continuum of our human experience. It is important to note that the subject at hand at this point is not simply a willingness to kill others: indeed, a person with a strong desire to live might well participate in murdering others as if by doing so he is ensuring his own life. Similarly, a person with a strong will to hasten his or her own death might refrain from projecting his death wish onto others. Even so, how we feel about our own existence plays an important role in determining how we relate to the lives of others. The desirable goal is to care about our own lives first and foremost and then to protect the lives of others. In most cases, people who are happy with their own lives are more likely to want to preserve the lives of others.

Exercise 1.2
An Exercise about Our Personal Willingness to See Others Murdered and Perhaps Ourselves Play Active Roles in the Process of Mass Killing

Close your eyes.

1. Think of minority peoples and see which people most prominently come up in your mind's eye.

   a. Now imagine a pendulum swinging back and forth between two extremes: your respect for the lives of others and your willingness to defend the lives of minority people (on the right), and your desire to see piles of corpses of this minority people and your readiness to participate in the mass killings of the minority group (on the left).

      Imagine the movement of the pendulum. Explore your thoughts and feelings. As we know, millions of people are willing to assist or take an active role in the murder of others. During the Holocaust, the Jewish people learned firsthand that large numbers of people from many different national groups were ready to slaughter them. So, too, members of many other groups have been murdered in the same manner. We all have an obligation to learn about ourselves and to determine whether we too could find ourselves among the murderers in such situations.

   b. Now think about a different minority group and perform the exercise again. Repeat the exercise using at least three to five different minority groups.

Applying the Exercises to Your Own Personal Development in Your Daily Life

1. What have I learned about myself that is relevant to my everyday life?
2. Are there things I would like to change about my personality or the way I conduct my daily life?
3. Would I like to set a clearer moral norm for myself with regard to what I will and will not permit myself to do under different circumstances, including conditions of war?

INDEPENDENT STUDY 2
PROJECTING ONTO OTHERS VERSUS TAKING RESPONSIBILITY
FOR OUR NEGATIVE FEELINGS

Exercises Relating to Projection

It requires a good deal of intellectual and moral strength for us to acknowledge that we bear responsibility for a bad relationship with someone in our lives.

Exercise 2.1
An Exercise about Difficult Relationships in Our Lives

Make a detailed table of people you hate, with whom you have a bad relationship, with whom you do not maintain a normal "give-and-take," or who make you feel threatened or hated. In the second column, indicate your beliefs about the other person's role in creating the distance, tension, or feelings of hatred between you. In the third column, indicate your role in creating the negative relationship. Completing this column will require much more effort on your part in order to overcome the natural tendency to evade your own share of responsibility for negative relationships and wrongdoing.

Exercise 2.2
An Exercise about Hostile Projection onto Members of Other Ethnic, Racial, National, or Religious Groups (including Subgroups of One's Own Religion)

The following table contains a list of ethnic and national groups. Indicate for each one your automatic feelings about it, including your sense of distance from or hatred for the group, your inclination to take active measures to distance yourself from it, and your readiness to use violence against its members.

National, Ethnic, and Religious Groupings	Sense of Distance or Hatred	Readiness to Act Forcefully to Distance Them	Readiness to Use Violence against Them
Christians			
Muslim Arabs			
Christian Arabs			
Shi'ite Arabs			
Sunni Arabs			

Ultra-Orthodox Jews			
Secular Jews			
Germans			
Turks			
Russians			
Americans			
Intellectuals			
Blacks			
Mexicans			
Asians			

Applying the Exercises to Your Own Personal Development in Your Daily Life

1. What have I learned about myself that is relevant to my everyday life?
2. Are there things I would like to change about my personality or the way I conduct my daily life?
3. Would I like to set a clearer moral norm for myself with regard to what I will and will not permit myself to do under different circumstances, including conditions of war?

INDEPENDENT STUDY 3
HUMILIATING PEOPLE

Exercise 3.1

An Exercise on Humiliating Others

Ask yourself the following question:

Was there ever a time you enjoyed humiliating someone?

INDEPENDENT STUDY 4
EXCESSIVE PURSUIT OF POWER

Introductory Exercises about Addiction to Power

The following exercises enable us to explore our tendencies to seek power and justify our use of power against others, as well as whether and to what extent we are prone to intoxications of power and excesses in our use of power.

Exercise 4.1
An Exercise about Which Positions of Leadership Draw You

In the table below, indicate in each context the roles that attract you the most. Do you prefer to be a leader, instructor, or supervisor or to fill another role?

1	2	3
Family Life	In the Workplace	In the Community and Society
a. Decision making	a. Decision making	a. Decision making
b. Financial management	b. Financial management	b. Financial management
c. Organization (child care, planning entertainment, vacations, family, other needs)	c. Organization	c. Organization

Note: Leadership abilities and roles in themselves should not be thought of as reflecting excessive aspirations for power.

Exercise 4.2
An Exercise about Our Desires to Hold Authority and Be Superior to Others

Working with the previous list of leadership roles (columns 1, 2, and 3—a, b, and c), try to recall situations in which you—inwardly or outwardly—were very pleased to be in control and perhaps even expressed your pleasure openly. Describe the levels of excitement, gratification at being the authority, self-importance, and superiority you experienced in each situation.

1a	
1b	
1c	

2a	
2b	
2c	
3a	
3b	
3c	

Exercise 4.3
An Exercise about More Intense Dictatorial, Humiliating,
and Aggressive Behaviors

Consider leadership positions you have held in the past. In your opinion, have you ever crossed the line into dictatorial or aggressive behavior toward others?

1a	
1b	
1c	
2a	
2b	
2c	
3a	
3b	
3c	

Applying the Exercises to Your Own Personal Development in Your Daily Life

1. What have I learned about myself that is relevant to my everyday life?
2. Are there things I would like to change about my personality or the way I conduct my daily life?
3. Would I like to set a clearer moral norm for myself with regard to what I will and will not permit myself to do under different circumstances, including conditions of war?

INDEPENDENT STUDY 5
DEHUMANIZATION, "THINGING," OR CATEGORIZING OTHER PEOPLE AS "THINGS," AND DEMONIZATION—ATTRIBUTING EVIL POWER AND INTENTIONS TO OTHERS

Exercise 5.1
An Exercise about Feelings of Disgust toward Members of Other Groups

The following table contains a list of national, religious, and ethnic groups. Rate the level of emotional antipathy or disgust you feel toward the members of each group from 1 (lowest) to 10 (highest); also rate how much importance you attribute to this group in comparison to your own group.

National, Ethnic, and Religious Groups	Level of Emotional Antipathy-Disgust	Importance Relative to My Own Group
Christians		
Muslim Arabs		
Christian Arabs		
Shi'ite Arabs		
Sunni Arabs		
Ultra-Orthodox Jews		
Secular Jews		
Germans		
Turks		
Russians		
Americans		
Intellectuals		
Blacks		
Mexicans		
Asians		

Exercise 5.2
An Exercise about Our Readiness to Discriminate against Members of Other Groups

If your government ordered you to discriminate against members of a particular group or people, do you believe you would obey?

Exercise 5.3
An Exercise about Our Readiness to Kill Members of Other Groups

If your government ordered you to kill the members of a particular group, what would be your most likely course of action?

Moreover, if your government threatened to kill you if you didn't kill members of a particular group, what would be your most likely course of action?

INDEPENDENT STUDY 6
HOW MUCH AM I PREPARED TO HURT OTHERS?

Exercise 6.1
An Exercise in Self-Analysis and Evaluation of Our Readiness to Harm or Kill Others in Accordance with the Actions of the Majority Population

What is my position? Am I prepared to resist or to follow orders? Answer the following questions:

- Would I be ready to kill if doing so were consistent with the actions of the majority of the population (as in Germany and Rwanda)?
- Would I be ready to believe in and acquiesce to the calls of leaders and commanders to slaughter, torture, and rape innocent people, including women, children, and the elderly?

Applying the Exercises to Your Own Personal Development in Your Daily Life

1. What have I learned about myself that is relevant to my everyday life?
2. Are there things I would like to change about my personality or the way I conduct my daily life?
3. Would I like to set a clearer moral norm for myself with regard to what I will and will not permit myself to do under different circumstances, including conditions of war?

INDEPENDENT STUDY 7
CONFORMING TO THE BEHAVIORS OF OTHERS

Exercise 7.1
An Exercise about Participating in the Ongoing Actions of the Majority around Us

To what extent do you believe you would conform to and join in on the behavior of all the people around you?

- If you are a psychiatrist who does not believe in electric shock therapy for most clinically depressed patients, but all the other psychiatrists in the hospital where you work are treating their depressed patients in this manner, will you follow suit?
- If all the other doctors around you are doing so, will you carry out a "medical" selection in a concentration camp—directing young inmates to the left for whatever period they survive as forced labor and the rest to the right for immediate execution?
- If everyone else is doing so, will you take over an apartment and appropriate for yourself the property of the Jews after the Gestapo has forced them out of their homes and sent them on their way?

INDEPENDENT STUDY 8
WHAT SHOULD I DO IF I AM A WITNESS TO EVIL?

Exercise 8.1
An Exercise about Witnessing Evil Atrocities

How do you think you would react to witnessing the following?

- A policeman being violent to a civilian?
- A group of dealers selling drugs?
- A student cheating on a final exam?
- A government minister taking a bribe?
- A professional athlete taking a bribe to fix the outcome of a game?
- A foreign government granting you a sizable sum of money (e.g., a scholarship) on the condition that you refrain from criticizing its denials of human rights violations?
- Taking a lucrative business contract on the condition that you pay out a bribe to the person controlling the deal?

INDEPENDENT STUDY 9
STANDING UP FOR YOUR OWN IDEAS AND VALUES

Exercise 9.1
An Exercise in Self-Analysis of Your Ability to Stand Up to Popular Opinion

It was once rumored that Solomon Asch's famous experiment involving short and long lines also was carried out on Israeli pilots—who typically are known for their strength of character and independent and practical thinking. The pilots were supposedly presented with photographs of aircraft and asked to identify Phantom and Mirage planes. A majority of the pilots were there as stooges and unanimously identified a Mirage as a Phantom, even though it was not. The real subjects were the rest of the pilots. It is said that the majority of the real subjects did the same. (Despite my best efforts over the years, I have never found documentation of this study in the literature, and it's likely that the story was made up.)

What is your opinion? If you were a pilot, how would you respond? How do you think you would have responded in the original long line/short line experiment? Do you think you would have identified a longer line as a shorter line in accordance with most of those around you?

Applying the Exercises to Your Own Personal Development in Your Daily Life

1. What have I learned about myself that is relevant to my everyday life?
2. Are there things I would like to change about my personality or the way I conduct my daily life?
3. Would I like to set a clearer moral norm for myself with regard to what I will and will not permit myself to do under different circumstances, including conditions of war?

INDEPENDENT STUDY 10
WHERE DO OUR INTERNATIONAL AGENCIES STAND ON GENOCIDE?

Exercise 10.1
An Exercise about the Behavior of Churches, International Companies, and Other International Bodies

Consider the following questions as they apply to various genocides:

- Did the Catholic churches and the international leadership of the Catholic Church respond to the Holocaust and to the Rwandan Genocide in an appropriate manner? What should they have done?
- Did the Allied powers do all they could to fight those who carried out genocides during World War II?
- Did the United States respond correctly to the Armenian Genocide, the Holocaust, or the Rwandan Genocide?
- Did large international companies that operated in Nazi Germany, such as IBM, take any position regarding the persecution and murders their customers in Europe were executing? Did athletic organizations or international entertainers?
- Have modern-day international bodies such as the United Nations, the Organization of African Unity, the European Union, and the North Atlantic Treaty Organization sent diplomats to intervene in the massacres of various peoples? Where yes and where no? Have they dispatched military forces?

INDEPENDENT STUDY 11
LETTING GO OF ONE'S WILDNESS IN A CROWD SITUATION

Exercise 11.1
An Exercise in Acting Wildly—Alone, in the Presence of a Small Number of Other People, and in Larger Groups

- Try to yell and act in a boisterous and unruly manner when you are alone in a room.
- Try the same type of behavior in the presence of one other person or a small group.
- Now join a group of people (or recall a past experience of this kind) who are marching noisily or celebrating in exhilaration the winning outcome of a sports event or are having a wildly good time at a carnival. Does your being in a collective context have any impact on your ability to yell and act rowdily?

INDEPENDENT STUDY 12 (FOR MEN)

Exercise 12.2
Where Do You Stand on Committing Rape? An Exercise about Our Readiness to Abuse and Rape under the Influence and Encouragement of a Group

- The scene develops without violence but in an alluring instinct-driven atmosphere that builds up progressively. Are you in "for the ride"?
- You are part of a group of adolescents or perhaps a group of young adults in a respectable university framework. A sensual young woman is flirting with the group and appears to be willing to have sexual relations with the members of the group one after the other. But now that the leader of the group has almost finished undressing her, she begins to cry and mumbles fearfully that she wants to go home. You are a young man, eager and excited, but nonetheless you see and understand her distress. What do you do?

INDEPENDENT STUDY 13
PAYOFF QUESTIONS: HOW YOU WILL BE IN A GROUP THAT TORTURES AND COMMITS MURDER?

So, in your final analysis, looking at who you were when you began this study and in light of all the thinking and exercises you have done in the course of reading this book, where do you feel you stand as regards your intended ways of reacting if and when an era of genocidal killing erupts in your life?

Exercise 13.1
An Exercise about Readiness to Participate in a Group That Tortures and Possibly Even Murders Others

Think about your behavior in the past. Have you ever allowed yourself to do things as a member of a group, or in the name of a belief or an ideology, that you would never have considered doing on your own? Imagine the following scenarios:

- You are living during the era of Nazi rule and are assigned the task of gathering Jews to send them on trains to the concentration camps. Would you carry out the order? In what manner?
- You are a Russian soldier living under Stalinist rule and are sent to expel the Chechens from their homes to send them to Siberia. Would you follow this order? In what manner?

- You are a devout Catholic who shares the theological beliefs of the Inquisition. Would you be capable of setting fire to the nonbelievers who deny your god?
- You are a member of the Communist Khmer Rouge in Cambodia. Would you be capable of killing, with your own two hands, the people identified as opponents of the regime?

Applying the Exercises to Your Own Personal Development in Your Daily Life

1. What have I learned about myself that is relevant to my everyday life?
2. Are there things I would like to change about my personality or the way I conduct my daily life?
3. Would I like to set a clearer moral norm for myself with regard to what I will and will not permit myself to do under different circumstances, including conditions of war?

INDEPENDENT STUDY 14
A CONCLUDING EXERCISE FOR REGULAR USE THROUGHOUT OUR LIVES TO STRENGTHEN OUR BEING DECENT PEOPLE

A Simple Exercise of Meditation and Choice for Everyday Life

This exercise is designed both for "ordinary people" and for generals and heads of state as well. It should be repeated on a regular basis (recommended monthly) throughout one's entire life.

- Have I developed an ethical outlook and personal guidelines for how aggressive I will or won't be in the different areas of my life—my academic and professional life, my relationships with neighbors, my business dealings, and so on?
- **Am I committed to not harm others and certainly not to destroy the lives of others?**

Appendix

Studies on Israeli Willingness to Commit Evil

In a series of psychological studies, Daphna Fromer and I examined the bases of cognitive willingness of Jewish Israelis to discriminate against others. The studies were conducted as simulations, and subjects were requested to play certain roles as explained below.

One study dealt with a fictitious population suffering from serious chronic illnesses in an unidentified country in Africa. Subjects were presented with a number of imaginary scenarios including an extreme program of "mercy killing."[1,2]

A second study dealt with an imaginary, yet not inconceivable, scenario in which most of Israel's Arab population was "transferred," or deported, across Israel's borders by a right-wing government.[3]

A third study examined attitudes toward the 1956 murders at Kfar Qasim (Kfar Kassem), which took place on the first day of the Sinai War. In this incident, Israeli soldiers murdered forty-nine unarmed Arab men, women, and children who were returning to their homes after work, unaware that an earlier curfew had been imposed.[4]

The subjects of the first two studies were Jewish Israeli students in the three helping professions of medicine, psychology, and social work. Subjects were selected on the assumption that students in these fields of treatment could be expected to be sensitive to the needs of others, particularly regarding the preservation of human life.

In the first study, students were instructed to imagine themselves as therapists—physicians, psychologists, or social workers—sent by the Israeli government to Africa and instructed to commit a series of increasingly unethical acts on chronically ill patients.

In the second study, the students were also asked to see themselves as therapists in the future. In this case a right-wing government in Israel orders them to implement a "selection" to identify those Arab Israelis who are medically unfit to endure the hardships of mass deportation in the oncoming expulsion of Arab Israelis that the government has ordered. Although the participants were being asked to protect—save—the weaker Palestinians from deportation, doing so meant they were participating, as professionals, in the program to deport the majority. Students who agreed to play their assigned roles determining which Arabs would and would not be expelled from the country thus became partners to expulsion. In effect, their willingness to follow manifestly unlawful orders made them accomplices to ethnic cleansing, which is defined as a crime against humanity under international law.

The subjects of the third study were Jewish Israelis visiting a museum in Tel Aviv to view Claude Lanzmann's nine-hour film *Shoah*.[5] As they stood in line, we asked them questions about the massacre of innocent Arabs perpetrated at Kfar Qasim.

THE STUDY REGARDING THE TREATMENT OF CHRONICALLY ILL IN AFRICA

In the study dealing with the treatment of chronically ill patients, the students were told that they had already completed their academic studies and were bona fide young professionals who had been sent to a country in Africa to assist the local ministry of health—in accordance with the Jewish and humanist tradition of extending aid to the ill and to developing countries. During the study, we made intentional use of phrases and concepts used by the Nazis during the Holocaust. The Nazis never spoke of "extermination" and "murder" but rather talked of mercy killing and a "Final Solution." They actually used the term "mercy killing" to refer to Operation T4—their very first program of mass extermination in which they murdered mentally disabled children, the handicapped, and the mentally ill—which included children who wet their beds and rebellious children whose behavior disturbed adults, who then classified them as "mentally ill."[6] We were assessing the readiness of our student subjects—all Israeli citizens studying helping professions decades after the Holocaust—to follow the instructions of their superiors to carry out a series of tasks, which began with questionable actions, to say the least, then increased in severity and ended up in fully lethal actions performed on those chronically ill patients diagnosed as having no chance of recovery.

Of course, we gave the young professionals explanations and justifications. In this way, we fulfilled one basic requirement of genocide perpetrators—to provide people "rational" explanations and justifications for their actions. We told our subjects that poverty in the African country was on the rise, that the resources available for treating the ill were declining, and that the local ministry of health had issued the orders in consultations with senior physicians at the Faculty of Medicine of the local university—it is always desirable for genocidal process to have the "approval" of high-ranking governmental, religious, or medical authorities. The sequence we used is that we first told the students that the health ministry had made a series of decisions to reduce treatment; then we told them the decision had become to discontinue treatment of the most critically ill patients; finally we said that a decision was made to "rescue the untreatable cases" from their suffering through "mercy killing" carried out by the medical establishment.

To what extent did our students agree to take part in the procedures we designed for them?

- Approximately 40 percent indicated that had they been there, they would have approved the program to discontinue treatment for the critically ill.
- Approximately 17 percent were ready to approve the implementation of a "selection" of patients to be killed through "mercy killing."
- 10 percent expressed a willingness to perform the "mercy killings" themselves.

Further discussion of these results follows below.

THE STUDY REGARDING THE EXPULSION OF ARABS FROM ISRAEL

In our study of "transfer," we told our subjects that a far right-wing government had been established in Israel and decided to remove all Arab inhabitants from Israeli territory "once and for all." We explained, however, that due to our own experience as a people who have endured great suffering and with a strong tradition of espousing high moral principles, we would not force emigration upon those Arabs who were too young, too old, or too ill to endure the hardships involved. Therefore, in order to carry out the "humanitarian" process of diagnosing and selecting the Arab inhabitants to be permitted to remain in Israel, the Israel Defense Forces (IDF) had drafted young professionals. The students were instructed to regard themselves as graduates in their respective fields who were ordered to classify, diagnose, and select those who would be exempt from deportation. As noted earlier, by agreeing to participate even in order to implement a benevolent act aimed at protecting the weak members of the Arab population, the subjects were actually agreeing to follow orders and take part in the transfer.

The result was that 34 percent of the subjects said that they were willing to do what was asked of them.

THE STUDY OF THE MASSACRE OF ARABS AT KFAR QASIM

As noted, the subjects of the third study were people who had come to see Claude Lanzmann's film *Shoah*. The study assumed that anyone willing to watch such a difficult movie for nine hours must by definition be more aware than others of the evil involved in murdering innocent people. On this premise, we were assessing their attitudes toward the murders committed at Kfar Qasim.[7]

As the subjects stood in line to purchase tickets for the movie, graduate student researchers approached and addressed them as follows: "Hi. I see you're buying tickets for the screening of *Shoah*. I'm a university student researcher. Would you be willing to answer four short questions for our study?"

If the respondents agreed, the research students would ask their questions, the last of which was our main research interest. We asked whether the subjects agreed with, supported, or accepted with understanding the murder of the forty-nine unarmed Arab inhabitants killed while returning to Kfar Qasim on the day of the outbreak of the Sinai War in 1956.

- Approximately 40 percent answered yes.
- Approximately 54 percent of the Holocaust survivors and others whom we identified closely with Holocaust commemoration answered yes.
- Approximately 26 percent of native-born Israelis who were not Holocaust survivors answered yes (a significant statistical difference from the previous finding).

THE PARADOX: GOOD AND BAD RESULTS

A number of important published studies of the willingness to perpetrate evil or to identify with perpetrators of evil that were conducted in the United States and elsewhere, including Stanley Milgram's study[8] and a study of the willingness of Americans to follow orders to kill women and children in the Vietnamese village of My Lai,[9] found that the percentage of subjects willing to do harm to others was almost double what we found in our studies in Israel. On this comparative basis, we concluded, both happily and sadly, that our own findings could be understood as both positive and negative, or "good" and "bad."

As a Jew and an Israeli, I am ashamed of each and every subject who consented to or approved the unjust acts examined in each of the three studies.

As a university professor of psychology and family therapy who has trained many therapists, and as a clinical supervisor for psychiatrists, psychologists, and social workers, I understood clearly that I would be obligated to discontinue the studies of any student, no matter how talented, who expressed attitudes that I identified as prejudiced and persecutory in their essence, such as the willingness to approve so-called mercy killing in the first experiment and certainly the readiness to execute the "treatment."

I would be similarly unable to tolerate and justify the responses of students who were willing to take part in the selection of Arab citizens who would be unable to endure the hardships of deportation from Israel. At the same time I could not make an unequivocal determination that they too had crossed such a red line that justified the cessation of their studies. I did not believe they had gone so far that there was justification for actually expelling them from a professional training program. In such cases, my own personal view is that I would severely reprimand such students and stress to them their obligation never to follow orders to implement programs that are prohibited under international law—even when serving within a military framework.

We submitted articles providing accounts of these experiments to several respected professional journals. We received some skeptical responses on a scientific level, as well as emotional responses from some Jewish editors who were very pained by the "bad" findings—that some Jews were willing to harm or take the lives of others. Some editors also said they understood that in Israel too one could identify a substantial level of destructive tendencies but nonetheless were hesitant about publishing the findings out of concern that they would be exploited for anti-Semitic purposes. In the end, however, all the editors who expressed concern and anguish over the studies ultimately agreed to publication.

On a scientific level, the editors of one of the journals to which we had submitted the first study for publication asked us to provide evidence that other instructors in the professions would agree with our assessment of the severity of the attitudes expressed by the students who approved the "mercy killing" program. In response we ran a supplementary study in which we asked thirty clinical instructors in the three relevant fields (medicine, psychology, and social work), at a variety of universities, how they would handle students in their respective professions who would agree to shorten the lives of their patients, even under the authority of the local health ministry. The vast majority of instructors were in agreement with us, as reflected in the following findings:

- 17 percent of the instructors indicated that they would discontinue the studies of students who agreed to stop the treatment of their patients, and 56 percent indicated that they would suspend but not expel them from their program of study.
- 80 percent indicated that they would discontinue the studies of the students who agreed to the program of "mercy killing."
- Between 63 and 73 percent of the instructors indicated that they would discontinue the studies of students in their respective fields who agreed to take part in deciding which Arabs should not be deported from Israel, and 23 percent indicated that they would suspend the students.

The articles documenting the experiments we had conducted appeared in five influential journals outside Israel, three of which are at the top of their respective fields of specialization. The journals that published the studies were

- *Holocaust and Genocide Studies* (at the time edited in Israel but published abroad as an international journal; see note 1)
- *American Journal of Orthopsychiatry*
- *Journal of Traumatic Stress* (see note 4)
- *IDEA: A Journal of Social Issues* (see note 2)[10]
- *Contemporary Family Therapy* (see note 3)

Those familiar with the field of Holocaust and genocide studies will appreciate the special significance of the publication of our first study in the first journal listed above. In later years, this same journal would be criticized for excessive focus on the Holocaust and neglect of its self-declared commitment (as reflected in its title) also to publish substantial scholarship on other cases of genocide and on fundamental aspects of the process of genocide.[11]

OPPOSITION TO PUBLICATION OF THE STUDIES IN ISRAEL

Not one of the studies, however, was ever published in a professional journal in Israel! The first two studies on treatment of the severely ill and forced migration of Arabs were not accepted by any scientific journal in Israel, despite our best efforts, and the third study on attitudes to the genocidal massacre at Kfar Qasim was also subject to heavy academic criticism. A bit of saving grace will be found in the fact that the first two studies were the subject of a number of write-ups in Israeli newspapers, such as *Haaretz* and *Maariv*, but all other Israeli publications refused to publish them.

We did try. We submitted articles in Hebrew to local professional journals. We knew there was a larger importance to such publication in Israel because journal articles are included in local academic databases that serve as a source for future generations of scholars investigating particular lines of research. The two Hebrew-language journals in Israel to which we submitted an article on the first two studies were *Megamot* ("Trends") and *Sihot* ("Dialogue"). *Megamot* based its rejection on the claim that the scientific structure of the experiment was flawed (obviously in contradiction to the judgments made by the editors of the English-language journals). The editors of *Sihot* went much further, and after first accepting the article, then cancelled it on the basis that they had determined that our findings were "falsified and deceitful"!

To a certain degree, the saga of our efforts to publish our findings in Israel reflects some of the less-flattering, though relatively well-known aspects, of Israeli society: undue aggressiveness, supercilious displays of power, and a willingness to humiliate others. Aluf Hareven has summed up this aspect of Israeli society in his book *Do Israelis Really Respect Human Dignity?*

Israel is a country where most Israeli leaders and citizens have yet to undergo a deep self-examination on the question of whether it is a state of human dignity or a state of human humiliation. Is Israel a society where approximately one million citizens live in families in which men are violent toward their wives? Are we a society in which the rates of violence and humiliation among our youth are among the highest in the developed world? Will we continue to oppress and humiliate the three million Palestinians living in the occupied territories and discriminate against Israel's million and a quarter Arab citizens? Will we continue our humiliating treatment of new immigrants from the Commonwealth of Independent States and Ethiopia? Will we continue to witness police officers humiliating citizens from weaker sectors of society, commanders humiliating soldiers, public servants humiliating citizens in need, Knesset members humiliating their colleagues, employers humiliating foreign workers, the mutual humiliation of fans of opposing sports teams, and the humiliating behaviors of Israelis while traveling abroad, staining Israel's good name?

Is Israel truly a state of human dignity? This question touches on the very essence of Israel as a Jewish state. Israel was established by Jews who aimed to free themselves of the shackles of exile and to free themselves of their oppression and humiliation as human beings. If, after more than fifty years of statehood, Israel remains a society in which a large portion of its citizens humiliate others—whether strangers or people we know familiarly—the profound meaning of this state of affairs is that we have not yet freed ourselves from the shackles of exile in our daily lives. However, for some of us, these shackles find expression in a reversal of roles: it is now the Jews who are humiliating other Jews and minorities. The state's most important achievement has been its development of military might in order to defend the existence of the Jewish state, but it is doubtful whether on this basis Israel has become a defender of human dignity—a Jewish, Israeli, and universal value of major importance—to qualify as an exemplary humanitarian state according to the vision of the prophets of Israel.[12]

In sum, the unwillingness of the academic-scientific establishment in Israel to accept and publish our findings about the readiness of Israelis to commit evil in our simulation studies indeed reflects a larger, real-life willingness of too many Jewish Israelis to commit evil acts.

FROM SCIENTIFIC STUDIES TO REAL LIFE: THE BRUTALITY OF SOME ISRAELIS

From the laboratory to real life. In addition to conducting studies on the willingness of Israelis to carry out harmful acts against others under laboratory conditions, we have also witnessed harmful actions in real life. We already discussed the mass murder of innocent citizens perpetrated at Kfar Qasim in 1956. This is probably the most prominent and best-documented case of its kind. The Kfar Qasim massacre also went to court, which not only convicted several of the perpetrators but also issued a truly historic ruling prohibiting the execution of manifestly unlawful orders in the IDF. There are also reports of other massacres carried out by Israelis over the years, though this is not the place to discuss them. It is important to remember that we, too, are capable of such actions.

In a study carried out under the direction of Professor Yoel Elizur of the Hebrew University, Nufar Yishai-Karin interviewed IDF soldiers in two companies stationed in Gaza during the First Intifada.[13] In a book on Israeli soldiers in the intifada, Elizur writes,

> The testimonies of soldiers . . . can be difficult to read and it has also been difficult to write up, as they depict processes of escalation that in some cases resulted in brutal behavior. The study is based on interviews with discharged IDF soldiers following their compulsory army service in the two armored infantry companies that were stationed in Gaza during the first Intifada. The interviewees described severe atrocities which appear to have been committed by some of them and which were successfully concealed from the military authorities, apparently without much difficulty.[14]

Elizur sums up the findings by devising a series of subgroups to characterize the soldiers according to their responses.[15] Summing up, some of the interviewees had undergone a process of brutalization, others had remained passive, and a minority had engaged in an active struggle to counter these dynamics.

- The callous or the impulsive:
  These soldiers freed themselves of all inner restraints without any difficulty, at times with enthusiasm, and displayed the most severe violence.
- Ideologists:
  These soldiers maintained that the Palestinians should be dealt with sternly but, "when push came to shove," "failed" in their efforts to implement their ideology because of inner inhibitions. For example, one interviewee experienced a sense of emotional shock when he saw a fellow soldier beating prisoners.

- Followers:
    These soldiers were drawn into the violent behavior by their commanders and/or fellow soldiers leading the brutalization.
- Restrained:
    These soldiers retained their self-control and kept to a red line that reflected a compromise between their personal morals and the reality of the situation on the ground.
- Soldiers with conscience:
    These soldiers felt moral responsibility not only to themselves but also to the other soldiers in their unit. From the beginning of their service, they experienced a sense of moral tension.

Nufar Yishai-Karin, who served in the IDF as a noncommissioned officer charged with counseling soldiers, interviewed eighteen soldiers and three officers from one company, most of whom she knew from her own military service. In a newspaper story published in the *Haaretz* weekend magazine, reporter Dalia Karpel described the soldiers as follows:

What characterizes the twenty-one interviewees? They include all kinds of people. Approximately half were Ashkenazi and the rest were from Sephardic backgrounds. Most were born in Israel to middle class parents. They were the sons of *moshavim* and *kibbutzim*, residents of mixed cities such as Jerusalem, Acre, and Ramla, but also from Herzliyah Pituach, Tel Aviv, and Ramat Hasharon [cities higher on the socioeconomic scale].

Testimony: "I went out on my first patrol. The people who I was with simply were shooting like mad. I also started to shoot too, like everyone else. Look, I can't say that it wasn't cool. I'd be lying to you if I didn't say it was gratifying. Suddenly, for the first time, you just grab your weapon, and you are not practicing in field training on some hut in the sand dunes and you have no commander looking over your shoulder on the shooting range. Suddenly, you are responsible for your own actions. You take your weapon, and shoot. You do whatever you want to do."[16]

According to Karpel, Yishai-Karin concluded that "the soldiers enjoyed an 'intoxication of power' no less than the pleasure of using violence," an inference that is frightening but extremely important for understanding human beings—indeed for understanding ourselves.

Elizur Explains the Aim of the Study[17]

The aim of the study that analyzed the narratives of the combat soldiers was to assess the manner in which young men, who had been given good educations by their parents and teachers and had displayed no signs of excessive aggression before being drafted into the IDF, were capable of undergoing a rapid transformation that resulted in their breeching the boundaries of the law and morality. As a result of socio-psychological processes that took place within the two companies, the perpetrators underwent a quick process of joining up and identifying with their comrades in arms that escalated into their shaking off previous moral codes and constraints they previously felt and developing new cultural codes that justified excessive violence toward Palestinians. The more the codes reflecting a "culture of brutality" took root within the military units, the more the soldiers committed what we consider war crimes. Their evil atrocities included physical injury and also acts of humiliation against women, children, prisoners, and civilians, as well as destruction of property, looting, mutilation, and outright murder.

Was this an exceptional phenomenon?

Although we would feel more comfortable believing that these were simply the actions of two rotten companies and not a microcosm of the IDF and Israeli society, the trials of soldiers from the Givati and Golani brigades during the First Intifada exposed similar atrocities for which the soldiers were tried and found guilty. Moreover, the excessive violence exercised by IDF soldiers was documented in reports on television and radio and in the print media in Israel and abroad.

In the trial of the Givati soldiers, the court found as follows:

> We were horrified to hear the testimony of army soldiers who witnessed humiliating scenes of bound, helpless prisoners being beaten within the military base, and who remained indifferent to what they saw and shut their ears to the screams of those being beaten. How can there be a situation in which combat soldiers from a top unit, who appear to us to have received a good education, experience such serious failures in their behavior, disavow all the morals instilled in them by their parents and teachers, undergo a psychological metamorphosis, and are willing and capable of inflicting such murderous beatings. The ultimate conclusion is that the order issued to the defendants was manifestly unlawful. For this reason, none will be able to make use of the defense of "just following orders."[18]

Why is it important to elaborate on these studies and such real-life phenomena in this book on genocide? Are we not degrading the image of our country? Elizur offers an emotionally charged and well-thought-out answer to this question:

> In order to prevent brutalization, we must study it as a universal human phenomenon that can explode within each of us. In the words of the biblical passage about Cain and Abel in the book of *Genesis*: "If thou doest well, shalt thou not be accepted? And if thou doest not well, sin lieth at the door." In other words, an awareness of the temptation and forces pushing us toward wrongdoing creates an inner space within each of us where a struggle between our instincts takes place and in which a commitment to moral responsibility to limit violence can take form. At the same time, projections of our wrongdoing on others and denial that we are capable of doing evil can result in self-righteousness along the lines of "We are all good" which neutralizes our awareness of our own actions.

Elizur also considers whether prevention of brutality is at all possible:

> What is the use of shining a light in the shadows and stirring up bad feelings if in any event we are unable to change anything? This question, which is rooted in existential despair over the human condition, expresses a sense of helplessness in the face of the powerful forces within Israeli, Palestinian, and international society and politics that shape the realities on the ground. This attitude often leads to a cynicism toward the naïve and innocent who still believe in the possibility of creating a link between policy and politics on the one hand and values on the other hand. Sadly, this attitude of cynicism and helplessness is likely to reinforce phenomena of observing wrongdoing from the sidelines. The cynical approach knocks out the possibilities of working from the ground up to change realities for the better in many areas of life based on the argument that they can change nothing.

Fortunately, the present study also reports a redeeming light at the end of the tunnel in showing that if and when there does arise an ethical leadership, soldiers respond accordingly. The clear significance of this fact is evident: we must demand a greater steadfastness from our leaders when it comes to the values of human dignity and the preservation of human life, values in which so many of us in Israel often take such great pride.

Thus, the leadership of one of the IDF companies changed, and at the initiative of its new commanders, its "culture," or codes, and its spirit evolved. Insofar as a "culture of professionalism" grew in the unit—a culture that required discipline and a controlled, calculated, and lawful use of military force—there was a notable decrease in the frequency and severity of the wrongdoings committed by the soldiers.

The late Dan Bar-On, a professor at Ben-Gurion University, dared to study, one by one, the children of Nazis who had perpetrated the Holocaust.[19] He sought to gain an understanding of this second generation's reactions to the atrocities committed by their parents. Had these individuals learned the truth about their parents and other family members? Had they been able to lead normal lives?

Later, Bar-On went on to study Israelis. He had no doubt that Israelis have committed various harmful acts against the Palestinians and that when faced with criticism—whether from within Israel or from human rights groups based outside the country—they often deny any wrongdoing or insist that those who committed it were exceptions. According to Bar-On, the truth is that brutalization processes take hold in many Israelis.[20] He also pointed out that the majority of people in Israeli society remain passive bystanders when injustices are perpetrated nearby and go on with their lives as usual.

The most important conclusion of these studies is that we Israelis—for all that we are historic victims, and for all that we enjoy a history and tradition as an enlightened people who are leaders in the development of concepts of justice and humanism—find it extremely difficult to recognize and acknowledge the evil that is also within us.

Notes

INTRODUCTION

1. Excerpt from Bertolt Brecht's poem "When Evil-Doing Comes like Falling Rain," in Bertolt Brecht, *Poems, 1913–1956* (New York: Eyre Methuen Ltd., 1976), 247.

2. R. J. Rummel, "The New Concept of Democide," in *Encyclopedia of Genocide*, ed. Israel W. Charny (Santa Barbara, CA: ABC-CLIO, 1999), 1:18–23.

3. Samantha Power, *"A Problem from Hell": America and the Age of Genocide* (New York: Basic Books, 2002), 504.

4. Judith Lewis Herman, *Trauma and Recovery: The Aftermath of Violence—from Domestic Abuse to Political Terror* (New York: Basic Books, 1997), x, 7–8.

5. Elie Wiesel, "Then and Now: The Experiences of a Teacher," *Social Education* 42, no. 4 (1978): 266–271.

6. Primo Levi, *The Drowned and the Saved* (New York: Vintage International, 1989), 12.

7. On the terminological differentiation between Holocaust and genocide, see the first book in this series: Yair Auron, *Reflections on the Inconceivable: Theoretical Aspects in Genocide Studies* (Ra'anana: Open University of Israel, 2014).

8. Israel W. Charny, "Genocide: The Ultimate Human Rights Problem," special issue on human rights, *Social Education* 49, no. 6 (1985): 448.

9. Charny, *Encyclopedia of Genocide*, 6–8; Auron, *Reflections on the Inconceivable.*

10. From a May 1988 Israeli television broadcast.

PREFACE

1. US Government, *Preventing Genocide: A Blueprint for U.S. Policymakers.* Genocide Prevention Task Force. Madeline K. Albright and William S. Cohen,

Cochairs, December 2008. This report may be downloaded free of charge at www
.ushmm.org, www.academyofdiplomacy.org, and www.usip.org.

2. David Scheffer, "Genocide and Atrocity Crimes," *Genocide Studies and Prevention* 1, no. 3 (2006): 229–250.

1 WHO ARE WE AS HUMAN BEINGS? HOW DO ORDINARY PEOPLE COMMIT VIOLENCE?

1. Natan Alterman, *Hatur HaShvii* [The Seventh Column] (Tel Aviv: HaKibbutz HaMeuchad, 1977), Book 1, 149–151 (excerpt from longer poem in Hebrew, translated by Israel W. Charny).

2. This poem was written for and presented at the book launch at Open University of Israel on June 22, 2011. It has since been published in the *California Courier* on November 17, 2011.

3. Elie Wiesel, *Shiva Yamim* (weekly magazine of Yediot Aharonot). Clipping available without a date—probably late 1970s (Hebrew).

4. Christopher Browning, *Ordinary Men: Reserve Battalion 101 and the Final Solution in Poland* (New York: Harper Collins, 1998).

5. Gustave M. Gilbert, *The Psychology of Dictatorship: Based on an Examination of the Leaders of Nazi Germany* (New York: Ronald Press, 1950); Douglas M. Kelley, *Twenty-Two Cells in Nuremberg: A Psychiatrist Examines the Nazi Criminals* (New York: Greenberg, 1947; New York: MacFadden, 1961); Israel W. Charny, "Normal Man as Genocider: We Need a Psychology of Normal Man as Genocider, Accomplice or Indifferent Bystander to Mass Killing of Man," *Voices: The Art and Science of Psychotherapy* 7, no. 2 (1971): 68–79; Israel W. Charny and Chanan Rapaport, *How Can We Commit the Unthinkable? Genocide: The Human Cancer* (Boulder, CO: Westview Press, 1982); Hans Askenasy, *Are We All Nazis?* (Secaucus, NJ: Lyle Smart, 1978).

6. Genocide scholar Leo Kuper coined the term "genocidal massacre" to refer to the more "minor" instances of genocide. See Leo Kuper, "Types of Genocide and Mass Murder," in *Towards the Understanding and Prevention of Genocide: Proceedings of the International Conference on the Holocaust and Genocide*, ed. Israel W. Charny (Boulder, CO, and London: Westview Press and Bowker Publishing, 1984), 32–47; Leo Kuper, "Other Selected Cases of Genocide and Genocidal Massacres: Types of Genocide," in *Genocide: A Critical Bibliographic Review*, ed. Israel W. Charny (London and New York: Mansell Publishing and Facts on File, 1998), 155–171; Erik Markusen, "Genocidal Massacres," in *Encyclopedia of Genocide*, ed. Israel W. Charny (Santa Barbara, CA: ABC-CLIO, 1999), 248.

7. Browning, *Ordinary Men*.

8. Gilbert, *The Psychology of Dictatorship*.

9. Kelley, *Twenty-Two Cells in Nuremberg*.

10. Israel W. Charny, "Genocide and Mass Destruction: Doing Harm to Others as a Missing Dimension in Psychotherapy," *Psychiatry* 49, no. 2 (1986): 144–157;

Israel W. Charny, "Evil in Human Personality: Disorders of Doing Harm to Others in Family Relationships," in *Handbook of Relational Diagnosis and Dysfunctional Family Patterns*, ed. Florence Kaslow (New York: Wiley, 1996), 477–495.

11. Kilton Stewart, "The Dream Comes of Age," *Mental Hygiene* 46 (1962): 230–237; G. William Domhoff, "Senoi Dream Theory: Myth, Scientific Method, and the Dreamwork Movement," 2003, http://dreamresearch.net/Library/senoi.html.

12. Jon Bridgman and Leslie J. Worley, "Genocide of the Hereros," in *Genocide in the Twentieth Century: Critical Essays and Eyewitness Accounts*, ed. Samuel Totten, William S. Parsons, and Israel W. Charny (New York: Garland Publishing Company, 1995), 3–48. Also see the latest edition, Samuel Totten and William S. Parsons, *Centuries of Genocide* (New York: Routledge, 2012), 15–25. On the extermination of the Hereros, see Yair Auron, *So That I Wouldn't Be among the Silent* (Ra'anana: Open University Press, 2010), 167–176. (Hebrew)

13. Leo Kuper, *The Prevention of Genocide* (New Haven, CT: Yale University Press, 1985).

14. Samuel Totten, "Pinochet, Augusto, and a New Legal Precedent toward Extradition in Charges of Genocide," in *Encyclopedia of Genocide*, 460–462.

15. Mark Curtis, "Democratic Genocide: Britain and the United States Aided Genocide in Indonesia," in *Encyclopedia of Genocide*, 355.

16. Professor Rudolph J. Rummel is a prominent scholar of genocide whose work has constituted a landmark contribution to the field. Below is a list of his publications ordered chronologically by year of publication, preceded by a summary of the subjects they explore.

1. First and foremost are his comprehensive works, which assemble and present painstakingly detailed statistics regarding genocides in different parts of the world (*Statistics of Democide, Statistics of Democide: Genocide and Mass Murder since 1900*).

2. He has also published a number of books examining specific instances of genocide perpetrated over the years by various national groups, including the Russians (*Lethal Politics: Soviet Genocide and Mass Murder since 1917*), the Germans (*Democide: Nazi Genocide and Mass Murder*), and the Chinese (*China's Bloody Century: Genocide and Mass Murder since 1900*).

3. Rummel also made great efforts to advance a broad-scale conceptualization of genocidal events. Among other things, he offers a new typology that enables us to distinguish between different instances of genocide and the many other instances of mass murder that have been carried out for other reasons, such as war, the conquest of territory, or the suppression of political opposition. To designate such murders, Rummel proposed the term "democide" (*demo* meaning people or community and *cide* meaning murder). The term has not been widely used. Some scholars, myself included, maintain that at this point in time it would be better to refrain from advancing a new term, as only in

recent years have we succeeded in firmly establishing the term "genocide" in the universal lexicon. For this reason, I recommend using "genocide" as a generic concept and, by providing additional discussion and detail, specifying different types of genocide. In any event, students and scholars of genocide should familiarize themselves with Rummel's ideas and his principled distinction between mass murder by governments and the intentional mass murder or extermination of a specific people.

4. Rummel's most important publications may very well be his studies of the element of power at the root of genocide and his comparative analyses of democratic and totalitarian regimes based on the axiom "Power corrupts, absolute power corrupts absolutely." (See "Power Kills: Absolute Power Kills Absolutely," in *Power Kills: Democracy as a Method of Nonviolence*).

5. An extensive review of Rummel's work can be found in the *Encyclopedia of Genocide*.

Rummel, Rudolph J. 1990. *Lethal Politics: Soviet Genocide and Mass Murder since 1917*. New Brunswick, NJ: Transaction Publishers.

———. 1991a. *Democide: Nazi Genocide and Mass Murder*. New Brunswick, NJ: Transaction Publishers.

———. 1991b. *China's Bloody Century: Genocide and Mass Murder since 1900*. New Brunswick, NJ: Transaction Publishers.

———. 1992. "Power Kills. Absolute Power Kills Absolutely." Special issue, *Internet on the Holocaust and Genocide* 38. Jerusalem: Institute on the Holocaust and Genocide.

———. 1994. *Death by Government*. New Brunswick, NJ: Transaction Publishers.

———. 1997a. *Statistics of Democide*. Charlottesville: University of Virginia, Center for National Security Law.

———. 1997b. *Power Kills: Democracy as a Method of Nonviolence*. New Brunswick, NJ: Transaction Publishers.

———. 1999. *Statistics of Democide: Genocide and Mass Murder since 1900*. New Brunswick, NJ: Transaction Publishers.

Rummel's work can also be accessed on his websites at www.hawaii.edu/powerkills and www.joyphim.org, as well as via his blog on democratic peace at freedomspace.blogspot.com.

Rummel's work has faced criticism, particularly by critics who want to assign greater importance to genocides committed by regimes classified as democracies, such as the United States. Although Rummel's work may or may not stand to benefit from revision on this point, this would not alter his basic conclusion that democratic regimes murder less than fascist regimes. With the exception of this point, I am unaware of any other significant criticism of Rummel's diverse scholarship. I also know of no other scholar who has labored over the comparative statistics of genocide to the extent that Rummel has.

Other scholars have attempted to assess the future chances of genocide in different types of societies. One such scholar is Barbara Harff, who served as a professor of political science at the US Naval Academy in Annapolis, Maryland, for many years, and who coined the term "politicide" to refer to murder motivated by differences of political opinion. See Barbara Harff, "No Lessons Learned from the Holocaust? Assessing Risks of Genocide and Political Mass Murder since 1955," *American Political Science Review* 97 (2003): 57–73; Barbara Harff and Ted Robert Gur, "Toward an Empirical Theory of Genocides and Politicides: Identification and Measurement of Cases since 1945," *International Studies Quarterly* 32 (1988): 359–371.

17. Rummel initially maintained that between 1900 and 1994, a total of 174 million people had been killed in the course of democidal and genocidal events combined. In 2005, he published new calculations and conclusions influenced by the publication of two extremely important books on Maoist China and by his own reassessment of the genocide that took place in the Congo. According to his revised conclusions, between 1900 and 1999, the number of people killed by democide and genocide was 262 million. The two influential books on Maoist China are Jung Chang, *Wild Swans: Three Daughters of China* (New York: Touchstone, 2003), and Jung Chang and Jon Halliday, *Mao: The Unknown Story* (New York: Knopf, 2005).

18. Rummel, "Power Kills. Absolute Power Kills Absolutely"; Rummel, *Power Kills: Democracy as a Method of Nonviolence.*

19. Rummel, "Power Kills. Absolute Power Kills Absolutely"; Rummel, *Power Kills: Democracy as a Method of Nonviolence.*

20. Erich Fromm, "Hitler: Who Was He and What Constituted Resistance against Him?," in *For the Love of Life* (New York: Free Press, 1986), 133 (based on radio interviews given in the late 1970s).

21. Stanley Milgram, on CBS News, *60 Minutes*, March 31, 1979.

2 THE FOUNDATIONS OF EVIL IN HUMAN NATURE

1. James Waller, *Becoming Evil: How Ordinary People Commit Genocide and Mass Killing*, 2nd ed. (New York: Oxford University Press, 2007).

2. Waller, *Becoming Evil*, 240.

3. Waller, *Becoming Evil*, 227.

4. Albert Camus, *Neither Victims nor Executioners*, trans. D. MacDonald (New York: Continuum, 1980).

5. All quotations from Lawrence Rees. Excerpted from Saguy Green, "How Could They Kill Small Children?," *Haaretz English Edition*, October 26, 2000, 9 (report on a BBC series titled *The Nazis: A Warning from History*, written and directed by Lawrence Rees).

6. L'Estrange was a British thinker who lived between 1661 and 1704. R. l'Estrange, *Seneca's Morals by Way of Abstract*, 13th ed. (London: Straham, Bettesworth, Tonson, Lintot, Molte & Brown, 1729). Originally published in 1623.

7. Hans Toch, "The Management of Hostile Aggression: Seneca as Applied Social Psychologist," *American Psychologist* 38 (1983): 1022–1025 (quote is from 1022).

8. Primo Levi, "Evil in the Mirror," *Haaretz*, January 7, 2005 (Hebrew).

3 EXAGGERATED SELF-DEFENSE, EXAGGERATED POWER, AND DEHUMANIZATION

1. Rudolph J. Rummel, *Power Kills: Democracy as a Method of Nonviolence.* New Brunswick: Transaction Publishers, 1997.

2. If you haven't guessed, this incident took place at my home in Jerusalem, and I can testify that the boy in the story was actually less mischievous than all of our other children. This "disturbed child" has since grown up into a very fine adult.

3. Evelin Lindner, *Making Enemies: Humiliation and International Conflict* (New York: Praeger Security International, 2009).

4. Barbara Coloroso, *Extraordinary Evil: A Brief History of Genocide* (Toronto: Viking Canada, 2007).

5. Donald W. Winnicott, "Hate in the Countertransference," *Voices: The Art and Science of Psychotherapy* 1, no. 2 (1965): 102–109.

6. Melanie Klein, *The Collected Writings of Melanie Klein*, 4 vols. (London: Hogarth, 1975).

7. Winnicott, "Hate in the Countertransference."

8. My own life experience has taught me that the fields of marital therapy and genocide studies are not at all mutually exclusive. Professionally I am known as an expert in both fields: marriage and genocide—and if saying so is done in good taste, it makes a good joke at parties. In my judgment the common denominator shared by the two professional fields is the sanctity of life and the realization of quality of life in the face of threats of harm and destruction. See my autobiographical chapter in a book that pays tribute to the pioneering psychologists responsible for developing the methods of family therapy. Israel W. Charny, "Marital Therapy and Genocide: A Love of Life Story," in *Voices in Family Therapy*, ed. Florence Kaslow (Beverly Hills: Sage, 1990), 69–90.

9. At this point I would like to state clearly that I am truly partial to married life. I personally have experienced both serious failure and success in this realm. Nonetheless, it is important to remember that a statistical majority of couples fail, resulting in divorce, chronic problems and unhappiness, or a prevailing sense of emptiness and boredom. For a discussion of different models of married life, see Israel W. Charny, *Existential/Dialectical Marital Therapy: Breaking the Secret Code of Marriage* (New York: Brunner/Mazel, 1992).

10. A large body of scholarship on marital therapy addresses the processes of mutual spousal projections. It is always worth reading the pioneering classic in this field by the late Henry Dicks, a psychiatrist at the well-known Tavistock Center for Couple Relationships in London. Intriguingly—at least for me—Dicks

also studied both marriage and the psychology of genocide (specifically of Nazi criminals jailed in European prisons) after probing deep into the subconscious processes at play in marital relationships. See Henry Dicks, *Marital Tensions: Clinical Studies towards a Theory of Interactions* (New York: Basic Books, 1967). I also recommend the work of a psychiatrist who takes marital therapy in the direction of achieving an understanding by both spouses regarding their respective roles in the mutual witch hunt and how to stop it. See Robert Taylor Segraves, *Marital Therapy: A Combined Psychodynamic and Behavioral Approach* (New York: Plenum, 1982).

11. I was first introduced to this view a number of years ago during a conversation with psychologist Bertram Karon of the University of Michigan. As a result of this talk, I made up my mind to study a group of patients hospitalized in a ward for schizophrenics at the Veterans Administration Hospital in Coatesville, Pennsylvania. With the help of the psychologist and the social worker of the ward, I studied whether, at the time they were hospitalized, the patients had stressful relationships, and whether they had been filled with anger and violent feelings against anyone. Our findings were quite surprising: in most cases we were able to identify this complex of emotions. Even if this does not constitute direct proof of the full sequence, it is nonetheless likely that these feelings played an important role in the patients' deterioration into the nonfunctioning state that required hospitalization. Other psychiatric literature describes schizophrenic patients' fears of becoming violent out of their own thoughts and desires. On this subject, see the classic touching account of Hannah Green, *I Never Promised You a Rose Garden* (New York: Penguin Books, 1964).

12. Robert A. Clark, "Friends and Aggression" (mimeographed paper) (Philadelphia: American Friends Service Committee, 1965).

13. Karen Horney, *The Neurotic Personality of Our Time* (New York: Norton, 1937); Karen Horney, *Self-Analysis* (New York: Norton, 1942).

14. This 1975 Oscar-winning film was based on Ken Kesey's 1962 novel *One Flew over the Cuckoo's Nest* (New York: Viking, 1962).

15. Theodor W. Adorno et al., *The Authoritarian Personality* (New York: Harper, 1950).

16. Philip G. Zimbardo et al., "The Psychology of Imprisonment, Privation, Power, and Pathology," in *Theory and Research in Abnormal Psychology*, ed. David Rosenhan and Perry Lomdon, 2nd ed. (New York: Holt, Reinhart and Winston, 1975), 270–287; Philip G. Zimbardo and Alan Fundt, *Candid Camera Classics in Social Psychology: Viewer's Guide and Instructor's Manual* (New York: McGraw-Hill, 1992). A recently published book by Zimbardo appraises the willingness of people to be drawn into committing evil acts under the appropriate circumstances. See Philip Zimbardo, *The Lucifer Effect: How Good People Turn Evil* (New York: Random House, 2007).

17. N. Christie, "Definition of Violent Behavior," in *International Course of Criminology: The Faces of Violence* (Maracaibo, Venezuela: University del Zulia, 1974), 1:25–34.

18. Christopher Browning, *Ordinary Men: Reserve Battalion 101 and the Final Solution in Poland* (New York: Harper Collins, 1998).

19. Rummel, *Power Kills*.

20. Cecil P. Taylor, *Good: A Tragedy* (London: Methuen, 1982).

21. Philip G. Zimbardo, Christina Maslach, and Craig Haney, "Reflections on the Stanford Prison Experiment: Genesis, Transformations, Consequences," in *Obedience to Authority: Current Perspectives on the Milgram Paradigm*, ed. Thomas Blass (Mahwah, NJ: Lawrence Erlbaum Associates, 2000), 193–237. Christina Maslach writes a section within this chapter titled "An Outsider's View of the Underside of the Stanford Prison Experiment," 214–220.

22. Blass, *Obedience to Authority*.

23. Israel W. Charny, *Fascism and Democracy in the Human Mind* (Lincoln: University of Nebraska Press, 2006).

24. Alex Alvarez, *Governments, Citizens, and Genocide: A Comparative and Interdisciplinary Approach* (Bloomington: Indiana University Press, 2001), 133–135; Israel W. Charny, "Dehumanization: Killing the Humanity of Another," in *Encyclopedia of Genocide*, ed. Israel W. Charny (Santa Barbara, CA: ABC-CLIO, 1999), 155–157.

25. René Lemarchand, "Rwanda and Burundi, Genocide," in *Encyclopedia of Genocide*, 508–513; Philip Gourevitch, *We Wish to Inform You That Tomorrow We Will Be Killed with Our Families* (New York: Farrar, Strauss and Giroux, 1998).

26. Alexander Laban Hinton, "Comrade Ox Did Not Object When His Family Was Killed," in *Encyclopedia of Genocide*, 135; Alexander Laban Hinton, "Explaining the Cambodian Genocide in Terms of Psychological Dissonance," *American Anthropologist* 98, no. 4 (1996): 818–831.

27. George Bach and Peter Wyden, *The Intimate Enemy: How to Fight Fair in Love and Marriage* (New York: William Morrow, 1969).

28. "'I Saw the Face of a Relative': Tuol Sleng Interrogation Center Museum," in *Encyclopedia of Genocide*, 423.

29. "Japanese Unit 731: Dread Medical Experiments That Preceded the Nazis," in *Encyclopedia of Genocide*, 413.

30. Israel W. Charny and Chanan Rapaport, "Toward a Genocide Early Warning System," in Charny, *How Can We Commit the Unthinkable?*, 283–331; Israel W. Charny, "Genocide Early Warning System (GEWS)," in *Encyclopedia of Genocide*, 253–265.

31. Chaim Schatzker, "The Teaching of the Holocaust: Dilemmas and Considerations," in *Reflections on the Holocaust: Historical, Philosophical, and Educational Dimensions*, eds. Irene G. Shur, Franklin H. Littell, and Marvin E. Wolfgang. Annals of the American Academy of Political and Social Science 450

(Philadelphia: American Academy of Political and Social Science, 1980): 218–226 (quote from 221).

32. Thomas Merton, "A Devout Meditation in Memory of Adolph Eichmann," reprinted in *Reflections* 2 and 3 (1967): 21–23.

4 "JUST LIKE EVERYONE ELSE": CONFORMITY AND THE LURE OF THE GOLDEN CALF

1. Ian Kershaw, *Hitler, 1936–1945: Nemesis* (New York: Norton, 2001); Michael Burleigh, *The Third Reich: A New History* (New York: Hill and Wang, 2000).

2. Eugen Tarnow, "Self-Destructive Obedience in the Airplane Cockpit and the Concept of Obedience Optimization," in *Obedience to Authority: Current Perspectives on the Milgram Paradigm*, ed. Thomas Blass (Mahwah, NJ: Lawrence Erlbaum Associates, 2000), 111–123.

3. See the appendix to this book, "Studies on Israeli Willingness to Commit Evil."

4. Pnina Blitz, "Parental Collusions in Destructiveness towards a Child as a Cause of Psychiatric and Emotional Disturbance" (unpublished MSW diss., Bob Shapell School of Social Work, Tel Aviv University, 1993). See chart: Pnina Blitz and Israel W. Charny, "Disorders of Incompetence and Pseudocompetence in Marital, Family, and Parental Relationships," in Israel W. Charny, "Evil in Human Personality: Disorders of Doing Harm to Others in Family Relationships," in *Handbook of Relational Diagnosis and Dysfunctional Family Patterns*, ed. Florence W. Kaslow (New York: Wiley, 1996), 477–495.

5. Habib Malik, "Can Christians and Muslims Relate in Peace?," Council for Christian Colleges and Universities," February 3, 2003, http://www.cccu.org/professional_development/resource_library/speech_can_christians_and_muslims_relate_in_peace (accessed September 16, 2003).

6. Edy Kaufman, with the assistance of Pedro Herscovici, "Argentina: The 'Dirty War' of Disappearances, 1976–1983," in *Encyclopedia of Genocide*, ed. Israel W. Charny (Santa Barbara, CA: ABC-CLIO, 1999), 655–657.

7. Michael R. Marrus and Robert O. Paxton, *Vichy France and the Jews* (New York: Basic Books, 1981).

8. Blass, *Obedience to Authority*.

9. Christopher Browning, *Ordinary Men: Reserve Battalion 101 and the Final Solution in Poland* (New York: Harper Collins), 1998.

10. Solomon E. Asch, "Opinions and Social Pressure," *Scientific American* 193, no. 5 (1995): 31–35; Solomon E. Asch, "Studies of Independence and Conformity: A Minority of One against a Unanimous Majority," *Psychological Monographs* 70, no. 416 (1956): 3–45.

11. Leon Festinger, *A Theory of Cognitive Dissonance* (Stanford, CA: Stanford University Press, 1957); Eddie Harmon-Jones and Judson Mills, eds., *Cognitive*

Dissonance: Progress on a Pivotal Theory in Social Psychology (Washington, DC: American Psychological Association, 1999). Daniel Kahnemann, a psychologist and a recipient of the Nobel Prize for economics, is despondent regarding the poverty of thinking and the self-deception that characterize human decision making and modes of thinking. According to Kahnemann, people invent facts and make decisions based on their own conceptions and believe that they have far greater influence on reality than they actually do. Overall, he maintains, people are more biased and focused on their own personal interests than on morals and the pursuit of justice. See Daniel Kahnemann, *Attention and Effort* (Englewood Cliffs, NJ: Prentice Hall, 1973); Daniel Kahnemann, "Psychology of Large Mistakes and Important Decisions," Seventh Oscar Van Leer Annual Lecture, Van Leer Institute, Jerusalem, September 7, 2003. Cognitive psychologist Anthony Greenwald argues that the organization of the human mind is similar to that of a totalitarian state and that people make sense of information by ignoring information with which they are not satisfied. They make believe, construct a world that seems better than it really is, and have no problem fabricating information in order to safeguard their interests. See Anthony G. Greenwald, "The Totalitarian Ego: Fabrication and Revision of Personal History," *American Psychologist* 35, no. 7 (1980): 603–618; Carol Travis and Elliot Aronson, *Mistakes Were Made (but Not by Me): Why We Justify Foolish Beliefs, Bad Decisions, and Hurtful Acts* (Orlando, FL: Harcourt, 2007).

12. Blitz, "Parental Collusions in Destructiveness towards a Child."

13. Leon S. Sheleff, *The Bystander: Behavior, Law, Ethics* (Lexington, MA: Lexington Books, 1978).

14. Michael Berenbaum, ed., *A Mosaic of Victims: Non-Jews Persecuted and Murdered by the Nazis* (New York: New York University Press, 1990); Michael Berenbaum, "The Holocaust, Non-Jewish Victims," in *Encyclopedia of Genocide*, 324–327.

15. Abraham M. Rosenthal, *Thirty-Eight Witnesses* (New York: McGraw-Hill, 1964).

16. Larry Getlen, "Debunking the Myth of Kitty Genovese," *New York Post*, February 16, 2014, http://nypost.com/2014/02/16/book-reveals-real-story-behind -the-kitty-genovese-murder.

17. Elie Wiesel, *The Town beyond the Wall* (New York: Atheneum, 1964).

18. John M. Darley and C. Daniel Batson, "'From Jerusalem to Jericho': A Study of Situational and Dispositional Variables in Helping Behavior," in *Experiencing Social Psychology: Readings and Projects*, ed. Ayala Pines and Christina Maslach (New York: Alfred Knopf, 1979), 149–156.

19. George M. Kren and Leon Rappoport, *The Holocaust and the Crisis of Human Behavior*, rev. ed. (New York: Holmes and Meier, 1994) (originally published in 1980).

20. Gustave Le Bon, *The Crowd: A Study of the Popular Mind* (London: F. Unwin, 1903) (translated from the French).

21. Elias Canetti, *Crowds and Power* (London: Phoenix, 2000).

22. American Psychiatric Association, *DSM-V: Diagnostic and Statistical Manual*, 5th rev. ed. (Washington, DC: American Psychiatric Association, 2013).

23. Browning, *Ordinary Men*.

24. Matthias Geyer, "An S.S. Officer Remembers: The Bookkeeper from Auschwitz," *Der Spiegel*, May 9, 2005 (translated from German by Christopher Sultan).

25. Jung Chang and Jon Halliday, *Mao: The Unknown Story* (New York: Knopf, 2005).

26. Chang and Halliday, *Mao*, 49.

27. Chang and Halliday, *Mao*, 397.

28. Chang and Halliday, *Mao*, 42.

5 SS FOOTSTEPS: PUTTING ON THE UNIFORMS OF CAMP GUARDS AND SACRIFICING OTHERS

1. See Zimbardo's publications above.

2. "The Jews of the Channel Islands," Holocaust Education and Archive Research Team, http://www.holocaustresearchproject.org/nazioccupation/channelislands.html (accessed June 9, 2008). Sources cited by this article include Lawrence Rees, *Auschwitz: The Nazis and the Final Solution* (London: BBC Books, 2005), and Martin Gilbert, *The Holocaust—the Jewish Tragedy* (London: Collins, 1986).

3. N. Christie, "Definition of Violent Behavior," in *International Course of Criminology: The Faces of Violence* (Maracaibo, Venezuela: University del Zulia, 1974).

4. Rudolph J. Rummel, "Khmer Rouge and Cambodia," in *Encyclopedia of Genocide*, ed. Israel W. Charny (Santa Barbara, CA: ABC-CLIO, 1999), 132–136; Ben Kiernan, "The Cambodian Genocide and Its Leaders," in *Encyclopedia of Genocide*, 129–132; Ben Kiernan, *How Pol Pot Came to Power: Colonialism, Nationalism, and Communism in Cambodia, 1930–1975* (New Haven, CT: Yale University Press, 2007).

5. "'I Saw the Face of a Relative': Tuol Sleng Interrogation Center Museum," in *Encyclopedia of Genocide*, 423.

6. Shimon Sachs, *Operation T4: The Extermination of the Disabled in the Third Reich* (Tel Aviv: Papyrus Publishing House, University of Tel Aviv, 1985) (Hebrew).

7. "Outstanding Leaders in American Intelligentsia Were Avid Supporters of the Eugenics Movement in the 1930s," in *Encyclopedia of Genocide*, 220.

8. William E. Seidelman, "Eugenics and the Holocaust," in *Encyclopedia of Genocide*, 215–217; Israel W. Charny, "Life Unworthy of Living," in *Encyclopedia of Genocide*, 404.

9. Vahakn N. Dadrian, "The Role of Turkish Physicians in the World War I Genocide of Ottoman Armenians," *Holocaust and Genocide Studies* 1, no. 2 (1986): 169–192.

10. "Japanese Unit 731: Dread Medical Experiments That Preceded the Nazis," in *Encyclopedia of Genocide*, 413.

11. Robert Jay Lifton, *The Nazi Doctors: Medical Killing and the Psychology of Genocide* (New York: Basic Books, 1986).

12. Israel W. Charny, *Fascism and Democracy in the Human Mind* (Lincoln: University of Nebraska Press, 2006); Erich Neumann, *Depth Psychology and a New Ethic* (New York: Putnam's, 1969).

13. Donald W. Winnicott, "Hate in the Countertransference," *Voices: The Art and Science of Psychotherapy* 1, no. 2 (1965).

14. Berel Lang, *Act and Idea in the Nazi Genocide: Religion, Theology, and the Holocaust* (Syracuse, NY: Syracuse University Press, 2003). A significant number of scholars of the Nazi regime maintain that the ritual surrounding Hitler reached quasi-religious proportions. The following poem, which was familiar to children in Germany, is one example of this phenomenon:

> Führer, my Führer, given me by God,
> Protect and preserve my life for long.
> You saved Germany in time of need.
> I thank you for my daily bread.
> Be with me for a long time, do not leave me,
> Führer, my Führer, my faith, my light,
> Hail to my Führer!

Source: Jean-Denis Lepage, *Hitler Youth, 1922–1945: An Illustrated History* (Jefferson, NC: McFarland and Company, 2008), 87.

15. René Girard, *Violence and the Sacred* (Baltimore: Johns Hopkins University Press, 1977).

16. Ron Jones, "The Third Wave," in *Experiencing Social Psychology*, ed. Ayala Pines and Christina Maslach (New York: Alfred A. Knopf, 1979). Jones's experiment was the basis for a successful television movie entitled *The Wave* in the early 1980s. The Israeli Ministry of Education's catalogue contains the following description of the movie: "A high school teacher in the United States conducts a daring experiment on his students, aiming to show them how, as was the case under Nazi rule, obedience, blind discipline to a dictator, and group control over the individual can be destructive and lead to the breakdown of social values and individual will." Jones made many television appearances followed by the production of the short television movie, a full-length feature film, and a book that became a best seller in Europe and served as required reading in German schools. The story has also been adapted for the stage, primarily by schools, in countries such as Holland, Germany, and Canada.

17. The US Holocaust Museum estimates that approximately 12,000 Jehovah's Witnesses were sent to the concentration camps and that between 2,500 and 5,000 died either in the camps or in prison.

18. Leo Kuper, "Theological Warrants for Genocide: Judaism, Islam, and Christianity," *Terrorism and Political Violence* 2, no. 3 (1990): 351–379.

19. State of Israel (2003), Knesset Library, (2003). Topics before the Public: Suicide Bomber, downloaded from the Internet on December 27, 2010. In July 2008, an Arab man from Sur Baher, an Arab neighborhood on the outskirts of Jerusalem, carried out a terrorist attack in central Jerusalem, killing eight and injuring fifty. The attacker's mother cried out immediately upon hearing that her son had been shot to death, "Shaheed!" (martyr). Later, despite the mother's reaction, which expressed her identification with the anti-Israeli act, the family made every effort to prove that the attacker was in fact not a terrorist and had no ties to ideological groups.

20. Israel W. Charny, *Fighting Suicide Bombing: A Worldwide Campaign for Life* (Westport, CT: Praeger Security International, 2007); Human Rights Watch, *Erased in a Moment: Suicide Bombing Attacks on Israeli Civilians* (New York: Human Rights Watch, 2002), https://www.hrw.org/reports/2002/isrl-pa/ISRAELPA1002.pdf.

21. Ernest Becker, *The Denial of Death* (New York: Free Press, 1973); Israel W. Charny, "Sacrificing Others to the Death We Fear Ourselves: The Ultimate Illusion of Self-Defense," in *How Can We Commit the Unthinkable? Genocide: The Human Cancer*, ed. Israel W. Charny and Chanan Rapaport (Boulder, CO: Westview Press, 1982), 185–211; Israel W. Charny, "Psychology of Sacrificing," in *Encyclopedia of Genocide*, 485–487.

22. Robert Jay Lifton, *The Broken Connection: On Death and the Continuity of Life* (New York: Simon and Schuster, 1979); Eric Markusen, "Psychology of Immortality: Robert Jay Lifton's Perspective on the Psychology of Immortality and Its Relevance for Genocidal Killing," in *Encyclopedia of Genocide*, 484–485.

23. Michael Berenbaum, *The World Must Know: The History of the Holocaust as Told in the United States Holocaust Memorial Museum* (Boston: Little, Brown, and Company, 1993).

24. Michael Berenbaum, "What Makes a Museum Great?," *Haaretz English Edition*, March 4, 2005, B5.

25. According to Calvin Hall, our dreams are primarily aggressive in content. Calvin S. Hall, *The Meaning of Dreams* (New York: Harper and Row, 1953).

26. George Bach and Peter Wyden, *The Intimate Enemy: How to Fight Fair in Love and Marriage* (New York: William Morrow, 1969).

27. I. Shlomo Kulscar, Shoshana Kulscar, and L. Szondi, "Adolf Eichmann and the Third Reich," in *Crime, Law, and Corrections*, ed. Ralph Slovenko (Springfield, IL: Charles Thomas, 1966), 16–52; I. Shlomo Kulscar, "De Sade and Eichmann," in *Strategies against Violence: Design for Nonviolent Change*, ed. Israel W. Charny (Boulder, CO: Westview, 1987), 19–33.

28. Israel W. Charny, "The Psychotherapist as Teacher of an Ethic of Nonviolence," *Voices: The Art and Science of Psychotherapy* 3 (1967): 57–66; Charny, *Fascism and Democracy in the Human Mind*; Jonathan Glover, *Humanity: A Moral History of the Twentieth Century* (New Haven, CT: Yale University Press, 1999); Avishai Margalit, *The Decent Society* (Cambridge, MA: Harvard University Press, 1996).

29. Lionel Rubinoff, "In Nomine' Diaboli: 'The Voices of Evil'," in Charny, *Strategies against Violence*, 34–67

30. Quoted in Rubinoff, "In Nomine' Diaboli," 60; From a letter by Niccolò Machiavelli to Francesco Guicciardini, dated May 17, 1521.

31. Becker, *The Denial of Death*.

32. Announcement of the Armenian National Committee of America.

33. Howard W. French, "China Lifts a Curtain: Private Shrine Tells of 1960's Madness," *International Herald Tribune*, May 30, 2005.

6 "I DID NOTHING WRONG": DENIAL AND IMPROPER MANAGEMENT OF EMOTIONS

1. Israel W. Charny, "A Classification of Denials of the Holocaust and Other Genocides," *Journal of Genocide Research* 5, no. 1 (2003): 11–34. I published an update of the above classification in *GPN: Genocide Prevention Now* 12 (winter 2012), http://www.genocidepreventionnow.org/Home/GPNISSUES/ Issue12Winter2012/tabid/193/ctl/DisplayArticle/mid/1161/aid/655/Default.aspx.

2. Steven T. Katz, *The Holocaust in Historical Context, vol. 1: The Holocaust and Mass Death before the Modern Age* (New York: Oxford University Press, 1994).

3. Deborah Lipstadt, *Denying the Holocaust: The Growing Assault on Truth and Memory* (New York: Free Press, 1993); Michael J. Bazyler, "Holocaust Denial Laws and Other Legislation Criminalizing Promotion of Nazism," *GPN: Genocide Prevention Now* 1 (February 2010), http://www.genocidepreventionnow.org/Home/ GPNISSUES/GPNBulletinLAWSAGAINSTDENIALSpecialSection9/tabid/164/ctl/ DisplayArticle/mid/971/aid/195/Default.aspx.

4. "Japanese Unit 731: Dread Medical Experiments That Preceded the Nazis," in *Encyclopedia of Genocide*, ed. Israel W. Charny (Santa Barbara, CA: ABC-CLIO, 1999), 423.

5. Israel W. Charny, "Innocent Denials of Known Genocides: A Further Contribution to a Psychology of Denial of Genocide," *Human Rights Review* 1, no. 3 (2000): 15–39.

6. George Orwell, *1984* (New York: Harcourt Brace and Company, 1949).

7. Robert Cribb, "Indonesia, Genocide," in *Encyclopedia of Genocide*, 355; Mark Curtis, "Democratic Genocide: Britain and the United States Aided Genocide in Indonesia," *Ecologist* 26, no. 5 (1996).

8. Samuel Totten, "Pinochet, Augusto," in *Encyclopedia of Genocide*, 460–462.

9. Carl Frankenstein, *The Roots of the Ego: A Phenomenology of Dynamics and of Structure* (Baltimore: Williams and Wilkins, 1966); Peter M. Gollwitzer and John A. Bargh, eds., *The Psychology of Action: Linking Cognition to Motivation to Behavior* (New York: Guilford Press, 1996).

10. Israel W. Charny, *Fascism and Democracy in the Human Mind* (Lincoln: University of Nebraska Press, 2006). On subconscious structural mechanisms

that lead us to excessive behavior, see Charny, "Discovering Applications of the Democratic Mind in Everyday Life," in *Fascism and Democracy in the Human Mind*, 254–303.

11. Peter Nathan, "Fascism Makes You Feel Good," in *The Psychology of Fascism* (London: Faber and Faber, 1943), 95–106.

12. This concept, known as the functionalist approach, is very much in accordance with a Hebrew maxim that one transgression leads to another. Every phase of action leads to the following phase and ultimately results in a willingness to go all the way. In respect of the Holocaust, this view is that the Nazis did not plan their steps from the outset but rather "grew" into them as they moved along. The competing approach in Holocaust research is the intentionalist school, which maintains that Hitler planned the Holocaust in advance in its entirety and then it was implemented in practice, beginning with his early hallucinations of large-scale massacres of Jews and continuing during his years in power. See Jack Nusan Porter, "Holocaust Controversies: A Point of View," in *Encyclopedia of Genocide*, 307–312.

13. D. M. Levy, "The Act as a Unit," *Psychiatry* 25 (1962): 295–314.

14. Marvin Zuckerman, *Sensation Seeking: Beyond the Optimal Level of Arousal* (Hillsdale, NJ: Erlbaum, 1979); C. S. Carver and M. F. Scheier, *On the Self-Regulation of Behavior* (Cambridge: Cambridge University Press, 1998).

15. E. Tory Higgins, "Value from Hedonic Experience and Engagement," *Psychological Review* 113 (2006): 439–460.

16. For more on the basic concepts of eros and thanatos, see any one of the many introductions to Freudian thinking.

17. Israel W. Charny, "The Ultimate Existential Meaning of Suicide Bombings: The Killing of Human Life," in *Fighting Suicide Bombing: A Worldwide Campaign for Life* (Westport, CT: Praeger Security International, 2007), 79–99.

18. Robert Adler, "Are We on Our Way Back to the Dark Ages?," *New Scientist* 2 (2005): 26–27; Roy F. Baumeister, *Meanings of Life* (New York: Guildford Press, 1991); Roy F. Baumeister, *Evil: Inside Human Violence and Cruelty* (New York: Freeman, 1997); Colin Feltham, *What's Wrong with Us? The Anthropology Thesis* (New York: Wiley, 2007).

19. Comments of Armenian foreign minister Vartan Oskanian before the UN General Assembly session marking the sixtieth anniversary of the liberation of the Nazi concentration camps, January 2005.

20. Gerhard Schroeder, chancellor of Germany, in a speech on the sixtieth anniversary of the liberation of Auschwitz, *Haaretz*, January 26, 2005 (Hebrew).

21. Deputy Foreign Minister Rabbi Michael Melchior, lecture delivered at Heikhal Shlomo in Jerusalem, September 27, 2002.

22. Benyamin Neuberger, "'Our Holocaust—and Others': The Holocaust Should Be Taught Along with the Other Cases of Genocide," *Haaretz English Edition*, April 28, 2006.

7 SUMMING UP: WHO ARE WE AND WHAT WILL BECOME OF US? TOWARD OUR INDIVIDUAL AND COLLECTIVE FUTURES

1. Marc Pilisuk and Lyn Ober, "Torture and Genocide as Public Health Problems," *American Journal of Orthopsychiatry* 46, no. 3 (1976): 388–392.

2. Carolyn Raffensberger and Joel Tickner, *Protecting Public Health and the Environment: Implementing the Precautionary Principle* (New York: Island Press, 1999); European Environmental Agency, *Late Lessons from Early Warnings: The Precautionary Principle, 1896–2000*, Environmental Issue Report No. 22, January 9, 2002, http://www.eea.europa.eu/publications/environmental_issue_report_2001_22 (accessed October 31, 2011); Elihu D. Richter and Richard Laster, "The Precautionary Principle, Epidemiology, and the Ethics of Delay," *International Journal of Occupational Medicine and Environmental Health* 17, no. 1 (2004): 9–16. According to the authors, this was the first medical publication to apply the precautionary principle to the topic of genocide. Elihu Richter et al., "Malthusian Pressures, Genocide, and Ecocide," *International Journal of Occupational and Environmental Health* 13, no. 3 (2007): 331–341; Elihu Richter and Jutta Lindert, "The Precautionary Principle and the Prevention of Genocide in Light of the U.S. Genocide Prevention Task Force" (presented at the Seventh Biennial Conference of the International Association of Genocide Scholars, Bosnia-Herzegovina, July 10, 2007). For a discussion of the Iranian threat, see Elihu D. Richter and Alex Barnea, "Tehran's Genocidal Incitement against Israel," *Middle East Quarterly* (2009): 45–51. Reprinted from *GPN: Genocide Prevention Now*, Institute on the Holocaust and Genocide in Jerusalem (http://www.genocidepreventionnow.com).

3. Barbara Harff, "No Lessons Learned from the Holocaust? Assessing Risks of Genocide and Political Mass Murder since 1955," *American Political Science Review* 97 (2003): 57–73; Barbara Harff and Ted Robert Gur, "Toward an Empirical Theory of Genocides and Politicides: Identification and Measurement of Cases since 1945," *International Studies Quarterly* 32 (1988): 359–371.

4. In 1977, I published the first proposal for a Genocide Early Warning System (GEWS) with Chanan Rapaport. See Israel W. Charny and Chanan Rapaport, *A Genocide Early Warning System: Establishing a Data Bank for Events of Genocide and Other Major Violations of Human Rights* (Jerusalem: Szold National Institute for Research in the Behavioral Sciences, 1977).

5. Franklin H. Littell, "Early Warning System (EWS)," in *Encyclopedia of Genocide*, ed. Israel W. Charny (Santa Barbara, CA: ABC-CLIO, 1999), 261–265 (includes "Franklin Littell's Writings on Early Warnings of Genocide," 262; Franklin H. Littell, "Early Warning," *Holocaust and Genocide Studies* 3, no. 4 (1998): 483–490.

6. Helen Fein, *Accounting for Genocide: National Responses and Jewish Victimization during the Holocaust* (New York: Free Press, 1979); Helen Fein, "Genocide: A Sociological Perspective," *Current Sociology* 38, no. 1 (1990): 1–126; Helen Fein, ed., *The Prevention of Genocide: Rwanda and Yugoslavia Reconsidered* (New York: Institute for the Study of Genocide, 1994).

7. Harff, "No Lessons Learned from the Holocaust?"; Harff and Gur, "Toward an Empirical Theory of Genocides and Politicide."

8. Gregory Stanton, "The 8 Stages of Genocide," *Genocide Watch*, 1998, http://www.genocidewatch.org/aboutgenocide/8stagesofgenocide.html.

9. "Security Council Passes Landmark Resolution—World Has Responsibility to Protect People from Genocide," Oxfam, press release, April 28, 2006; World Health Organization, World Summit Outcome, Document 15, September 2005; Gareth Evans and Mohammed Sahnoun, "The Responsibility to Protect," *Foreign Affairs* (November–December 2002).

10. Ian Williams, "Ban Ki Moon and R2P," *Foreign Policy in Focus*, August 3, 2009.

11. "Responsibility to Protect—an Idea Whose Time Has Come and Gone?," *Economist*, July 23, 2009.

12. Steven K. Baum, *The Psychology of Genocide: Perpetrators, Bystanders, and Rescuers* (New York: Cambridge University Press, 2008).

13. Alexander Laban Hinton, *Annihilating Difference: The Anthropology of Genocide* (Los Angeles: University of California Press, 2002); Alexander Laban Hinton, *Genocide: An Anthropological Reader* (London: Blackwell, 2002); Alexander Laban Hinton, *Why Did They Kill? Cambodia in the Shadow of Genocide* (Berkeley: University of California Press, 2005).

14. Alex Alvarez, *Governments, Citizens, and Genocide: A Comparative and Interdisciplinary Approach* (Bloomington: Indiana University Press, 2001); Alex Alvarez, *Genocidal Crimes* (New York: Taylor and Francis, 2009).

15. Steven Leonard Jacobs, *Confronting Genocide: Judaism, Christianity, Islam* (Lanham, MD: Lexington Books, 2009).

16. David A. Hamburg, *Preventing Genocide: Practical Steps toward Early Detection and Effective Action* (Boulder, CO: Paradigm Publishers, 2008).

17. Samuel Totten and Paul R. Bartrop, eds., *Dictionary of Genocide*, 2 vols. (Westport, CT: Greenwood Press, 2008).

18. The first comprehensive directory of academic degree programs and courses on the Holocaust and genocide was edited by Marc I. Sherman and is available at "Directory of Academic Programs Full Listing," *GPN: Genocide Prevention Now*, http://www.genocidepreventionnow.org/Home/Holocaustandgenocidereviewhgr/DirectoryofAcademicProgramsandCourses.aspx.

19. Eric Reeves, website on Sudan research, analysis, and advocacy: www.sudanreeves.org.

20. Konrad Lorenz, *On Aggression* (New York: Harcourt, Brace and World, 1966).

21. Baum, *The Psychology of Genocide*, 237.

22. Michael Berenbaum, *The World Must Know: The History of the Holocaust as Told in the United States Holocaust Memorial Museum* (Boston: Little, Brown, and Company, 1993), 332, 335.

23. Peter Baker and Jim Yardley, "Pope Francis, in Congress, Pleads for Unity on World's Woes," *New York Times*, September 24, 2015, http://www.nytimes.com/2015/09/25/us/pope-francis-congress-speech.html.

24. Flora Lewis, "A Geopolitical New Deal: Realism Means Helping the World," *International Herald Tribune*, October 28, 2001.

25. See Robert Spencer, "Hamas: 'We Love Death like Our Enemies Love Life!,'" *Jihad Watch*, July 31, 2014, http://www.jihadwatch.org/hamas-we-love-death-like-our-enemies-love-life.This author also notes that the concept is widely used by Islamic terrorists: "This is just another statement of the Islamic jihadists' oft-repeated desire for death. A Muslim child preacher taunted those he has been taught to hate most: 'Oh Zionists, we love death for the sake of Allah, just as much as you love life for the sake of Satan.' Jihad mass murderer Mohamed Merah said that he 'loved death more than they loved life.' Nigerian jihadist Abubakar Shekau said: 'I'm even longing for death.' Ayman al-Zawahiri's wife advised Muslim women: 'I advise you to raise your children in the cult of jihad and martyrdom and to instill in them a love for religion and death.' And as one jihadist put it, 'We love death. You love your life!' And another: 'The Americans love Pepsi-Cola, we love death.' That was from Afghan jihadist Maulana Inyadullah."

26. See BBC News, "Islamic State 'We Love Death as You Love Life,'" YouTube, www.youtube.com/watch?v=zlfagPS6490: "John Simpson examines the successes of Islamic State and the consequences for those affected."

27. Hannah Arendt, *The Life of the Mind*, vol. 1: *Thinking* (New York: Harcourt, Brace Jovanovich, 1978). Quotation accessed from Wikiquotes and can be found in countless other compilations of quotations.

28. J. K. Rowling, *Harry Potter and the Sorcerer's Stone* (New York: Scholastic, Arthur A. Levine Books, 1998).

APPENDIX: STUDIES ON ISRAELI WILLINGNESS TO COMMIT EVIL

1. Israel W. Charny and Daphna Fromer, "A Study of the Readiness of Jewish/Israeli Students in the Health Professions to Authorize and Execute Involuntary Mass Euthanasia of 'Severely Handicapped' Patients," *Holocaust and Genocide Studies* 5, no. 3 (1990): 313–335.

2. Israel W. Charny and Daphna Fromer, "A Study of the Readiness of Jewish/Israeli Students in the Health Professions to Authorize and Execute Involuntary Mass Euthanasia of 'Severely Handicapped' Patients," *IDEA: A Journal of Social Issues* 9, no. 1 (September 25, 2004).

3. For a summary of the two last studies referred to above and an additional study of the children of perpetrators of the Holocaust, see Israel W. Charny, "To Commit or Not to Commit to Human Life: Children of Victims and Victimizers—All," *Contemporary Family Therapy* 21, no. 5 (1990): 407–426.

4. Israel W. Charny and Daphna Fromer, "A Study of Attitudes of Viewers of the Film 'Shoah' toward an Incident of Mass Murder by Israeli Soldiers (Kfar

Kassem, 1956)," *Journal of Traumatic Stress* 5, no. 2 (1992): 303–318. See also Ruvik Rosenthal, ed., *Kafr Kassem: Myth and History* (Tel Aviv: Hakibutz Hameuchad, 2000) (Hebrew).

5. Claude Lanzmann, *Shoah: An Oral History of the Holocaust* (New York: Pantheon, 1985).

6. Shimon Sachs, *Operation T4: The Extermination of the Disabled in the Third Reich* (Tel Aviv: Papyrus Publishing House, University of Tel Aviv, 1985) (Hebrew); Henry Friedlander, *The Origins of the Nazi Genocide: From Euthanasia to the Final Solution* (Chapel Hill: University of North Carolina Press, 1995).

7. Editorial comment: As noted, I, the author, classify the killings at Kfar Qasim as a "genocidal massacre," but the editor of the original book published by Open University believes that the term "massacre" is more accurate and felt a need to add this comment.

8. Stanley Milgram, *Obedience to Authority: An Experimental View* (New York: Harper and Row, 1974); Stanley Milgram, *Obedience* (a film) (University Park, PA: Penn State Audio-Visual Services [distributor], 1965). A recently published special issue of the prestigious home journal of the American Psychological Association was dedicated in its entirety to corroborating, expanding, and deciphering Milgram's work. See, especially, Jerry M. Burger, "Replicating Milgram: Would People Still Obey Today?," *American Psychologist* 64, no. 1 (2009): 1; Thomas Blass, "From New Haven to Santa Clara: A Historical Perspective on the Milgram Obedience Experiments," *American Psychologist* 64, no. 1 (2009): 44.

9. Herbert C. Kelman and V. Lee Hamilton, *Crimes of Obedience: Towards a Social Psychology of Authority and Responsibility* (New Haven, CT, and London: Yael University Press, 1989).

10. In 2004, fourteen years after its original publication, we were asked to republish our article on the first experiment in this digital online journal. See note 2.

11. Steven L. Jacobs, "Holocaust and Genocide Studies: The Future Is Now," *Center News: Center for Holocaust, Genocide, and Peace Studies* [University of Nevada, Reno] 3, no. 2 (1998): 10–13.

12. Aluf Hareven, *Do Israelis Really Respect Human Dignity?* (Jerusalem: Israel Democracy Institute, 2003), 47–48 (Hebrew).

13. Yoel Elizur and Nufar Yishai-Karin, "How Does a Situation Happen? Wrongdoing by I.D.F. Soldiers in the Intifada," *Alpayim* 31 (2007): 25–54 (Hebrew); Yoel Elizur, "Participation in Atrocities among Israeli Soldiers during the First Intifada: A Qualitative Analysis," *Journal of Peace Research* 46, no. 2 (March 2009): 251–2267.

14. Yoel Elizur, ed., *The Blot of a Light Cloud: Israeli Soldiers, Army, and Society in the Intifada* (Tel Aviv: Kibbutz Hameuchad Press, 2012) (Hebrew) (quoted from draft of book shortly before publication).

15. Elizur and Yishay-Krien, "How Does a Situation Happen?"

16. Dalia Karpel, "Hamedovevet (The One Who Makes People Talk)," *Haaretz Weekend Magazine*, September 21, 2007 (Hebrew).

17. This and subsequent Elizur quotes come from his book *Salt of the Earth: Israeli Soldiers, Army, and Society in the Intifada* (Jerusalem: Kibbutz Meuchad and Van Leer Institute, 2012) (Hebrew).

18. Excerpt from the ruling in the August 22, 1988, trial of the soldiers from the Givati Brigade for the murder of Hani al-Hashimi of Jabaliya refugee camp.

19. Dan Bar-On, *Legacy of Silence: Encounters with Children of the Third Reich* (Cambridge, MA: Harvard University Press, 1989).

20. Dan Bar-On, *The "Others" within Us: A Socio-psychological Perspective on Changes in Israeli Identity* (Beersheba: Ben-Gurion University of the Negev, 2005) (Hebrew).

Bibliography

Adler, Robert. "Are We on Our Way Back to the Dark Ages?." *New Scientist* 2 (2005): 26–27.

Adorno, Theodor W., Else Frenkel-Brunswik, Daniel Levinson, and Nevitt Sanford. *The Authoritarian Personality*. New York: Harper, 1950.

Alterman, Nathan. *Ha-tur ha-Shvi'i* (The Seventh Column). Book 1. Tel Aviv: Kibbutz Hameuchad, 1976–1977 (Hebrew).

Alvarez, Alex. *Governments, Citizens, and Genocide: A Comparative and Interdisciplinary Approach*. Bloomington: Indiana University Press, 2001.

———. *Genocidal Crimes*. New York: Taylor and Francis, 2009.

American Psychiatric Association. *Diagnostic and Statistical Manual*. 4th rev. ed. Washington, DC: American Psychiatric Association, 1994.

Asch, Solomon E. "Studies of Independence and Conformity: A Minority of One against a Unanimous Majority." *Psychological Monographs* 70, no. 416 (1956): 3–45.

———. "Opinions and Social Pressure." *Scientific American* 193, no. 5 (1995): 31–35.

Askenasy, Hans. *Are We All Nazis?* Secaucus, NJ: Lyle Smart, 1978.

Auron, Yair. *Sensitivity to the World's Suffering: Genocide in the 20th Century*. Tel Aviv: Kibbutzim College of Education, 1994 (Hebrew).

———. *The Pain of Knowledge: Holocaust and Genocide Issues in Education*. New Brunswick, NJ: Transaction Publications, 2005.

———. *So That I Wouldn't Be among the Silent*. Ra'anana: Open University Press, 2010 (Hebrew).

———. *Reflections on the Inconceivable: Theoretical Aspects in Genocide Studies*. Ra'anana: Open University Press, 2010 (Hebrew).

Bach, George, and Peter Wyden. *The Intimate Enemy: How to Fight Fair in Love and Marriage*. New York: William Morrow, 1969.

Bar-On, Dan. *Legacy of Silence: Encounters with Children of the Third Reich*. Cambridge, MA: Harvard University Press, 1989.

———. *The "Others" within Us: A Socio-psychological Perspective on Changes in Israeli Identity*. Beersheba: Ben-Gurion University of the Negev, 2005 (Hebrew).

Baum, Steven K. *The Psychology of Genocide: Perpetrators, Bystanders, and Rescuers*. New York: Cambridge University Press, 2008.

Baumeister, Roy F. *Meanings of Life*. New York: Guildford Press, 1991.

———. *Evil: Inside Human Violence and Cruelty*. New York: Freeman, 1997.

Bazyler, Michael J. "Holocaust Denial Laws and Other Legislation Criminalizing Promotion of Nazism." *GPN: Genocide Prevention Now* 1 (February 2010). http://www.genocidepreventionnow.org.

Becker, Ernest. *The Denial of Death*. New York: Free Press, 1973.

Berenbaum, Michael, ed. *A Mosaic of Victims: Non-Jews Persecuted and Murdered by the Nazis*. New York: New York University Press, 1990.

———. *The World Must Know: The History of the Holocaust as Told in the United States Holocaust Memorial Museum*. Boston: Little, Brown, and Co., 1993.

———. "The Holocaust, Non-Jewish Victims." In *Encyclopedia of Genocide*, 324–327. Santa Barbara, CA: ABC-CLIO, 1999.

———. "What Makes a Museum Great?" *Haaretz English Edition*, March 4, 2005, B5.

Berktay, Halil. "Armenia—Genocide Denied." *Dateline*, Australian Television, by Matthew Carney, October 9, 2002.

Blass, Thomas, ed. *Obedience to Authority: Current Perspectives on the Milgram Paradigm*. Mahwah, NJ: Lawrence Erlbaum Associates, 2000.

———. "From New Haven to Santa Clara: A Historical Perspective on the Milgram Obedience Experiments." *American Psychologist* 64, no. 1 (2009): 44.

Blitz, Pnina. "Parental Collusions in Destructiveness towards a Child as a Cause of Psychiatric and Emotional Disturbance." Unpublished MSW dissertation, Bob Shapell School of Social Work, Tel Aviv University, 1993.

Brecht, Bertolt. *Poems 1913–1956*. New York: Eyre Methuen Ltd., 1976.

Bridgman, Jon, and Leslie J. Worley. "Genocide of the Hereros." In *Genocide in the Twentieth Century: Critical Essays and Eyewitness Accounts*, edited by Samuel Totten, William S. Parsons, and Israel W. Charny, 3–48. New York: Garland Publishing Company, 1995. See also the latest edition: *Century of Genocide*, edited by Samuel Totten and William S. Parsons. New York: Routledge, 2015.

Browning, Christopher. *Ordinary Men: Reserve Battalion 101 and the Final Solution in Poland*. New York: Harper Collins, 1998.

Burger, Jerry M. "Replicating Milgram: Would People Still Obey Today?" *American Psychologist* 64, no. 1 (2009): 1.

Burleigh, Michael. *The Third Reich: A New History*. New York: Hill and Wang 2000.

Camus, Albert. *Neither Victims nor Executioners*. Translated by D. MacDonald. New York: Continuum, 1980.

Canetti, Elias. *Crowds and Power*. London: Phoenix, 2000.

Carver, C. S., and M. F. Scheier. *On the Self-Regulation of Behavior*. Cambridge: Cambridge University Press, 1998.

Charny, Israel W. "The Psychotherapist as Teacher of an Ethic of Nonviolence." *Voices: The Art and Science of Psychotherapy* 3 (1967): 57–66.

———. "The Psychology of Genocide." *International Problems* 10, no. 1–2 (1971): xxxxi–xxxxvii (Hebrew).

———. "Normal Man as Genocider: We Need a Psychology of Normal Man as Genocider, Accomplice or Indifferent Bystander to Mass Killing of Man." *Voices: The Art and Science of Psychotherapy* 7, no. 2 (1971): 68–79.

———. "Genocide: The Ultimate Human Rights Problem." Special issue on human rights. *Social Education* 49, no. 6 (1985).

———. "Genocide and Mass Destruction: Doing Harm to Others as a Missing Dimension in Psychotherapy." *Psychiatry* 49, no. 2 (1986): 144–157.

———. "Marital Therapy and Genocide: A Love of Life Story." In *Voices in Family Therapy*, edited by Florence Kaslow, 69–90. Beverly Hills, CA: Sage, 1990.

———. "To Commit or Not to Commit to Human Life: Children of Victims and Victimizers—All." *Contemporary Family Therapy* 21, no. 5 (1990): 407–426.

———. *Existential/Dialectical Marital Therapy: Breaking the Secret Code of Marriage*. New York: Brunner/Mazel, 1992.

———. "Evil in Human Personality: Disorders of Doing Harm to Others in Family Relationships." In *Handbook of Relational Diagnosis and Dysfunctional Family Patterns*, edited by Florence Kaslow, 477–495. New York: Wiley, 1996.

———. "Disorders of Incompetence and Pseudocompetence in Marital, Family and Parental Relationships." In Israel W. Charny, "Evil in Human Personality: Disorders of Doing Harm to Others in Family Relationships." In *Handbook of Relational Diagnosis and Dysfunctional Family Patterns*, edited by Florence W. Kaslow, 477–495. New York: Wiley, 1996.

———. Editor in chief. *Encyclopedia of Genocide*. Associate editors: Rouben Paul Adalian, Steven L. Jacobs, Eric Markusen, Samuel Totten; bibliographic editor: Marc I. Sherman; forewords by Archbishop Desmond M. Tutu and Simon Wiesenthal. Santa Barbara, CA: ABC-CLIO, 1999.

———. "Dehumanization: Killing the Humanity of Another." In *Encyclopedia of Genocide*, 155–157. Santa Barbara, CA: ABC-CLIO, 1999.

———. "Genocide Early Warning System (GEWS)." In *Encyclopedia of Genocide*, 253–265. Santa Barbara, CA: ABC-CLIO, 1999.

———. "Life Unworthy of Living." In *Encyclopedia of Genocide*, 404. Santa Barbara, CA: ABC-CLIO, 1999.

———. "Psychology of Sacrificing." In *Encyclopedia of Genocide*, 485–487. Santa Barbara, CA: ABC-CLIO, 1999.

———. "Innocent Denials of Known Genocides: A Further Contribution to a Psychology of Denial of Genocide." *Human Rights Review* 1, no. 3 (2000): 15–39.

———. "A Classification of Denials of the Holocaust and Other Genocides." *Journal of Genocide Research* 5, no. 1 (2003): 11–34.

———. *Fascism and Democracy in the Human Mind.* Lincoln: University of Nebraska Press, 2006.

———. *Fighting Suicide Bombing: A Worldwide Campaign for Life.* Westport, CT: Praeger Security International, 2007.

Charny, Israel W., and Shamai Davidson, eds. *The Book of the International Conference on the Holocaust and Genocide: Conference Program and Proceedings.* Tel Aviv: Institute on the Holocaust and Genocide, 1984.

Charny, Israel W., and Daphna Fromer. "A Study of the Readiness of Jewish/Israeli Students in the Health Professions to Authorize and Execute Involuntary Mass Euthanasia of 'Severely Handicapped' Patients." *Holocaust and Genocide Studies* 5, no. 3 (1990): 313–335.

———. "The Readiness of Health Profession Students to Comply with a Hypothetical Program of 'Forced Migration' of a Minority Population." *American Journal of Orthopsychiatry* 60, no. 4 (1990): 486–495.

———. "A Study of Attitudes of Viewers of the Film 'Shoah' toward an Incident of Mass Murder by Israeli Soldiers. Kfar Kassem, 1956." *Journal of Traumatic Stress* 5, no. 2 (1992): 303–318.

Charny, Israel W., and Chanan Rapaport. *A Genocide Early Warning System: Establishing a Data Bank for Events of Genocide and Other Major Violations of Human Rights.* Jerusalem: Szold National Institute for Research in the Behavioral Sciences, 1977.

———. *How Can We Commit the Unthinkable? Genocide: The Human Cancer.* Boulder, CO: Westview Press, 1982.

———. "Toward a Genocide Early Warning System." In *How Can We Commit the Unthinkable? Genocide: The Human Cancer,* edited by Israel W. Charny and Chanan Rapaport, 283–331. Boulder, CO: Westview Press, 1982.

Christie, N. "Definition of Violent Behavior." In *International Course of Criminology: The Faces of Violence,* 1:25–34. Maracaibo, Venezuela: University del Zulia, 1974.

Clark, Robert A. "Friends and Aggression" (mimeographed paper). Philadelphia: American Friends Service Committee, 1965.

Coloroso, Barbara. *Extraordinary Evil: A Brief History of Genocide.* Toronto: Viking Canada, 2007.

Cribb, Robert. "Indonesia, Genocide in." In *Encyclopedia of Genocide,* 355. Santa Barbara, CA: ABC-CLIO, 1999.

Curtis, Mark. "Democratic Genocide: Britain and the United States Aided Genocide in Indonesia." *Ecologist* 26, no. 5 (1996). See also in *Encyclopedia of Genocide,* 355. Santa Barbara, CA: ABC-CLIO, 1999.

Dadrian, Vahakn N. "The Role of Turkish Physicians in the World War I Genocide of Ottoman Armenians." *Holocaust and Genocide Studies* 1, no. 2 (1986): 169–192.

Darley, John M., and C. Daniel Batson. "'From Jerusalem to Jericho': A Study of Situational and Dispositional Variables in Helping Behavior." In *Experiencing Social Psychology: Readings and Projects*, edited by Ayala Pines and Christina Maslach, 149–156. New York: Alfred Knopf, 1979.

Dicks, Henry. *Marital Tensions: Clinical Studies towards a Theory of Interactions.* New York: Basic Books, 1967.

Domhoff, G. William. "Senoi Dream Theory: Myth, Scientific Method, and the Dreamwork Movement." 2003. http://dreamresearch.net/Library/senoi.html.

Elizur, Yoel. "Participation in Atrocities among Israeli Soldiers during the First Intifada: A Qualitative Analysis." *Journal of Peace Research* 46, no. 2 (March 2009): 219–235.

———. *Salt of the Earth: Israeli Soldiers, Army, and Society in the Intifada.* Jerusalem: Kibbutz Meuchad and Van Leer Institute, 2012 (Hebrew).

Elizur, Yoel, and Nuphar Yishay-Krien. "How Does a Situation Happen? Wrongdoing by I.D.F. Soldiers in the Intifada." *Alpayim* 31 (2007): 25–54 (Hebrew).

Eugenics Committee of the United States of America. "Outstanding Leaders in American Intelligentsia Were Avid Supporters of the Eugenics Movement in the 1930s." In *Encyclopedia of Genocide*, 220. Santa Barbara, CA: ABC-CLIO, 1999.

European Environmental Agency. *Late Lessons from Early Warnings: The Precautionary Principle, 1896–2000.* Environmental Issue Report No. 9. January 22, 2002. http://www.eea.europa.eu/publications/environmental_issue_report _2001_22.

Evans, Gareth, and Mohammed Sahnoun. "The Responsibility to Protect." *Foreign Affairs* (November–December 2002).

Fein, Helen. *Accounting for Genocide: National Responses and Jewish Victimization during the Holocaust.* New York: Free Press, 1979.

———. "Genocide: A Sociological Perspective." *Current Sociology* 38, no. 1 (1990): 1–126.

———, ed. *Genocide Watch.* New Haven, CT: Yale University Press, 1992.

———, ed. *The Prevention of Genocide: Rwanda and Yugoslavia Reconsidered.* New York: Institute for the Study of Genocide, 1994.

Feltham, Colin. *What's Wrong with Us? The Anthropology Thesis.* New York: Wiley, 2007.

Festinger, Leon. *A Theory of Cognitive Dissonance.* Stanford, CA: Stanford University Press, 1957.

Frankenstein, Carl. *The Roots of the Ego: A Phenomenology of Dynamics and of Structure.* Baltimore: Williams and Wilkins, 1966.

French, Howard W. "China Lifts a Curtain: Private Shrine Tells of 1960's Madness." *International Herald Tribune*, May 30, 2005.

Friedlander, Henry. *The Origins of the Nazi Genocide: From Euthanasia to the Final Solution.* Chapel Hill: University of North Carolina Press, 1995.

Fromm, Erich. *For the Love of Life.* New York: Free Press, 1986.

Geyer, Matthias. "An S.S. Officer Remembers: The Bookkeeper from Auschwitz." *Der Spiegel.* May 9, 2005.

Gilbert, Gustave M. *The Psychology of Dictatorship: Based on an Examination of the Leaders of Nazi Germany.* New York: Ronald Press, 1950.

Gilbert, Martin. *The Holocaust—the Jewish Tragedy.* London: Collins, 1986.

Girard, René. *Violence and the Sacred.* Baltimore: Johns Hopkins University Press, 1977.

Gollwitzer, Peter M., and John A. Bargh, eds. *The Psychology of Action: Linking Cognition to Motivation to Behavior.* New York: Guilford Press, 1996.

Gourevitch, Philip. *We Wish to Inform You That Tomorrow We Will Be Killed with Our Families.* New York: Farrar, Strauss and Giroux, 1998.

Green, Hannah. *I Never Promised You a Rose Garden.* New York: Penguin Books, 1964.

Green, Saguy. "How Could They Kill Small Children?" *Haaretz English Edition,* October 26, 2000.

Greenwald, Anthony G. "The Totalitarian Ego: Fabrication and Revision of Personal History." *American Psychologist* 35, no. 7 (1980): 603–618.

Hall, Calvin S. *The Meaning of Dreams.* New York: Harper and Row, 1953.

Hamburg, David A. *Preventing Genocide: Practical Steps toward Early Detection and Effective Action.* Boulder, CO: Paradigm Publishers, 2008.

Hareven, Aluf. *Do Israelis Really Respect Human Dignity?* Jerusalem: Israel Democracy Institute, 2003 (Hebrew).

Harff, Barbara. "No Lessons Learned from the Holocaust? Assessing Risks of Genocide and Political Mass Murder since 1955." *American Political Science Review* 97 (2003): 57–73.

Harff, Barbara, and Ted Robert Gur. "Toward an Empirical Theory of Genocides and Politicides: Identification and Measurement of Cases since 1945." *International Studies Quarterly* 32 (1988): 359–371.

Harmon-Jones, Eddie, and Judson Mills, eds. *Cognitive Dissonance: Progress on a Pivotal Theory in Social Psychology.* Washington, DC: American Psychological Association, 1999.

Higgins, E. Tory. "Value from Hedonic Experience and Engagement." *Psychological Review* 113 (2006): 439–460.

Hinton, Alexander Laban. "Explaining the Cambodian Genocide in Terms of Psychological Dissonance." *American Anthropologist* 98, no. 4 (1996): 818–831.

———. "Comrade Ox Did Not Object When His Family Was Killed." In *Encyclopedia of Genocide,* 135. Santa Barbara, CA: ABC-CLIO, 1999.

———. *Annihilating Difference: The Anthropology of Genocide.* Los Angeles: University of California Press, 2002.

————. *Genocide: An Anthropological Reader*. London: Blackwell, 2002.

————. *Why Did They Kill? Cambodia in the Shadow of Genocide*. Berkeley: University of California Press, 2005.

Horney, Karen. *The Neurotic Personality of Our Time*. New York: Norton, 1937.

————. *Self-Analysis*. New York: Norton, 1942.

Human Rights Watch, *Erased in a Moment: Suicide Bombing Attacks on Israeli Civilians*, 2002. http://www.hrw.org/en/reports/2002/10/15/erased-moment-0.

"'I Saw the Face of a Relative': Tuol Sleng Interrogation Center Museum" (feature story from press reports). *Encyclopedia of Genocide*, 423. Santa Barbara, CA: ABC-CLIO, 1999.

Jacobs, Steven Leonard. "Holocaust and Genocide Studies: The Future Is Now." *Center News: Center for Holocaust, Genocide, and Peace Studies* [University of Nevada, Reno] 3, no. 2 (1998): 10–13.

————. *Confronting Genocide: Judaism, Christianity, Islam*. Lanham, MD: Lexington Books, 2009.

"Japanese Unit 731: Dread Medical Experiments That Preceded the Nazis" (feature story from press reports). *Encyclopedia of Genocide*, 413. Santa Barbara, CA: ABC-CLIO, 1999.

Jones, Ron. "The Third Wave." In *Experiencing Social Psychology*, edited by Ayala Pines and Christina Maslach, 203–211. New York: Alfred A. Knopf, 1979.

Jung, Carl. *Wild Swans: Three Daughters of China*. New York: Touchstone, 2003.

Jung, Carl, and Jon Halliday. *Mao: The Unknown Story*. New York: Knopf, 2005.

Kahnemann, Daniel. "Psychology of Large Mistakes and Important Decisions." Seventh Oscar Van Leer Annual Lecture, Van Leer Institute, Jerusalem, September 7, 1973.

————. *Attention and Effort*. Englewood Cliffs, NJ: Prentice Hall, 1973.

Karpel, Dalia. "Hamedovevet (The One Who Makes People Talk)." *Haaretz Weekend Magazine*, September 21, 2007 (Hebrew).

Katz, Steven T. *The Holocaust in Historical Context*. Vol. 1: *The Holocaust and Mass Death before the Modern Age*. New York: Oxford University Press, 1994.

Kaufman, Edy, with the assistance of Pedro Herscovici. "Argentina: The 'Dirty War' of Disappearances, 1976–1983." In *Encyclopedia of Genocide*, 655–657. Santa Barbara, CA: ABC-CLIO, 1999.

Kelley, Douglas M. *Twenty-Two Cells in Nuremberg: A Psychiatrist Examines the Nazi Criminals*. New York: Greenberg, 1947; New York: MacFadden, 1961.

Kelman, Herbert C., and V. Lee Hamilton. *Crimes of Obedience: Towards a Social Psychology of Authority and Responsibility*. New Haven, CT: Yale University Press, 1989.

Keren, Nili. "Evil in the Mirror." *Haaretz English Edition*. January 7, 2005.

Kershaw, Ian. *Hitler, 1889–1936: Hubris*. New York: Norton, 2000.

————. *Hitler, 1936–1945: Nemesis*. New York: Norton, 2001.

Kesey, Ken. *One Flew over the Cuckoo's Nest*. New Jersey: Viking, 1962.

Kiernan, Ben. "The Cambodian Genocide and Its Leaders." In *Encyclopedia of Genocide*, 129–132. Santa Barbara, CA: ABC-CLIO, 1999.

———. *How Pol Pot Came to Power: Colonialism, Nationalism, and Communism in Cambodia, 1930–1975.* New Haven, CT: Yale University Press, 2007.

Klein, Melanie. *The Collected Writings of Melanie Klein.* 4 vols. London: Hogarth, 1975.

Kren, George M., and Rappoport, Leon. *The Holocaust and the Crisis of Human Behavior.* Rev. ed. New York: Holmes and Meier, 1994 (originally published in 1980).

Kulcsar, I. Shlomo. "De Sade and Eichmann." In *Strategies against Violence: Design for Nonviolent Change*, edited by Israel W. Charny, 19–33. Boulder, CO: Westview, 1987.

Kulcsar, I. Shlomo, Shoshana Kulscar, and L. Szondi. "Adolf Eichmann and the Third Reich." In *Crime, Law, and Corrections*, edited by Ralph Slovenko, 16–52. Springfield, IL: Charles Thomas, 1966.

Kuper, Leo. "Types of Genocide and Mass Murder." In *Towards the Understanding and Prevention of Genocide: Proceedings of the International Conference on the Holocaust and Genocide*, edited by Israel W. Charny, 32–47. Boulder, CO, and London: Westview Press and Bowker Publishing, 1984.

———. *The Prevention of Genocide.* New Haven, CT: Yale University Press, 1985.

———. "Theological Warrants for Genocide: Judaism, Islam, and Christianity." *Terrorism and Political Violence* 2, no. 3 (1990): 351–379.

———. "Other Selected Cases of Genocide and Genocidal Massacres: Types of Genocide." In *Genocide: A Critical Bibliographic Review*, edited by Israel W. Charny, 155–171. London and New York: Mansell Publishing and Facts on File, 1998.

Lang, Berel. *Act and Idea in the Nazi Genocide: Religion, Theology, and the Holocaust.* Syracuse, NY: Syracuse University Press, 2003.

Lanzmann, Claude. *Shoah: An Oral History of the Holocaust.* New York: Pantheon, 1985.

Lapid, Pinhas. "A Dress Rehearsal for the Holocaust." *Bar Ilan University Bulletin* (summer 1974): 14–20 (Hebrew).

Le Bon, Gustave. *The Crowd: A Study of the Popular Mind.* London: F. Unwin, 1903 (translated from the French).

Lemarchand, René. "Rwanda and Burundi, Genocide." In *Encyclopedia of Genocide*, 508–513. Santa Barbara, CA: ABC-CLIO, 1999.

Lepage, Jean-Denis. *Hitler Youth, 1922–1945: An Illustrated History.* Jefferson, NC: McFarland and Company, 2008.

Levi, Primo. *The Drowned and the Saved.* New York: Vintage International, 1989.

Levy, D. M. "The Act as a Unit." *Psychiatry* 25 (1962): 295–314.

Lewis Herman, Judith. *Trauma and Recovery: The Aftermath of Violence—from Domestic Abuse to Political Terror.* New York: Basic Books, 1997.

Lifton, Robert J. *The Broken Connection: On Death and the Continuity of Life*. New York: Simon and Schuster, 1979.

———. *The Nazi Doctors: Medical Killing and the Psychology of Genocide*. New York: Basic Books, 1986.

Lindner, Evelin. *Making Enemies: Humiliation and International Conflict*. New York: Praeger Security International, 2009.

Lipstadt, Deborah. *Denying the Holocaust: The Growing Assault on Truth and Memory*. New York: Free Press, 1993.

Littell, Franklin H. "Early Warning." *Holocaust and Genocide Studies* 3, no. 4 (1998): 483–490.

———. "Early Warning System (E.W.S.)." In *Encyclopedia of Genocide*, 261–265. Santa Barbara, CA: ABC-CLIO, 1999.

Lorenz, Konrad. *On Aggression*. New York: Harcourt, Brace and World, 1966.

Malik, Habib. "Can Christians and Muslims Relate in Peace?." Council for Christian Colleges and Universities." February 3, 2003. http://www.cccu.org/professional _development/resource_library/speech_can_christians_and_muslims_relate_in _peace.

Margalit, Avishai. *The Decent Society*. Cambridge, MA: Harvard University Press, 1996.

Markusen, Eric. "Genocidal Massacres." In *Encyclopedia of Genocide*, 248. Santa Barbara, CA: ABC-CLIO, 1999.

———. "Psychology of Immortality: Robert Jay Lifton's Perspective on the Psychology of Immortality and Its Relevance for Genocidal Killing." In *Encyclopedia of Genocide*, 484–485. Santa Barbara, CA: ABC-CLIO, 1999.

Marrus, Michael R., and Robert O. Paxton. *Vichy France and the Jews*. New York: Basic Books, 1981.

Merton, Thomas, "A Devout Meditation in Memory of Adolph Eichmann." Reprinted in *Reflections* 2–3 (1967): 21–23.

Milgram, Stanley. *Obedience* (a film). University Park: Penn State Audio-Visual Services [distributor], 1965.

———. *Obedience to Authority: An Experimental View*. New York: Harper and Row, 1974.

Nathan, Peter. "Fascism Makes You Feel Good." In *The Psychology of Fascism*, 95–106. London: Faber and Faber, 1943.

Neuberger, Benyamin. "Our Holocaust—and Others'." *Haaretz English Edition*. April 28, 2005. http://www.haaretz.com/print-edition/opinion/our-holocaust-and-others-1.186432.

Neumann, Erich. *Depth Psychology and a New Ethic*. New York: Putnam's, 1969.

Orwell, George. *1984*. New York: Harcourt Brace and Company, 1949.

Oxfam. "Security Council Passes Landmark Resolution—World Has Responsibility to Protect People from Genocide." Press release, April 28, 2006.

Pilisuk, Marc, and Lyn Ober. "Torture and Genocide as Public Health Problems."
    American Journal of Orthopsychiatry 46, no. 3 (1976): 388–392.
Porter, Jack Nusan. "Holocaust Controversies: A Point of View." In *Encyclopedia of
    Genocide*, 307–312. Santa Barbara, CA: ABC-CLIO, 1999.
Power, Samantha. *A Problem from Hell: America and the Age of Genocide.* New
    York: Basic Books, 2002.
Raffensberger, Carolyn, and Joel Tickner. *Protecting Public Health and the
    Environment: Implementing the Precautionary Principle.* New York: Island
    Press, 1999.
Rees, Lawrence. *Auschwitz: The Nazis and the Final Solution.* London: BBC Books,
    2005.
Reeves, Eric. *A Long Day's Dying: Critical Moments in the Darfur Genocide.*
    Toronto: Key Publishers, 2007.
"Responsibility to Protect—an Idea Whose Time Has Come and Gone?." *Economist,*
    July 23, 2009.
Richter, Elihu, and Richard Laster. "The Precautionary Principle, Epidemiology,
    and the Ethics of Delay." *International Journal of Occupational Medicine and
    Environmental Health* 17, no. 1 (2004): 9–16.
Richter, Elihu, and Jutta Lindert. "The Precautionary Principle and the Prevention
    of Genocide in the Light of the U.S. Genocide Prevention Task Force." Presented
    at the Seventh Biennial Conference of the International Association of Genocide
    Scholars, Bosnia-Herzegovina, July 10, 2007.
Richter, Elihu, Rony Blum, Tamar Berman, and Gregory H. Stanton. "Malthusian
    Pressures, Genocide, and Ecocide." *International Journal of Occupational and
    Environmental Health* 13, no. 3 (2007): 331–341.
Richter, Elihu, and Alex Barnea. "Tehran's Genocidal Incitement against Israel."
    Middle East Quarterly (2009): 45–51.
Rosenthal, Abraham M. *Thirty-Eight Witnesses.* New York: McGraw-Hill, 1964.
Rosenthal, Ruvik, ed. *Kafr Kassem: Myth and History.* Tel Aviv: Hakibutz
    Hameuchad, 2000 (Hebrew).
Rubinoff, Lionel. "In Nomine Diaboli: The Voices of Evil." In *Strategies against
    Violence: Design for Nonviolent Change*, edited by Israel W. Charny, 34–67.
    Boulder, CO: Westview, 1987.
Rummel, Rudolph J. *Lethal Politics: Soviet Genocide and Mass Murder since 1917.*
    New Brunswick, NJ: Transaction Publishers, 1990.
———. *Democide: Nazi Genocide and Mass Murder.* New Brunswick, NJ:
    Transaction Publishers, 1991.
———. *China's Bloody Century: Genocide and Mass Murder since 1900.* New
    Brunswick, NJ: Transaction Publishers, 1991.
———. "Power Kills. Absolute Power Kills Absolutely." Special issue. *Institute on the
    Holocaust and Genocide* 38. Jerusalem: Institute on the Holocaust and Genocide.

————. *Death by Government*. New Brunswick, NJ: Transaction Publishers, 1994.

————. *Statistics of Democide*. Charlottesville: University of Virginia, Center for National Security Law, 1997.

————. *Power Kills: Democracy as a Method of Nonviolence*. New Brunswick: Transaction Publishers, 1997.

————. *Statistics of Democide: Genocide and Mass Murder since 1900*. New Brunswick: Transaction Publishers, 1999.

————. "The New Concept of Democide." In *Encyclopedia of Genocide*, 324–327. Santa Barbara, CA: ABC-CLIO, 1999., 18–23.

————. "Khmer Rouge and Cambodia." In *Encyclopedia of Genocide*, 34–67. Santa Barbara, CA: ABC-CLIO, 1999.

Sachs, Shimon. *Operation T4: The Extermination of the Disabled in the Third Reich*. Tel Aviv: Papyrus Publishing House, University of Tel Aviv, 1985 (Hebrew).

Schatzker, Chaim. "The Teaching of the Holocaust: Dilemmas and Considerations." In *Reflections on the Holocaust: Historical, Philosophical, and Educational Dimensions*, ed. Irene G. Shur, Franklin H. Littell, and Marvin E. Wolfgang. *Annals of the American Academy of Political and Social Science* 450. Philadelphia: American Academy of Political and Social Science, 1980.

Segraves, Robert Taylor. *Marital Therapy: A Combined Psychodynamic and Behavioral Approach*. New York: Plenum, 1982.

Seidelman, William E. "Eugenics and the Holocaust." In *Encyclopedia of Genocide*, 215–217. Santa Barbara, CA: ABC-CLIO, 1999.

Sheleff, Leon. *The Bystander: Behavior, Law, Ethics*. Lexington, MA: Lexington Books, 1978.

Stanton, Gregory. "The 8 Stages of Genocide." *Genocide Watch*. http://www.genocidewatch.org/aboutgenocide/8stagesofgenocide.html.

Stewart, Kilton. "The Dream Comes of Age." *Mental Hygiene* 46 (1962): 230–237.

Tarnow, Eugen. "Self-Destructive Obedience in the Airplane Cockpit and the Concept of Obedience Optimization." In *Obedience to Authority: Current Perspectives on the Milgram Paradigm*, edited by Thomas Blass, 111–123. Mahwah, NJ: Lawrence Erlbaum Associates, 2000.

Taylor, Cecil P. *Good: A Tragedy*. London: Methuen, 1982.

Totten, Samuel. "Pinochet, Augusto, and a New Legal Precedent toward Extradition in Charges of Genocide." In *Encyclopedia of Genocide*, 460–462. Santa Barbara, CA: ABC-CLIO, 1999.

Totten, Samuel, and Paul R. Bartrop, eds. *Dictionary of Genocide*. 2 vols. Westport, CT: Greenwood Press, 2008.

Totten, Samuel, and William S. Parsons, eds. *Century of Genocide*. New York: Routledge, 2015.

Travis, Carol, and Elliot Aronson. *Mistakes Were Made (but Not by Me): Why We Justify Foolish Beliefs, Bad Decisions, and Hurtful Acts*. Orlando, FL: Harcourt, 2007.

US Government. *Preventing Genocide: A Blueprint for U.S. Policymakers.* Genocide Prevention Task Force. Madeline K. Albright and William S. Cohen, Cochairs, December 2008.

Waller, James. *Becoming Evil: How Ordinary People Commit Genocide and Mass Killing.* 2nd ed. New York: Oxford University Press, 2007.

Wiesel, Elie. *The Town beyond the Wall.* New York: Althenium, 1964.

———. *Shiva Yamim* (weekly magazine of *Yediot Aharonot*). N.d., probably late 1960s (Hebrew).

———. "Then and Now: The Experiences of a Teacher." *Social Education* 42, no. 4 (1978): 266–271.

Williams, Ian. "Ban Ki Mon and R2P." *Foreign Policy in Focus.* August 3, 2009.

Winnicott, Donald W. "Hate in the Countertransference." *Voices: The Art and Science of Psychotherapy* 1, no. 2 (1965): 102–109.

World Health Organization. World Summit Outcome, Document 15, September 2005.

Zimbardo, Philip G., Craig Haney, W. Curtis Banks, and David Jaffe. "The Psychology of Imprisonment, Privation, Power, and Pathology." In *Theory and Research in Abnormal Psychology*, edited by David Rosenhan and Perry London, 270–287. 2nd ed. New York: Holt, Reinhart and Winston, 1975.

Zimbardo, Philip G., and Alan Funt. *Candid Camera Classics in Social Psychology: Viewer's Guide and Instructor's Manual.* New York: McGraw-Hill, 1992.

Zimbardo, Philip G., Christina Maslach, and Craig Haney. "Reflections on the Stanford Prison Experiment: Genesis, Transformations, Consequences." In *Obedience to Authority: Current Perspectives on the Milgram Paradigm*, edited by Thomas Blass, 193–237. Mahwah, NJ: Lawrence Erlbaum Associates, 2000.

Zimbardo, Philip G. *The Lucifer Effect: How Good People Turn Evil.* New York: Random House, 2007.

Zuckerman, Marvin. *Sensation Seeking: Beyond the Optimal Level of Arousal.* Hillsdale, NJ: Erlbaum, 1979.

Index

List of Learning Exercises for the Reader about Our Own Readiness to Do Harm to Others

(listed in the order of appearance in the book)

1. Exercises about our will to live or die, and our wishes toward others, 171–172: an exercise about our will to live, 172; an exercise about our personal willingness to see others murdered, and perhaps ourselves play active roles in the process of mass killing, 173

2. Exercises relating to projection, 174–175; an exercise about difficult relationships in our lives, 174; an exercise about hostile projection on to members of other ethnic, racial, national, or religious groups (including subgroups of my own religion), 174–175

3. Readiness to humiliate others: an exercise on humiliating others, 175

4. Introductory exercises about addiction to power, 175–176; an exercise about which positions of leadership draw you, 176; an exercise about our desires to hold authority and be superior to others,176; an exercise about more intense dictatorial, humiliating, and aggressive behaviors, 177

5. Exercises about dehumanization, "thinging," categorizing other people as "things," and demonization—attributing evil power and intention to others, 178–179; an exercise about feelings of disgust toward members of other groups, 178; an exercise about our readiness to discriminate against members of other groups, 178; an exercise about our readiness to kill members of other groups, 179

About the Author and the Institute on the Holocaust and Genocide in Jerusalem

Israel W. Charny is an American and Israeli who is widely known in the United States, Europe, and Israel, particularly as a leader in genocide studies and prevention and also for his work as a clinical psychologist and family therapist.

His commitment to genocide scholarship dates back to the mid-1960s; by the mid-1970s he formulated for himself the two goals that ever since have identified his work: continuation of his own research into the psychology of genocide, denials of genocide, communication techniques for disseminating information about genocide, genocide early warnings; and contributions to the development of a discipline of genocide studies. He is also well known as a founder and first president of the Israel Family Therapy Association, a past president of the International Family Therapy Association, and a cofounder and past president of the International Association of Genocide Scholars.

He has written a score of well-received books on family therapy and on genocide. Three of the works have been awarded Outstanding Academic Book of the Year by the American Library Association: *Genocide: A Critical Bibliographic Review* (1988), *Encyclopedia of Genocide* (1999–2000), and *Fascism and Democracy in the Human Mind* (2006). Two other books are also forthcoming from Rowman & Littlefield: *A Democratic Mind: Psychology and Psychiatry with Fewer Meds and More Soul* and *Psychotherapy for a Democratic Mind: Treatment of Intimacy, Tragedy, Violence, and Evil.*

In 2011 he was honored with a Presidential Prize by the president of Armenia "in recognition of his decades-long academic work and activities contributing to international recognition of the Armenian Genocide and his researches of denials of genocides."

In 1980 Charny established the Institute on the Holocaust and Genocide in Jerusalem with Nobel laureate author and Holocaust survivor Elie Wiesel and the late Professor Shamai Davidson, a psychiatrist and psychoanalyst who at the time was director of a psychiatric hospital and himself focused on the treatment of Holocaust survivors. In 1982, Charny and his associates organized the first International Conference on the Holocaust and Genocide. This pioneering conference marked a turning point in awareness of the subject of genocide, which until that point the academic world had neglected. The conference and then the institute appear to mark the first linked usages of the terms "Holocaust" and "genocide." The institute, which Charny has directed since its establishment, may also have been the first official institution to focus on this linkage.

Charny was one of four cofounders of the International Association of Genocide Scholars, together with Helen Fein, Robert Melson, and Roger Smith, and was subsequently elected to serve as its vice-president (in 2003) and president (2005–2007). From 2010 to 2012 he was editor of the website www.genocidepreventionnow.org, which hosted *GPN: Genocide Prevention Now*, a web magazine supported by the Carnegie Foundation of New York and designed to develop a new kind of journalism that combines news of developments in genocide studies with academic-level research articles.

For many years Charny was an associate professor of psychology at Tel Aviv University's School of Social Work. He later served briefly as a professor of psychology at Ben-Gurion University's School of Social Work and in 1992 was invited by the Hebrew University of Jerusalem to serve as a professor of psychology and family therapy and to set up and direct (1993–1997) a new division within the Department of Psychology and the Martin Buber Center, the Program for Advanced Studies in Integrative Psychotherapy, which became the School of Psychotherapy.